Azul editores®

First edition for English translation: February 2016

© Ana Cecilia González

© Azul Editores®

© Felipe Montes, Fábrica Literaria, S.C. San Pedro Garza García,
Nuevo León, México.

Plaza Río, Ave. San Pedro 801 L8 y L9. Colonia Fuentes del Valle
San Pedro, C.P. 66224

contacto@fabricaliteraria.com

www.fabricaliteraria.com

Translator- Helen Rowland

Photography- Jaime Espinosa

E-book conversion- Carmen Macossay

Impreso en México.

Printed in México

Ana Cecilia González

When life is not forever...

03/06/16

To Carol,
Enjoy your journey,
It's a privilege and a
great gift to be
alive,

love,
Ana Cecilia

Azul editores

DEDICATION

I dedicate the story of my life especially to

my parents, Enrique Luis and Sandra Patricia.

To my great motivators, Ana Paula and Daniel.

To my sisters, Sandra Patricia and Marcela Sofía,

and to my brother, Enrique Luis.

To my grandparents, Enrique and Nena, Esaú and Chagüita,

To my nephews and nieces, my best cheerleaders.

ACKNOWLEDGMENTS:

Thank you to my mentor, Sofía Segovia,
for her unconditional support.

To Morena, who marked the beginning of this project.

To Carmen and Lorena, who helped me
not to lose sight of my objective.

To my Soul Mates, who were beside me all the way.

To Lilia and José Luis, who have been my
constant source of spiritual strength.

To my doctors who have been standing
by me every step of the way.

To *Ráfel*, who has been at my side since my arrival.

Table of Contents

WHEN LIFE IS NOT FOREVER...

●INTRODUCTION

Dear Ana Cecilia and Readers,
*It is a genuine privilege for me to write this brief note of introduction
to this courageous book. I came to know Ana Cecilia in the adult
segment of her incredible journey. As has been true of her entire life,
at the time of our intersection she faced a personal medical scenario
that was essentially an unknown. There are very few adult patients
in the entire world living with a single ventricle. Even more rare is
the sub-category of patients who underwent the earliest attempts of a
Fontan operation, lived, thrived, but then deteriorated. At the time of
her most recent surgery, just as earlier in her life, Ana Cecilia faced
the choice of agreeing to a largely unproven (revision) operation;
complex, lengthy, risk laden, but with the hope of a better future.
In agreeing to the surgery, she continued in her role as not only a
patient, but a pioneer.*

*I am inspired by the human will to live and experience life. It
sustains me as a congenital heart surgeon when we fall short in our
aspiration to help. In my career that now approaches 25 years and
15,000 operations, I am humbled by the intrepid spirit and courage
of patients like Ana Cecilia. She and all patients remind us that "Life
is not forever" for any of us. Life and the joys of living are transient
and precious and to be revered.*

Charles D. Fraser, Jr., M.D.
Surgeon-in-Chief
Clayton Chair in Surgery
Donovan Chair and Chief,
  Congenital Heart Surgery
  Texas Children's Hospital
Professor of Surgery and Pediatrics
  Baylor College of Medicine

CHARLES D. FRASER, JR., MD

Ana Cecilia,

Thirty years have passed since I first met you, and for all that time, not once have I seen you give up when faced with the adversities you've encountered in your life.

You are one of the oldest people alive who have survived the congenital heart condition known as Single Ventricle, associated with many more cardiovascular defects which you have had since birth. There are very few human beings with your illness who, after more than 40 years of life, are still fighting fearlessly to make the most of each moment of their lives.

As we have discussed on many occasions, the difficulties and highly complex surgical interventions have never managed to defeat you. On the contrary, I remember each one of them, and they all made you grow, when faced with the possibility of an unsuccessful surgery and subsequent death. It sometimes seemed to me that you relished the sheer thrill of meeting head-on the adversities which you had to deal with.

Not only did you grow up under a constant threat to your life: besides that, you decided to give life to another human being, even against the recommendations of many of u,s who were only too aware of the high risk resulting from pregnancy. Given your particular conditions, a Caesarean was in no way a straightforward choice; and yet, now, more than two decades later, you can enjoy your daughter whom you brought into this world many years ago. Your dogged certainty and your unflinching conviction have always helped you to keep fighting for your life.

I have no doubt in my mind that, during these years, there have been many moments of near-despair and somber nights of private gloom, but they have never managed to break your will to live. Your faith has been firm and your perseverance indestructible.

Patients like yourself help the doctors learn from their experiences and pass them on to other patients, so that they too can be helped to face the long, arduous roads of their own sicknesses.

It was a privilege for me to have encountered you. You helped me recognize the fortitude of the human being, as I watched you recover from innumerable crises and setbacks, one after the other. God granted you the strength not to let yourself be defeated by pain. You taught me that, in order to survive, there is no other way.

May God continue to guide you in the years to come. I pray that you preserve peace in your soul, the smile that you have always had on your face, and the unshakable serenity which characterizes you. I hope that, by your example, you may continue to help many sick people cope with pain and ill health, in order for them to live a full life. May your example be constant proof that a person can be happy in spite of the cruel hand dealt by sickness. May your heart live forever and may you continue on this beautiful voyage that you began fifty years ago!

Dr. Jose Luis Assad

José Luis Assad Morell M.D.
University of Nuevo León
Medical School Monterrey, Mx.
With Suma Cum Laude Honors

Member of the American Collage DR. JOSE LUIS ASSAD
of Cardiology Society of Cardiac
Angeography and intervention

Head of Heart Institute at
Christus Muguerza Monterrey, Mx.

●CONDEMNED TO DIE

When I learned to walk hand-in-hand with Death whilst holding on tightly to Life with the other hand, I began to live life to the fullest.

I was sentenced to death at birth. So are we all, but my faulty heart left me in no doubt about it right from the moment I arrived in this world.

Death and I have come face to face many times, but we averted our eyes and turned our backs on each other. One day, when we were very close, we made a pact: I would walk alongside Death with my hand in hers, and with the other one, I would hold on to Life. I am still wary of her, but now, when she approaches, I am no longer afraid, and I feel at peace. She knows my hand won't let go of life and I'll enjoy it right up to my last breath.

I've been living this story for fifty years and wanting to tell my story for twenty-five of them. I know the exact time, because my daughter was ten months old when I had to be separated from her, not knowing whether I would ever see her again. I was on my way to my first open-heart surgery in the city of Houston, Texas. The prognosis was not encouraging, the chances of success, very slight. I was having trouble breathing and my strength was failing; my heart was giving up, but I certainly wasn't.

It was while I was in Intensive Care that I started to write. It was all I could do to convince the nurses that I needed pen and paper at two o'clock in the morning. Luckily for me, it's not easy to say "no" to someone who was in such bad physical shape as I was.

●HOW ARE YOU STILL ALIVE?

Science makes a diagnosis, but only faith and hope make a forecast.

EIGHT MONTHS OLD

When I arrived in Houston at the age of twenty- four, accompanied by my husband, I realized that the life I had lived, a normal one, just like any healthy person, was indeed met with surprise and astonishment. In the hospital there, for all the vast experience of its medical team, nobody had ever before seen a grown woman of my age, with my particular malformation, who had no previous surgical intervention, not to mention a woman who was the mother of a young daughter. No one could understand how on earth I was still alive!

"You had a child? How was that possible? How could you risk giving birth?" asked Doctor Michael Nihill, when he noted the scar from my Caesarean.

"I asked God for it and He granted it to me," was my reply.

For me, it was simple, but for him, it meant reviewing once more, all the investigations which had been carried out, the statistics which had emerged, and he was compelled to question everything he had learned during his years of training and medical practice.

The doctor looked perturbed. He cleared his throat before pronouncing that he had never seen anything like this. Very simply, it was totally beyond belief.

He asked to see more information about my case. The hospital had been in possession of my medical records since I was eleven months old. The doctor was so taken aback that he read assiduously every paper he could lay his hands on. It was by now a very old file, a dingy yellow color and with some pages written by hand.

●MY MEDICAL RECORDS

In many moments of my life, the only thing that has held me together has been my inner strength.

Now that he had my file in his hands, Doctor Nihill could familiarize himself with more details; that I was born in 1964 with a congenital heart condition, a malformation called "transposition of the great vessels and single ventricle, as well as pulmonary stenosis." This meant that the natural two-way circulation of blood, as in the case of a normal heart, was, in my case, not separate. Instead of a normal four-chambered heart, my heart had only three chambers. Because there was only one ventricle, the blue and red blood became mixed inside one common chamber and the body received blood which was low in oxygenation. This malformation causes cyanosis, which means, the act of turning blue. Besides this, there is a very large amount of blood in the single ventricle, which regularly fails at a very early age.

By then, I had studied the subject myself, and I knew that the death rate for young adults born with a single ventricular heart which has gone untreated, is very high. After talking for a while with the doctor, many questions and doubts entered my mind with regard to what happened next. My tiredness, cyanosis and shortage of breath were painfully obvious.

"My doctor in Monterrey said I needed surgery, that I'm not oxygenating well. What will happen if I don't get an operation now?" I asked the doctor.

"There is no time to waste. It's surprising that your physical state is as good as it is, but the truth is your heart is very tired and you're in desperate need of attention."

"Maybe my case isn't so bad, or somehow my body has found its own balance. Until just recently, I'd never really suffered from shortage of breath. I feel quite healthy, really!"

The doctor just smiled in a mixture of admiration and downright amazement.

"The truth is that you are an extremely unique case. Seventy per cent of people with your condition die before they turn seventeen. You have a left-side single ventricle anatomy, and that has helped you. When the anatomy is of the right ventricle, fifty per cent of patients die at about four years of age. The most common causes are arrhythmia, heart failure and sudden death. Actually, it's incredible to see you looking so well, even though you might not believe me."

"All of that is news to me. At least, I had no idea I could be one of those few cases."

"It'll be hard to find anyone else like you, believe me. By the way, how's the baby? Was it a normal birth?"

"Oh yes, doctor, she was born healthy, albeit very tiny, but without any complications."

"You are such a special case, I'm sure there's lots you could tell us. We want to hear your story, take care of you and keep an eye on your daughter. Well, we cardiologists and surgeons have a lot to discuss before we can decide on any kind of solution, but there is absolutely no doubt that you need an operation."

"How urgent is it?"

"We'll try to schedule it for in four or five days time. Whatever you do, don't leave town!"

My husband and I exchanged glances and kept quiet. Neither of us had been expecting to hear this. We hadn't imagined that my health problems could be due to me having such a delicate heart.

Later, I phoned my parents to tell them that I wouldn't be going back to Monterrey any time soon. We talked about who we could ask to take care of Ana Paula, as I had to have my parents near me, and, in any case, there was no way they were going to leave me on my own. The following day, they joined me in Houston.

Some years later, I went for a medical check-up and I was just sitting there waiting to be called in, along with my parents, Sandra, my sister, and my brother, Enrique Luis. I overheard a conversation which got my attention. Two men and a woman were vehemently discussing the state of health of a family member. The woman was bemoaning the person's fate and couldn't understand why this relative had to suffer so much.

This got me thinking, and I realized that this is how we sometimes live our lives. We feel so sorry for what happens to others or ourselves, or for what doesn't happen to us, or for what might or might not have been. We spend so much time complaining about everything, that we seem to miss the real point, which is that we need to learn from these events, instead of letting these valuable opportunities to become better people just pass us by. I have to say that, in my case, it was different. I don't remember one moment in my life when I consciously complained about having been born with a heart problem which would, after all, significantly limit my everyday life. I just accepted it as something normal and, anyway, we're all different, and each of us can be prone to some ailment, whereas others are not, for whatever reason. In any case, my parents made a point of not letting me feel sorry for myself.

I was eight years old when I first became aware of my congenital heart condition. Whilst not understanding how the world worked, I did decide then and there to live life intensely, seeing as it appeared that I wasn't going to live for ever, like everyone else. Comparing myself with other people was a waste of time. I had what I had, and I was who I was. The problem was when people, especially my parents, treated me differently. They wanted to protect me from things, and I couldn't see why I needed protection. Their intention was not to give me special treatment, but it was inevitable with so many visits to the doctor's.

I was constantly being taken to the doctor's. My teachers were told about my physical condition and made certain allowances for me which I never asked for and which I never really understood. I felt so well, I just thought it was ridiculous to treat people as if they were sick when they so obviously weren't. That was my life, and those were my feelings during my childhood and adolescence. It hardly ever occurred to me to use this to my advantage, except, perhaps, when I wanted to annoy my brother and sister when we were little, if they happened to have said something about my nails or the color of my lips.

My mother tells me that whenever I used to get sick, I was the one who would stay cheerful and put a smile on my face and make jokes with whoever came to visit me. The inner strength that kept me going was my will to live. I fought as hard as I could not to feel bad and to get better as quickly as I could. I believed that sickness was all in the mind, so, if I didn't think about it, then it didn't exist.

If I had seen myself as a sick person or someone with a physical limitation, I'm sure I wouldn't be here now to tell my story. My positive thinking didn't allow my body to get sick or to experience sickness. This wasn't by chance- it was, and is, choice, a change of mentality.

It's what I am, and not what I have, that makes me who I am.

A series of unlikely events has allowed me to continue here. Perhaps it had to be this way, so that I could convince others that life was important. What I instinctively knew as a young girl, I now know and can confirm unequivocally- enjoying the journey and being grateful brings about great changes in our lives.

●BIRTH

Should you ever doubt true love, just remember what a mother is capable of doing for her child.
MY PARENTS

My mother has always been a very beautiful woman. Even as a little girl, she attracted attention. She met my father when she was barely fourteen. He was a handsome young man, tall and slim. Even today, you can appreciate how good-looking he was in his youth, just like my mother. They both had five younger siblings. They make a lovely couple.

They were young when they got married; she was just nineteen and he was twenty-six. Recently, they celebrated fifty years of marriage. Thanks to some old films we found, we could see that the love they showed for each other back then, and the way they looked at each other, can still be seen, even today.

When I remember some of the difficult moments in their relationship that I was a witness to, those occasions when life really puts you to the test, I do admire how they managed to overcome the stress of having to deal with me while, at the same time, bringing up their other children.

We went through some tough times financially, and my mother would sew clothes for my sister and me. She always dressed us like princesses. It was she who spurred my father on to better himself, and he never failed to be a great example, both as a human being and in his professional life.

My father was the protective husband and provider, and my mother saw to it that everything ran smoothly in the home, thanks to her being a good organizer. With her lively mind, and being such a capable woman, she unfailingly supported my father and helped him become the successful man he is today. She always regretted that my grandfather wouldn't let her continue her studies, on the grounds that she was going to get married. I know my mother could have been the great architect she always dreamed of being. Today, she is totally at home with the new technology and is often known to share her knowledge with the other family members.

They began their married life with all the excitement and anticipation of any young couple in love, and they could never have imagined what their life together would be like within just a couple of years. Their first child was Sandra, a beautiful little girl whose eyes radiated light and joy, and the first grandchild on both sides of the family. I was born fifteen months later.

It had been a normal full-term pregnancy. When I was first placed in my mother's arms, she saw a lovely little girl, albeit with a skin tone somewhat darker than expected. Not that that was necessarily a bad thing; it was just that she didn't understand where the dark complexion came from, seeing that both my parents are fair-skinned. My arrival was, in any case, a great blessing, and they were delighted with their second daughter.

After four or five days, my mother noticed that I seemed unusually tired for a newborn baby. My breathing would become very accelerated and I would just stop eating. Comparing me with my sister, mother knew that something was not right. As she was still convalescing, my father and my maternal grandmother, Chagüita, took me to see a doctor, and were told I was suffering from a heart murmur, which didn't seem to be a cause for concern and explained the purplish colour I had at birth and the darkish skin tone. For one or two days, everyone felt more reassured, as it didn't appear to be anything serious.

My parents were worried, and exhausted by having to wake up frequently to feed me, and then seeing my little body panting so hard, whilst turning purple with the mere effort of eating. They embarked on a never-ending search for other doctors' evaluations. My mother was scared and confused; hardly surprising, since she had no experience of children with heart problems, nor had there been any history of such cases in the family.

I was baptized just a few days after my birth on December 12th.1964. My parents' great friends, Oscar and Dora, acted as my godparents, and they shared the family's concerns about my health. They were always ready to offer comfort in the early years, as it became more and more evident that there was something seriously wrong. Childless themselves in those days, they relished their role as godparents and looked upon me as their first daughter. Even though they did have two children of their own some years later, they always looked on me fondly as their first daughter, another member of the family, and that very special friendship has endured right up to today.

The days went by, and signs of my increasing tiredness were becoming more obvious. I was feeding every hour, but would get so exhausted in a matter of minutes that I would stop eating and fall asleep, leaving me hungry all the time. Understandably, I cried constantly. Then I would wake up again, desperately start drinking from the bottle, only to be too tired to continue and fall asleep again. These were without doubt extremely trying times for my mother, who was only twenty-one, and who had an eighteen-month-old daughter to attend to. My father had to go to work, of course, and so things became increasingly tense within the family home.

After various weeks of searching for answers, they decided to take me to Mexico City, helped by my dear Uncle Esaú, himself a doctor and working on his specialty there. He was always a great support, right up to the end of his life.

We made the long journey by train, as the cost of the airfare was prohibitive. I was now four months old. My sister was left in the loving care of my grandparents, Chagüita, which is what my maternal grandmother was affectionately called, and Grandma Nena, my father's mother. Even so, it was heart-wrenching for my parents to be separated from Sandra for the very first time. When we finally arrived in Mexico City, I was admitted into the Children's Hospital, where I was eventually to stay for a full ten weeks.

My mother was welcomed into the home of two aunts on my father's side, whom, in fact, she had never met before, but who offered her a place to sleep and a comfortable home. Meanwhile, my father returned to his work in Monterrey.

Aunts Leonor and Virginia Montfort lived together and led busy lives, being out at work all day, not leaving much time for chatting with my mother or strengthening family ties. They were also quite a lot older than her, but at least she could arrive home each night and prepare herself a hot meal, exchange a few words with them, and generally enjoy a taste of normal home life to relieve her from the stress of the day, so they were a true blessing for her in those very difficult times.

In the mornings, the aunts would drive my mother to hospital on their way to work. Visiting hours were strictly adhered to: ten o'clock in the morning and four o'clock in the afternoon, each visit lasting no more than one hour. Whenever possible, one of the aunts would pick up my mother from the hospital to take her home; otherwise, she would take a taxi. She would sit patiently, hour after hour, in the waiting room, sometimes making the wait more tolerable by devoting herself to silent prayer. If there weren't any other patients' relatives to talk to, she would just focus on the hands of the clock on the wall until they arrived at ten on the dot, at which time she would get up and head straight for the doors of the nursery in the Intensive Care Unit. This pattern was repeated in the afternoon, day after day, week after week.

She couldn't stay with me, as the nursery was full of cribs for the other young patients. I can imagine her desperation, sitting there in the waiting room, counting the minutes and hours till she was allowed to be at my side for just a moment, before once more having to abandon her child to strangers. Who was there to console her in those endless days?

She ate what she could in the hospital, spending as little money as possible, and enduring the hours till four o'clock finally came around. She listened at length to people's tales of woe. The relatives cried and bemoaned their fate, whilst my mother did what she could to stay strong, even offering comfort herself to many. She shared with them her faith and her trust in God, if only to lift their spirits. Nearly all of them were older but, even so, they listened to her and, in return, supported her with kind words.

All of this period seemed eternal. Without yet knowing the full extent of my sickness, she knew it was serious. The stories she heard in the waiting-room were heart-wrenching; she had no choice but to hope and trust that the diagnosis for her daughter would not be so bad after all.

The doctors wouldn't release me, as I was very much underweight. I had so little strength for sucking at the bottle that they had to feed me with a dropper. I was very thin, and so, all the doctors insisted that, until I gained some weight, they couldn't do the necessary tests, let alone allow me to go home.

These were weeks of sadness and anguish for each one of us; all, in our own different ways, were suffering from the sense of abandonment. My mother was missing her elder daughter, a little girl bounding with energy and good health, full of life, who was now out of reach, hundreds of miles away from her, while she had to spend her days alone in a waiting-room, with neither daughter nor husband. My father was alone in Monterrey, without his wife and his two daughters. Sandra was with her grandparents, but missing the everyday life she shared with her parents and little sister, although, fortunately, my father did take the time to go and see her every day after work. And then there was me; in the nursery, surrounded by strangers. I was so tiny, and hardly realized what was going on, but I was aware that those I loved most in this world had, for some reason, left me there, alone.

The waiting was awful. Everyone desperately hoped for some good news as to what my future held, and were trusting that somehow I would get better. My mother's pain and exhaustion were relieved, to some extent, by my father's visits on weekends. He would take a bus every Friday after work, and travel through the night to be with my mother and me on Saturday and Sunday. When the weekend was over, back he would go through the night to arrive in Monterrey by six o'clock Monday morning, just in time to have a shower and go to work.

One of the things that I admire about my mother was what she did around the time of her birthday, which happened to fall during this long and wearisome episode. She decided to use some of the birthday money she had been given by my grandparents to buy a bus ticket to

Monterrey and to be with Sandra for two days. This would be her best birthday present ever, just to be with her daughter. It took courage to make that journey, as it meant leaving me in the care of the doctors and nurses, so when it was time to leave, it was amidst tears and sobs that she begged them to look after me and spoil me with lots of cuddles in her absence. I was oblivious to what was happening, but a mother feels that, if she's not there, her child can't possibly be fine. Even so, in spite of these misgivings, she knew that, of course, I would come to no harm and wouldn't even realize that she wasn't there, being still very young. And so, she put on a brave face and set out on her trip to Monterrey on Tuesday March 16th, 1965, to be with Sandra on the Wednesday and Thursday.

By the time Friday came around, back she was, as always, at her post in the hospital, waiting to see me once again. Her trip had filled her with much-needed energy and strength to keep her going a bit longer.

After almost six weeks of observation in hospital and performing a complete catheterization and angiocardiogram, the doctors were ready to meet with my parents and explain the nature of my sickness: I had only one ventricle with transposition of great vessels. Unfortunately, the technology in those days and the understanding of my complex heart condition were not enough to permit any corrective surgery, so the only recommendation was to wait and see.

The prognosis was far from encouraging: as regards life expectancy, the chances were that I would not live many more years, ten at the most; I would, possibly, not even have the strength to walk; my growth would be stunted, and I would perhaps have to spend all my days confined to a crib.

This pronouncement was so utterly devastating; it was more than anyone could bear. My mother heard what they were saying and just cried and cried, refusing to believe any of it, unable to process the words.

"I don't understand anything of what you're saying. Wait and see? Wait for what? What can we expect? Is she going to die? How much time has she got left? What are we going to do? I don't understand you!" shouted my mother amidst tears of desperation.

"All we can do is wait and see how she evolves. Don't build up your hopes, as your daughter's physical condition is extremely complex."

My father held on to my mother, trying to console her. She couldn't stop crying. The news was far more terrible than she'd ever imagined.

All those dreams and plans and longings which any parent cherishes for his or her children seemed to vanish in the blink of an eye. Their daughter's life was to be cut short. Now they had two choices: either to sink into the depths of feeling sorry for themselves, or to enjoy every moment they could, while they still had her, and give her the best possible life. Their hearts weighed down by sadness, and yet holding on to a tiny glimmer of hope for a miracle, they bundled me up, and we all returned to Monterrey two weeks later, when I'd finally managed to gain a little weight and thereby have permission to be discharged.

FIRST YEARS

If you want to appreciate the flower, learn to ignore the thorns.
SANDRA AND I.

My parents decided to hope for the best in the midst of so much pain and fear of the unknown. Thanks to their enormous faith in God, they stayed strong and trusted that I would be fine. They never stopped fighting for their little girl: this tiny warrior who seemed ready to stand up to any obstacle. They believed in me, they had faith in God, and I proved to them that they were right to do so.

A short time ago, I visited Doctor Charles D. Fraser Jr., Chief of the Department of Congenital Heart Surgery at Texas Children's Hospital, and his words confirmed to me the enormous role that the parents play: "The atmosphere and love that surrounded you were instrumental, in many ways, to your arriving at the point where you are today. Someone trusted that your future would be marvelous. Your family, and the circumstances you grew up in, contributed greatly to the fortunate position you find yourself in now today."

I am sure that much of my physical and emotional health is a direct result of how I was raised and of the confidence which my parents and relatives exuded. Very often, words are just that: words. However, thoughts and convictions, as well as the showing by example, can be perceived without a word being spoken; of that I have no doubt. Besides, I know that my way of being was a gift from God, which prepared me for the struggle I would have to face.

God provided me with the tools. We are all born with the necessary equipment to face our difficulties in the best way possible. What we do with these tools is what, ultimately, makes the difference. Any path, however unlike that of everyone else´s, has both its difficulties and its unique beauty. I am sure that it is impossible to get good results from negative thoughts. In time, I began to understand that the words I used determined who I was and where I was going.

When my godparents told me what my parents went through after I was born, I realized the far-reaching power of faith when all seems lost. Thanks to their absolute certainty that God would not abandon them, they were capable of standing firm, never doubting that the prognosis could indeed change.

My father devoted himself to supporting my mother. He let nobody see his fears, his pain, his anguish. He protected her at all times, making sure she didn't feel alone. He made it his priority to provide strength to his wife as she cared for their two daughters. Sometimes, I think my mother's inner strength stems from the mutual courage she and my father gave each other, both in their own way, and, between the two of them, they provided me with an environment where I could enjoy a normal life. The fact that they never gave up on me made all the difference.

When I reached eleven months and just weighed a mere eight kilos, my parents decided to take me to Houston for a second opinion. The months prior to this had been tough, mainly because they found it so difficult to feed me; however, I was a lively, restless little thing who just wanted to play. The doctors presented them with a more thorough diagnosis. The situation was basically the same: I had transposition of the great vessels and single ventricle, as well as pulmonary stenosis.

Years later, I found out that this stenosis was a stroke of luck. It was a hard growth that had formed on the lungs which prevented the blood from flowing to the lungs with what would be an abnormal, and thereby harmful, force. Since there was only one ventricle, the force with which the heart pumped the blood to the lungs was much greater. Thanks to the stenosis, the lungs were protected. Today, any patient with a similar problem undergoes an operation soon after birth which, in effect, achieves something resembling that stenosis.

At that moment, this seemed to be just one more threat to my health. My oxygenation was around eighty per cent, instead of the expected hundred per cent; the doctors concluded, however, that I looked quite good, all things considered. They discharged me from hospital on the understanding that I would undergo strict medical observation; and yet, not even in Houston was there any possibility of a completely corrective surgery or even any special medication for me.   "Mr. and Mrs. Gonzalez, we shall have to wait and trust that Ana Cecilia's body will hold up and stay alive until medical science finds a solution."

"But what's the general prognosis for children like her?" asked my mother.

"Most start to experience problems just before puberty. Some don't even live that long. We trust that her case is different. Each one is."

We returned home, and so my parents began the long saga of trying to keep me healthy and well-fed. My mother had to coax me into eating, which was quite an art in itself. She would try to give me my favorite foods in the hope that I would gain weight. In spite of my round, chubby face, I was still very thin.

I was two years old when Enrique Luis was born. I don't recall that day, but I do remember the great fun it was, before too long, having him as my little brother. My mother now had her hands full with two daughters, one aged three and the other aged two, and a newborn baby. She thanked God that he was calm and healthy.

Each child presented his or her own challenge. Mine was the issue of my feeding. Sandra and I would sit at the same table, with the same amount of food in front of us, and I always ended up eating less than half of mine.

"Look, Ana Cecilia! How delicious! Eggs with ham and beans, just what you like. Let's see who eats theirs up first, you or Sandra."

"Mmm. Looks wonderful! I'm going to win! " I shrieked. I would start to wolf down my food, as I was very competitive and always wanted to win. But in no time at all, I was exhausted and had to admit defeat.

"I don't want any more, Mommy. I don't mind if Sandra wins. I've had enough egg. I'll let her win."

My mother would try and feed me, but it was no use. I simply didn't want any more food. For Sandra, these contests were of no importance. She only joined in because my Mom asked her to. She didn't argue and didn't mind if she won or lost. She just wanted to keep everyone happy and help her little sister.

Peace isn't a state of mind;
it is that tranquillity and trust
that only dwell within the soul.
MY MOTHER, ENRIQUE LUIS AND I

MY FIRST MEMORY

A bad childhood memory can stay in your heart for years. Heal it, so that it doesn't affect your journey through life.

My first memory of suffering and pain was when I was four years old. I was having my usual medical check-up in Mexico City, where I was hospitalized for a few days. My mother and godparents, Oscar and Dora, went to see me in visiting hours which were from ten to eleven in the morning and four to five in the afternoon. They gave me a doll which was all the latest rage-it had a cord on its back which, when pulled, made it start to cry. It nestled perfectly into my little arms. The time came for my visitors to leave, and I shouted and pleaded with them to stay, but to no avail. The further away they went, the more I cried.

I can still see so clearly in my mind's eye the image of them going away, but it was only many years later when I could appreciate how they must have felt on having to leave me. For me, it meant just one thing -I had been abandoned.

I leaned back in my crib, crying inconsolably, hugged my doll and started to pull the cord so that she would cry with me. When I became tired from shedding so many tears, I made her cry, and so we continued until I fell asleep. Later on, some doctors came to see me. One of them took hold of my doll.

"What's she called?"

"Dora, like my auntie," I said without hesitation.

Dora had only been with me a few hours, but I was already very fond of her. While the doctor was playing with the doll, he pulled the cord so hard, it came off, and Dora stopped crying.

"You've broken her! Fix her! Give her to me!"

"Hang on, don't worry. I'll mend it right away."

"Let me have her. I want her to cry."

"Look. I'll take her with me, and tomorrow I'll bring her back, all mended."

I felt as if he had wrenched from me a part of my heart, that tiny part that wasn't broken. I held out my arms, begging for the doll.

"Don't take her! Give her to me!"

It was useless. He wanted to repair the damage, even if it meant leaving me without Dora. He tried to win me over by giving me a popsicle, and then he left, taking my doll with him.

And so I spent the night, missing Dora terribly, as she was the only one who could share my imprisonment in that crib, the only one I could hug. I cried and felt sad, alone and abandoned once again. Even today, as a grown woman, I can recall only too well my loneliness that night. I tried not to sob like the other children, in the hope that, if I was a good girl, they would take me out of my crib and let me run around and explore my surroundings, but it didn't work.

The next day, the doctor arrived holding my doll, which he hadn't been able to fix, so, unable to give me back the doll whose tears made me feel better, he gave me another popsicle instead. I hugged Dora and vowed I would never lend her to anyone, ever again. It just wasn't the same now that I had no one to take turns with me to cry.

I tried to explain this to my parents when they came to see me.

"Mommy, I want Dora to cry again, and the doctor broke her."

"Doctors are here to make you well, not to break toys. Did you break it?"

"No, Mommy, it wasn't me. It was the doctor."

She took me out of the crib to have a little walk. She didn't seem too interested in the subject of Dora and, actually, neither was I when I was with my mother. Whenever my parents arrived, I felt my rescuers had arrived, my liberators. How painful it was when they left. I shouted and kicked to stop them putting me back in the crib, which was too deep for me to escape from without help.

"We'll be back soon, we won't be long. Don't cry, we're not going to leave you," my mother tried to reassure me.

"Why are you leaving me here? Don't go! You're mean! Mean! It wasn't me that broke Dora, Mommy!" I shouted and sobbed as they walked away.

My mother tells of how my father would cling on tightly to her hand and, once they were out of view, the tears she'd been holding back would burst out like a tidal wave, as she sobbed uncontrollably.

"I can't stand this. How can I tell her she's very sick, that I don't want to leave her, that I'm not a bad mother and I love her with all my heart and soul?" she cried out.

My father would try to console her as best he could, holding back his own grief, as off they went, wrapped in each other's arms.

When you are young, a few days can seem like weeks. Now, I know it was just a few days that I was there, and not the eternity that I imagined. Still, no one could ever understand how very painful those moments were for that small child.

FOUR YEARS OLD.

*MY FRIEND ANTONIA PRESENTED
ME WITH A REPLICA OF DORA
FOR MY FIFTIETH BIRTHDAY.*

VISITS TO MY GRANDMOTHER'S

Sometimes, fear is like a dragon.
When you confront it, you realize
it was a figment of your imagination.

I was five when my kindergarten organized a special school assembly. We were going to represent the origins of our national flag. "My chance to be a true performer," I thought. That day, I woke up very excited. From when we were very little, my mother had instilled in us the habit of getting our clothes ready at night for the following day, so the first thing I saw was my costume laid out on the stool of my dressing-table.

My mother did my hair and placed little flowers entwined in my braids. My costume was perfect for the occasion, as we had to wear indigenous dress, and I loved my sandals, as my mother always made sure they were not open at the front, so no one could see my toenails which were knobbly and purple.

The teacher arrived, placed us in our positions for the performance and told us to take off our shoes, as we had to be barefoot and absolutely still. The mere thought of this filled me with horror; no one must see my toenails.

Years later, I would understand why my nails were like that. But, back then, just being a child and trying to understand why my nails were so different from everybody else's, I could only conclude that I was adopted. There was no other explanation that I could think of, as, otherwise, how was it possible that I was so different from my parents and siblings? Whenever I felt cold, my skin transformed: it became totally purple, and my lips and nails turned practically black. Needless to say, it didn't escape my attention that the other children couldn't help noticing and staring. Not only that, each doctor I saw seemed to feel he had the right to take all the time in the world to examine them very closely. They would take my hand and apply pressure on my nails to see if they changed color when they let go.

Nobody asked me if I was OK with this. At every appointment, the first thing the doctors did was to examine me. They placed their stethoscopes all over my chest, and touched me as if I were a toy, all the while talking to my parents. Nobody asked my permission to lift up my blouse in order to listen to my heart. They touched me without ever considering whether I wanted them to or not. It's true, I was only five or six years old, but my mother had inculcated in me a certain modesty, which made me feel decidedly uncomfortable. It would have been so easy for them to ask if I minded, to check with me first. I'd also been taught to be respectful so I kept quiet and obeyed, notwithstanding the clear sensation of being abused.

My clothes were removed so that they could measure, weigh and evaluate me. Doctors put wires on my chest and legs when they wanted to perform an electrocardiogram. They rubbed a cold gel all over my torso so they could stick some suction caps on me, which hurt. All I saw was wires and more wires on every part of my body.

"Doctor, I don't like that. It hurts."

"Don´t move. Keep still or else we'll have to do it all again."

"I want to take this off - it stings, it hurts, it's cold."

"Nurse, take hold of her hands to prevent her from moving, will you? Now, little girl, you don't want to stay like that all day, do you, without moving? Well, do you?"

"No," I would say as tears rolled down my cheeks.

"Right then. Don't move."

They left me on the examining couch, nearly naked, with nothing on but my little lacy panties, while the doctors left the room to discuss the case with my parents. They didn't even bother to close the door. They just left me there: no clothes on and within view of anyone who passed by. I was just there. Nobody took any notice of me, nobody covered me up; I was just a child, a sick little girl, exposed and abandoned. Today, I can understand that all the adults there were scared, and were thinking of all manner of things except explaining to me what was happening, considering my feelings, my modesty. And it most certainly never occurred to them to ask me if I minded them examining my body. For them, I was just another case to be investigated, another life to save-they couldn't see the frightened little girl who was feeling so very much abused.

Horrible images passed through my mind as I sat there, exposed. It occurred to me that maybe I was the daughter of a strange creature, like Godzilla of the TV cartoons. Well, her nails were like mine: big, knobbly and ugly. Besides, her skin was very dark, just like mine was occasionally. Perhaps that explained the never-ending interest of the doctors in my case. Now, I could speak, of course, unlike that gigantic animal. I could communicate and really, to all intents and purposes, I was just like all the other humans. And yet, I was different: my skin became transformed and I turned another color.

I felt a great need to hide my nails from view so that the others wouldn't find out the truth about me. And what was that truth? I didn't know; I just knew that my nails revealed that I had another strange identity, one that I found hard to come to terms with. I wanted to feel like I was a part of my family, to belong, just like my brother and sister did, and yet, I could never help feeling that there was something different about me.

Admittedly, it was rather odd to be the daughter of a dinosaur, but, at that age, I honestly believed it to be true. How else could I explain so many differences? They were the only creatures who had fingers and toes like mine. My brother and sister would just look at me; sometimes, when we'd fallen out, usually through my own fault, they would make fun of my fingers. That was so humiliating! I felt so betrayed. The good thing was that they never ever did that in front of the other children. It all stayed within the family.

My Mom scolded them if she ever saw them laughing at me or making jokes about my fingers. Still, she wasn't always around when I needed her. She couldn't be there to come to my defence whenever a child at school was unkind to me, and I usually kept it to myself. It was only in the privacy of our home that I could run to my parents and tell tales, and then they would scold my poor brother and sister who, I knew, adored me.

I was so naughty that, sometimes, their only way to take revenge was to make fun. Nowadays, I can see how many of my tantrums and fits of anger were caused by my feelings of insecurity. I wanted to stand out, be the center of attention, make sure I had a place amongst these humans whom I shared my life with,, and not with the monsters who I imagined might well be my biological parents. I just didn't understand what was happening to me; deep down inside, I felt there was something different about me, and because of that insecurity, I would not let anyone or anything get the better of me.

That's why, on the day of my school presentation, I was acutely aware of each one of my toenails, and especially the ones on my big toes. When the other children's families walked around our tableau, what I had most feared actually happened. They didn't see the beautiful hair arrangement my mother had so painstakingly done for me, or the pretty little flowers so perfectly scattered here and there. Oh no! All they saw were my feet! I wanted to disappear, to hide my feet, just like the ostrich hides its head and then moves it from side to side, trying to bury it in the sand so no one would see it. My plan, unfortunately, was foiled by my teacher, who returned me to my original place.

"Stand up straight and don't move!"

There I was again, stripped and vulnerable, forced to stand there while everyone looked me up and down, just like the doctors did each time they examined me. And, like the obedient little girl that I was, I stayed absolutely still, like a marble statue.

That was when I closed my eyes tightly and resorted to the escape route that always came to my rescue when something was hurting. It was like the disappearing act of the famous escape artist, Houdini. I did this with the doctors, the people at school, and with my friends. By concentrating really hard, , I "vanished". My motionless body was still in position for all to see, but what they didn't know was that I was no longer in the school tableau. In the blink of an eye, I was standing in front of my grandmother Chagüita's house. There was no need for me to knock, as she opened the door straightaway, as if expecting me, and hugged me warmly.

Sometimes, she opened the front door, and, passing through, I could smell the scent of newly-polished wooden furniture. Everything in the house was neat and tidy, and her perfume wafted in the air, wherever I went. There were no magical creatures there; the smells and colors were as they had always been, and it was there that I found what I so desperately needed just then: a big hug from my grandmother, - a big hug from her, which I could enjoy just by closing my eyes.

When she opened the garage door, which was round the back of the house, we went through a small passage way before entering the main house. It always smelt of egg yolk and cardboard boxes. I could never forget that smell.

There was a small room where she kept the eggs that came from my grandfather's poultry farm. He always took her the biggest ones, and she sold them cut-price to cake shops or gave some to the nuns. The poultry farm had her name: Chagüita's Egg Farm. I supposed that, since she was the owner, she could decide who to sell, or simply give, the eggs to.

It was so special for me to help her put the eggs into the right cartons. She taught me how to do it ever so carefully, as they were so fragile. At these times, all my restless energy was momentarily tamed, so I could do my job with the greatest of care. I separated the cracked eggs from the good ones, and also the large eggs, as they were most likely double yolks and had to be put in a separate carton.

I felt so close to Chagüita in these moments. She made me feel useful and, more importantly, up to the task of helping her with one of the most delicate operations: not letting any eggs slip out of my hands and smash on the floor.

She never failed to have my hot chocolate waiting for me, along with a scrumptious doughnut. She would carry this to our working area and I would take a sip and put a few eggs in their right place. This was the best way for me to relax: just being with her. When I was there, I had no need to compete with anyone, I could move around freely; I felt enveloped, protected, loved, pain-free, and there was no need for me to fight off intrusive looks and cruel words.

The time came to leave and, as always, I snuggled into her arms, which she wrapped round me like a blanket of pure human warmth. I kissed her goodbye, and she made me feel the way only grandmothers can.

"You look beautiful, you are the prettiest girl in the whole wide world!" she said.

When all the children's parents had finished walking around, I opened my eyes, only to see that everyone had left, and we were finally allowed by the teacher to return to our classroom. If I hadn't gone with my grandmother, I could not have borne the weight of all those stares, nor have the strength to get through the rest of the day.

FIVE YEARS OLD.

●CRUEL ANSWERS

To give thanks for everything I have is one of the best lessons I have learned from my parents.

In spite of any difficulties I might have had, I was always a very happy child, and roared with laughter if anything struck me as funny. However, as the years passed by, I understood that when we are children, there is so much to discover, that we express our opinions and thoughts just as they occur to us. We can be cruel, and we ask questions out of curiosity, not worrying about the long-term effects of our comments; we don't realize that, when we target someone as different, we can affect them or mark them for the rest of their lives. I haven't forgotten the sensation of having those children and parents looking at my feet and hands. I was so painfully conscious of my purple nails, shaped like drum sticks. Today, I'd like to hug that little girl, dry her tears as they roll down her cheeks, and tell her that this, unlikely as it may seem, will eventually pass.

I couldn't go to my parents to complain and tell them how I felt. That was a battle I alone could fight: something that was part of me that I had to face on my own and sort out by myself if I wanted to survive. Anyway, I could just hear my mother's reply: "Too bad. That's just what you've been dealt with. What do you want me to do about it? You have to learn to live with what you've got and be grateful."

Of course, my Mom's reaction reflected her own pain. Feeling powerless to protect me from the harsh realities I was confronting, forced her to come out with comments that seemed harsh and cold, but her love was always unconditional. I'm sure that, as soon as her back was turned, she would hide somewhere, out of sight, to dry her own tears, and I do know that whatever she said to me, she would repeat the exact same words to herself. That was her private cross to bear.

And so, that's exactly what I did; I learned and grew and tried to keep laughing. My mother was right. Her response to me was very wise and helped me get on with life. I learned that, inside us, are voices that are best ignored, and we should just let ourselves be guided by the inner silence. Also, my own suffering made me acutely sensitive to other people's pains, and I could so easily empathize with them. I became my siblings' best protector, too. I may have fought with them at home but outside, if anyone was mean to them, I would be the first to spring to their defence.

Sandra and I were always given the same presents. If someone bought her a doll, I got one too, to avoid any conflicts. The one I remember most was Juanita Perez, a lovely doll, and there was a specialist store in the center of town where they sold clothes for her, so it was there that Granny Chagüita often took us to buy new garments for Juanita's wardrobe.

Sandra was happy just to dress her doll, arrange her hair and put her shoes on. I imitated everything she did. I wanted to do what she did and have what she had. This created quite a problem for her, as she didn't get the chance to have her own things without feeling overshadowed by her younger sister. I had so much fun with Sandra, as she was creative and always inventing new ways of making things prettier. She beautified, decorated, sketched and painted everything. I tried to do the same, but I soon had to give up. My talents in that area were definitely limited!

Granny Nena taught us to make clothes for our dolls. We often enjoyed an afternoon at her house, learning to sew, cook, carve and paint furniture, and we spent hours playing Lotto. Sandra enjoyed these visits, especially as they gave her the chance to create and make things by hand.

I often pestered Sandra to join me as I explored new places; I just couldn't stay still. I loved investigating and discovering things. For me, that was fun. She was so much calmer than me, enjoying her home and playing with her tea sets. If it hadn't been for her, I might not have learned to take some things quite so calmly.

The fact that I had a brother who I could play outside with was a big help. It was my idea that we climb up the electricity poles to get a bird's eye view of the town. We couldn't actually get up very high, but, even so, we persevered. We climbed on rooftops, went investigating the nearby hill and played hide 'n seek.

Nowadays, he says I was the "troublemaker" of the family, and I suppose he's right. If he ever got into trouble, it was usually me that was behind it all.

I had to tell him everything. I couldn't stand him not knowing we were going to have a baby sister. Two days before Christmas, 1970, I went to wake him up.

"Come on, our Christmas present has arrived early. Get up quickly!"

"What is it? What is it? Tell me!" he shouted, really excited, no doubt imagining some toy truck or bicycle.

We ran downstairs, giggling nervously, and there she was: my sister Marcela, a beautiful girl, just three days old. Her hair was like little rays of sunshine, her eyes huge, round emeralds. She looked like a precious little doll. Marcela gave me the chance to play at being Mommy. I used to pretend that she was my daughter and I took care of her so tenderly, carrying her and feeding her. I enjoyed her so much. I don't know if she was exactly what my brother was hoping for, but I only know that for me she was the greatest Christmas present I could ever have imagined.

THERE IS NO STRENGTH MORE POWERFUL THAN THE WILL TO LIVE.
MARCELA, MY MOTHER AND I.

Besides this, I was always looking for ways to help the family whenever I could. I loved it when my mother had garage sales to make a few pennies from clothes or toys we had outgrown, but which were still in excellent condition. I loved collecting the money and particularly relished selling for the modest price of five or ten pesos some article my mother had paid up to a hundred pesos for. We were getting rid of things we couldn't use, and were helping others at the same to buy things at a bargain price.

Similarly, I always enjoyed helping stray dogs. I wanted to feed them, and I would insist on them all having their own names. This got me into trouble with my parents as we were constantly surrounded by these little animals every day at home. It seemed important to me to help them because, if I didn't, then probably no one would. Such was my insistence that my parents finally gave in and let me have the first of many little dogs we would enjoy. Motita was this little dog's name, and she bore some resemblance to a white French poodle, and was very playful indeed.

My mother often employed someone to help with the housework and look after us children when she wasn't there. The person I have fondest memories of, as we went through so much together, was Rosa.

I must have given Rosa her fair share of headaches. She was dark-skinned, had a round face and was a little on the plump side. She had a mass of curly hair, which was always covered with a pink and white polka dot headscarf. She seemed to tower over me.

"Rosa, you look just like the lady on the box of hot cakes: Aunt Jemima."

"Yes, that's me. I used to spend my time making hot cakes, which was when they took that photo of me. But now I have to look after you," she would say, as she chased my brother and me around the house to give us tickles.

My mother asked her to be especially watchful, to make sure I didn't get tired. But once my mother had gone out, there was no holding me down! I was into everything. Luckily for me, Rosa had the eye of a hawk and stopped me from getting into a lot of mischief. If it hadn't been for her, I'd probably have spent all my childhood being grounded.

"Don't climb on the roof, or your Mom'll tell you off!"

"Don't worry, Rosa. We'll be careful. We won't fall."

"Ana Cecilia! Don't run! You'll get tired and your lips will turn blue!"

"I'm not going to get tired. I can do this!"

I didn't put any limits on myself and used all the strength my body could muster in order to enjoy life. And if my body did happen to get tired, just so that I could keep on doing what I wanted to do, I could always call on my special resource that never let me down: my lust for life!

When we played Catch in the back yard, I was always the one to go first. I would chase after Sandra and Enrique Luis, but it was so hard to catch up with them. More often than not, Rosa would arrive, scoop me up and run with me in her arms so that I would win the race. It was such fun having her in the house!

I loved her very much. Enrique Luis and I invented a song we used to sing just to get her mad, so she'd give in and play with us. We'd go to the kitchen, perch ourselves at the breakfast bar while she was washing the dishes, and then we'd start:

"Rosa with pink balls on her head. Rosa with lots of balls on her head."

In a flash, she would turn round, we'd run away screaming, and she'd go after us until she caught us and punished us with lots of tickles. Well, the truth is, she' would tickle Enrique Luis like crazy, but, with me, she was always much more careful and just hugged me tight before letting me go.

Rosa was also my confidante. I told her I didn't enjoy summer because I had to wear sandals, which showed my ugly nails.

"Can I wear socks with my sandals?"

"No, no, it doesn't look nice. The main thing is to keep nice and cool. Just ignore the people when they start looking at your nails. They'll so often say things without thinking. You've got lovely hands and feet. Don't take any notice of them."

She also told me I looked a lot like my parents, which went a long way to convince me that I wasn't adopted after all. When I told her I thought I was the daughter of dinosaurs, or some strange creature, she laughed until her stomach hurt, and then she hugged me very lovingly and explained that that simply wasn't possible, so, little by little, I put it out of my mind.

FACING UP TO THE DIAGNOSIS

●I OPENED MY EYES

I chose to focus less on the dangers and hardships which lay across my path, and more on the chance of overcoming them, until I reached my destination.

Shortly after Marcela was born, the family moved to Mexico City due to my father's work, and we lived there for just eighteen months. It was now so much easier to have my regular check-ups at the Children's Hospital.

By this time, I was in second grade of Primary School and was a regular eight-year-old who enjoyed climbing, jumping, playing hide 'n seek and exploring the world around me. I didn't want to miss out on anything that the other children did, but the only difference was that, in my case, I was always exhausted by the end.

One day, my parents and I were coming back from another of those very disagreeable check-ups, and I asked them why they were always taking me to the doctor's instead of letting me play with my brother and sisters. And why, I wanted to know, did the doctors always insist on examining my nails so closely?

I wanted to believe that my nails were simply big and round, just like my Dad's. I knew they had nothing to do with me being Godzilla's daughter, as by this time, Rosa had dismissed that idea from my head. I now believed I was indeed my parents' child, and I loved it when anyone told my Mom that I looked like her or my father or one of the grandparents. So, what was going on? Why was it only me they took to the doctor's and not their other children?

"I don't understand why you let them do so many things to me. You know I don't like it! The doctors put all this cold gel on my chest, and then they leave these nasty marks. They hurt me and I'm tired of being the only one that has to go. Why is that?"

My Dad stayed quiet, and it was my Mom who answered.

"When you were born, you started to turn a dark purple color, so we took you to the doctor's to see what was going on. They realized that your heart is different from that of other children. You have a heart problem."

"But why is it different? I can't feel anything."

"You have a small complication, which is why you tire so easily, and it's why your nails are a bit thick and round-looking and turn blue like they do."

With my typical optimism, I immediately refused to believe it and reacted by trying to find a more logical reason than this very complicated one I was hearing. I wasn't Godzilla's daughter, I wasn't adopted, so there was no sense in what they were saying... at least, not yet.

"My nails are just like Daddy's, aren't they, Daddy? They're big like his, Mommy!"

He smiled.

"Of course, don't worry, darling. I'm sure that's what it is."

At that moment, a whole new chapter of my life story opened out before me. Some things started to make sense. At that age, it's difficult to imagine the reasons why we can be so different from others. But there it was! I was different from my sisters, and my brother, and my friends. It is certainly not easy for parents to have to try to explain to their children the details of this very complex heart condition, and even harder for a child to understand.

"Nobody knows how many years it'll take for you to get well again. The doctors say you have to take great care, so you don't start to feel bad. That's why we take you to so many check-ups", my mother continued.

I started to cry.

That day was probably the first and last time my parents saw me cry from the shock and anguish of knowing I was sick, that I was different from everyone else. They were amazed that I could actually understand that my heart was not normal, and I could finally find an explanation for so many things that, even at my young age, had already affected me so much.

"So that's why I always turn blue when I'm cold, and my fingernails and toenails and lips go nearly black? Is that why, Daddy?"

"Yes, it is. That's why you have to take great care when you get a cold. You must always listen to everything your mother and the doctors say, because if you do, you'll live a healthy life for many, many years to come."

Today, I must say, I admire my parents for how bravely they spoke to me. It must have been so hard to broach this subject and give this kind of news to their young daughter. I'm just in awe of how they could go on talking, whilst having to watch me cry my eyes out, and they still managed not to break down. Surely, only the immense love of a mother and a father could possibly explain this.

As I tried to digest what they were telling me, many questions popped into my mind. Am I going to die? What does "being sick" really mean? Will I never be able to grow into a woman, get married and have children? What'll happen if I die?

"Do my brother and sisters know about this, Mommy? Have you told them yet? Do Chagüita and Abuelita already know?"

"Your brother and sisters don't know yet. You can tell them if you like, but I think it's better if you don't mention any of this to your friends. There's no point in them knowing, is there? And yes, Chagüita and Abuela do know already."

"But I don't want everyone to know I'm sick!"

When I arrived home later that day, I told my mother I wanted to speak to Chagüita. My mother must have wondered what was going through my little head, and why I felt this sudden need to speak to her mother.

"Hello, Chagüita. Did you know I've got a heart problem?"

"Not really. Why? What's the matter?" she answered, not wanting to say more than was necessary.

"Well, it's just that I have this heart condition, and that's why my nails are ugly. Did you know that? Why didn't you tell me? Everyone seems to know except me!"

"Now, just a moment. The truth is that even the doctors didn't actually know what your problem was, but now they do, and they've told your parents. Don't worry. You'll be fine. We'll take good care of you. You'll see. You won't even notice anything wrong, as long as you follow the doctors' instructions."

"But you knew…"

I handed the phone over to my mother and went to bed. Deep down, I felt betrayed by my greatest ally: Chagüita, my haven, my one refuge where I could escape to and feel safe, and who I loved so much, had not said anything to me about all this.

I got into bed and pulled my blanket up around my ears. I turned to look at Sandra, who was decorating her notebook to take to school the next day.

"Sandra, did you know why I've got these knobbly, blue nails?"

"No. Why?"

"Because I've got a heart problem."

"Oh, are they going to operate on you so you get better? That's what some people do, and they're fine after that."

"I don't know. The doctors haven't said. Chagüita and Abuelita already knew, but I didn't."

"Well, you must pray a lot, and you'll see that God will make you better."

"Will you help me?"

"Of course I will."

She stopped what she was doing and got into bed with me. We started to pray. This was something we usually did with the family when we would get together in the evening in the downstairs library. We would read a passage from the Bible and say a prayer before going to sleep. But that night was different; it was just Sandra and I who prayed. She led the prayers and I followed suit. My big sister, at the grand age of nine, was alongside me, and I knew she was my ally, my friend, my trustworthy companion. We finally fell asleep, peaceful in the knowledge that everything would be fine.

That day, for the very first time since I can remember, I didn't lay out my clothes for the following day. Something had changed. I'd become aware of a reality that hadn't existed for me before.

49

My grandmother Chagüita was so concerned, she phoned me the next day to tell me she'd fly to Mexico City, just to be with me. I was so thrilled that I overlooked the fact that she had hidden my illness from me. Her visits to our house were always fun: she took us out, gave us pocket money to buy sweets, and played board games with us. Never a dull moment!

FEW DAYS AFTER I FOUND OUT ABOUT MY HEART.

I WON'T LIVE FOR EVER

A great part of the pain and fear
we feel dwells only in our thoughts.

What does an eight-year-old girl do when she discovers she won't live forever, how she imagines other children will?

I started to die by living each day intensely.

Right from the moment my parents spoke to me, far from feeling sorry for myself, I decided to show everybody that there was nothing I couldn't do. Not an easy task, for sure. Although they didn't realize it, my parents had introduced me to the presence in my mind of the ghost of death, which would stay with me for the rest of my life considerably.

Years later, when medical research had advanced, a doctor left me with no doubt as to the seriousness of a diagnosis like mine in those days, when life expectancy was, frankly, extremely low. There is no known person alive who has lived the years that I have and, much less, with the quality of life that I have enjoyed.

I do believe that, sometimes, not knowing too much about a subject can enable you to create your own expectations.

CHAGÜITA AND ME

GRAND PARENTS CHAGUITA AND ESAU

●I LEARNED TO LISTEN TO MYSELF

Nothing is impossible when the will is strong.

What could possibly lie in store for a girl like me: restless, naughty and full of the will to live?

It wasn't long before I took to heart what my parents had told me, and, with my head full of girlish dreams, I tried to live a normal life and have great fun at the same time. I certainly kept my mother busy! Her problem now wasn't so much taking care of my faulty heart, which, of course, she never stopped doing, but it was more keeping a close eye on my physical well-being.

While we were living in Mexico City, I was also given the chance of exploring my more maternal instincts, thanks to my baby sister Marcela, who slept in the same room as the now six-year-old Enrique Luis. Every morning, I would take her out of her crib, change her diaper and dress her. I loved doing this and feeling I was helping my Mom, too. Marcela used to get so excited when she heard my alarm sound at six thirty, as she knew I'd go straight to her room to say hello.

The high altitude of Mexico City must have affected me, though I can't say I noticed. I had lots of friends and, more often than not, I would spend my afternoons playing with them. I would surreptitiously look for ways to make sure that whatever we did wouldn't put a strain on me physically, although I never mentioned my condition to them, and I tried not to think too much about what my parents had told me.

When the eighteen months were over, we left Mexico City, as planned, and settled back into our old house which happened to be in a side-street where nearly all the neighboring children were around our age. To one side was a big school: El Colegio Mexicano (The Mexican School). We didn't go to school there, but we used to see the nuns walking through the gardens and the children having fun in the schoolyard.

My Mom would ask us children to go and play outside so she could give the house a good clean and help us feel more at home. I loved going to play in the yard. Some decorators started work on various jobs, and I would look on, absolutely fascinated at how they painted and worked on the wood and used their drills.

Curiosity always got the better of me. One day, Sandra and Enrique Luis were in the garden playing with Marcela, and so, I decided to go to the laundry room to see what the decorators were doing.

"How pretty you are," one of them said. "How old are you?"

"I'm eight. And you?"

"I'm eighteen. Hey, do you want to do some painting? I can teach you if you want."

"Oh yes, I'd love to paint. Let me paint the wall!" I answered excitedly.

"OK. But first you have to give me a kiss."

I felt sick in my stomach. I knew I couldn't trust this man, but I did want to paint and to see what kissing was like. He had really nice eyes and I, in my naturally inquisitive way, just wanted to find out about these things. Who knew if anyone else would ever want to kiss me when I was older, me with my ugly nails? This would be my very first kiss, and I was pretty enough to get a grown-up, handsome young man to feel attracted to me.

Television programs in those days would always finish with the loving couple kissing at the end of the movie. My father would usually turn the TV off when he saw us watching this. It seems ironic that parents can say more to you by what they don't say. I was bursting with curiosity as to what a kiss was really like.

I agreed, so he lifted me up and stood me on top of the washing-machine. Then, taking my head in his hands, he suddenly gave me a big, sloppy kiss, covering my little mouth with his big wet lips.

"Ugh! That's horrible. I don't want to paint now!"

I tried to free myself from his grip.

"Hang on a minute. Let me give you another kiss, and I'll bring you lots of candies tomorrow."

"No, I don't want to. Let me get down, or I'll tell my Mommy. Leave me alone. I don't want to paint!"

I managed to set myself free and jumped down. He tried to convince me it was all right and I shouldn't be scared.

"Tomorrow, I'll bring you a bagful of candies, but don't say anything to your mother or you won't get anything. And anyway, if you tell on me, I'll just say you wouldn't let us get on with our work and it was all your fault."

Terrified, I ran to look for my brother and sisters, and that was the last time I got anywhere near the decorators. It took that one moment for me to understand the meaning of a bribe and how my curiosity could get me into serious trouble.

The next day, my mother wanted us to go outside again while the house was being cleaned. This time, I resisted strongly, hiding behind her back, while peeping out to see if that man had turned up for work. Yes, there he was! He slyly showed me the bag of candies to tempt me outside, but that was the last thing I wanted to do. I kept hiding behind my mother as she gave the workers their instructions for the day.

"Ana Cecilia! Stop hiding behind me and go outside, will you?"

"No, Mommy. I don't want to."

"Well, if you don't, you'll be punished and have to stay in your room all afternoon."

"I don't care!" and I swiftly went off to my room, duly punished but, thankfully, out of harm's way.

There was no way I could tell my mother what had really happened. I was full of guilt, as the young man had convinced me that I was bothering them, and maybe it was me who had asked for the kiss after all. I would be punished, and he would get away scot-free. I'd rather stay in my room playing with Juanita Perez and not venture out, even if it did mean missing out on the candies - oh, those sweet delights that lure so many innocent children away!

"I'd better forget about those candies, or else I'll be punished and then they won't let me go out later on," I told myself over and over again.

Now I can see how very much I would have loved to be able to tell my mother!

It must be said that, from a very early age, I had developed the habit of talking to myself, looking for ways to get out of sticky situations, and so tapping into my own resources to keep me on the right path.

If I had had then the maturity I have now, I would have said to myself:

"Ana Cecilia, how smart you are! You knew that something wasn't right, and you had the good sense to get out in time. Well done for listening to that inner voice which has always spoken to you. Your wisdom -way beyond your years- saved you from a man who wanted to abuse your innocence. You have somehow known how to take care of yourself, in spite of being very daring and and willing to take risks."

●IMAGINATION

Sometimes it's better not to think so much.
Let ourselves be guided by our inner silence.

When I knew that my heart was damaged, I realized that no longer were there only three people in that car holding my parents and myself that fateful day; now there were four of us. My ghost was my constant companion from then on. At the age of ten, I stopped seeing it as something threatening – on the contrary, now I could see that it gave me strength and courage to keep going with what life I had left in me. Even more than that, there were often times when it became my only playmate.

I supposed that a playmate would need a name, one that didn't already exist or, at least, didn't sound too familiar to me, as it was, after all, a ghost. I pondered over this for some time, as I didn't know whether my new friend was a boy or a girl, so,finally, I tried to invent one that would be good for either. After much deliberation, I decided on "Ráfel": not "Rafael" or "Rafaela". It was perfect. Never could I have imagined what I would discover about this name, years later.

At night, after a long day spent running, jumping and playing, I would go to bed and imagine to myself what death was like. Sometimes, I wanted so badly to speak to *Ráfel* and for him to answer me, but if ever he did, it was just in my imagination. I asked myself, "If I die, will I be able to see my family getting on with their lives? What will it feel like to be dead? Will nothing hurt anymore?" I saw myself as a kind of guardian angel for my family, invisible but ever-present, helping them and keeping them out of harm's way, in the same way that *Ráfel* accompanied me.

On occasions, I decided to stop breathing and die, even going so far as to practice it in the garden. I would walk along, then make believe that the air wasn't entering my lungs, and I would fall down on the ground, as if I had fainted. I held my breath for a while, until

I could stand it no longer and had to breathe in again. It wasn't long before my pet dog, Motita, arrived and licked me all over my face. I could almost see *Ráfel* laughing at me.

"Oh, let me die in peace! Leave me alone!" I'd say to poor Motita, who only wanted to play.

● WATER

*I know that my strength isn't physical:
it comes from the will of the soul.*
NINE YEARS OLD WITH MY FRIEND MORENA

One of my favorite outdoor activities, but one which made me suffer at the same time, was swimming. I loved water. The neighbors opposite our house had a swimming pool, and we'd go there to swim whenever we could. The problem was getting out of the water: it was so difficult for my body to warm up again, that my lips and nails turned completely blue, and my teeth wouldn't stop chattering for a long time.

We also went to my grandfather's ranch, where there was what seemed to me to be an enormous pool. It had no heating, so the water was generally very cold. For me, the problem wasn't so much getting in as getting out of the water. My head would start to hurt unbearably. I became dizzy and felt sick. I often felt that I'd never recover from this awful feeling which, no doubt, was a sign I was suffering to some degree from hypothermia.

"Go away. I don't want to play just now. This pain is terrible. Please leave me alone. I can't stand this headache. I want to get warm, and you only make me feel colder," I'd say to *Ráfel* in my imagination, but *Ráfel* wasn't going anywhere.

The only way I could feel a bit better was by covering myself with the biggest towel I could find, lie down and feel some relief, thanks to the heat of the sun on my body, as well as that from the hot, dry cement on one side of the pool.

I never told my mother anything about how bad I felt. That would mean acknowledging the fact that I was suffering, and then she wouldn't let me get in the water. She must have seen how my body reacted, but I don't know if she fully realized the extent of my torture.

●KITES

Never underestimate the positive or negative
effect that your words can have in the life of a child.

My father taught us how to make kites. The month of February was ideal for flying them. He took us out early on a Sunday morning to look for long, dry reeds, which he then cut with his penknife. We bought tissue paper in our favorite colors, and thread and ribbon for the tail. I nearly always chose purple with some orange decoration. Once back home, we'd make glue out of flour and water. Now, decorating was the fun part.

We cut out our paper following the lines traced by my father on the back. He cut two pieces of reed which we put in the form of a cross. Then we would join the tips with smaller reeds and fasten them all together with the thread, cover it all with glue, and stick on the tissue paper ever so carefully until it was completely. Then, we had to wait before we could attach the string.

"How're you going to do yours, Sandra? How're you going to decorate it? I want to do mine exactly the same."

I always wanted to copy Sandra, who spent ages decorating hers, cutting out tiny flowers of different colors from the tissue paper and sticking them on to the tail until it looked just perfect.

"I'm going to cut out a little yellow circle for the center of the flower and put pink petals round it. Then, I'll make the stem from green paper, and I'll add a leaf as well."

I did my best to copy her idea, but it was too fiddly for me, so, inevitably, Sandra ended up helping Enrique Luis and me. She absolutely loved anything to do with decoration, cutting and drawing and could work miracles with scissors and paper. My kites could never compare to hers, but it didn't matter, so long as they flew.

"Kites at the ready; let's fly them!" my father would declare when the glue had finally dried.

For these outings, my mother stayed home with Marcela who was now two or three years old. So, it was just the four of us who would climb into the car, holding on to our kites, and off we would go to some wide, open space. What an adventure that was!

Sandra painstakingly took great care of her kite so it wouldn't get damaged. She hated letting go of it, as it truly was a work of art. I was happy so long as mine flew high up into the air. My father helped us to get our kites off the ground before handing them over to us. What we treasured most of all was, of course, the time we spent with him. He dedicated his Sundays to making and flying kites with us, and this was priceless. The world wrapped itself round the four of us, and nothing and nobody else existed.

As Enrique Luis and I loved flying kites, when we couldn't go with father, we'd climb up on the roof of the house and we'd make our own with left-over sticks and paper. From our vantage point up there, we flew them over the fence of the school next door. We wrote on little pieces of paper and sent telegrams, fastening them on to the string, and carefully moving them along until they reached the head of the kite.

My mother had no idea where we were, and I doubt whether she would have given us permission to fly kites from off the roof. We were too young to realize the danger of falling off and hurting ourselves. So, we just played and I was certainly strong enough to do that, and more. Besides, I supposed that *Ráfel* became so bored with us flying kites that he went away, and I didn't miss him at all. I was with my brother, and this was much more fun. *Ráfel* only appeared when my life was at risk.

● *Ráfel*

There is no way to dull the light of one
who shines from his own light.

Ráfel showed up in my life when I was eight, but, at some point, I realized that, somehow, he must have been by my side right from birth. I looked on him as something like a ghost that got near to me when I was in danger. In those moments, I felt him very close, almost threatening. At other times, especially when I was still little, I would play with him and he was my imaginary friend.

I never had any doubt in my mind that *Ráfel* existed. When I used to talk to myself, I would imagine him answering and voicing his opinion. I came to the conclusion that he was a good ghost, but was waiting for the right time to take me away with him. Was he the ghost of death or life? I couldn't say, but what I did know was that, each time my life was threatened, his presence could clearly be felt at my side. And so, there came a moment when we made a pact: he wouldn't take me anywhere so long as I was strong enough to stay alive. And there was to be no cheating!

I must admit that there were times when he scared me, especially when I felt I was losing the battle, as my health was in jeopardy. Other times, I could feel him smile at me kindly, looking after me, but even so, I always felt that element of distrust, or, more likely, fear.

When I grew up, *Ráfel* was no longer my playmate; he was simply a ghost, who nearly always appeared when I was frightened for my health. Years could go by without me feeling his presence at all.

●NEIGHBORS

*Even though you're in a hurry,
each moment is precious. Enjoy it.*

I was the girl with purple nails, "skinny and freckle-faced" according to my brother. Flirty and funny, even from being a little girl, I wanted to sport the "off-the-shoulder" look on the clothes that my mother made on her sewing machine. Woe betide anyone who dared to imply I couldn't do something; I stood up for my rights and for those of anyone who might be downtrodden, as if my life depended on it. It wasn't unusual for me to get into hot water through speaking up. I turned problems into challenges, not obstacles.

Where we lived was perfect, in my eyes. The roads weren't paved, so it was as if we were in the heart of the countryside. The view was spectacular wherever we looked: from the many plots of land which lay empty to the huge garden belonging to the school next door. These abandoned plots of land were my playground for many years. We played softball, soccer, and catch, or we rode around on our bicycles. When it came to hide 'n seek, no place was off limits as a hiding place, so we might spend hours searching for those of the other team. Sometimes, for a change, we'd just sit by the front door and play board games or simply chat.

"Mommy, I'm going out to get all the neighbors to play softball. Enrique Luis, you go and tell the girls, and I'll tell the boys. Come on! If you're not quick, you won't play. Come on, Sandra! Let's go!"

"Hang on, I haven't finished knitting my scarf. Give me five minutes."

"You're not going to finish knitting a scarf in five minutes, you make them so long! And, anyway, in five minutes, the others might say they don't want to play. Hurry up!"

"OK. I'm coming. 'Bye Mom. I'm going with Ana Cecilia to play outside."

"Take care!" shouted my mother from her bedroom, where she had her sewing-machine.

My girl cousins lived around the corner and, since all the neighbors' children, even the newly-arrived ones, were roughly the same age, we all enjoyed the same games, so we made up a formidable team of eight or nine little terrors. When I was tired of running, I would always try to have a change of activity, but I never ever wasted the afternoons, as long as there was fun to be had.

"I don't want to play that now: let's play hide 'n seek instead," I'd say.

"But we're winning. Why would you want to change the game now?" Marc would ask.

" 'Cause I'm tired. Who says we play hide 'n seek?"

"I'm in," volunteered Rolf, from across the way.

"Us too," chimed in my cousins, Luly and Karen.

"You see? Everyone wants to play hide 'n seek!"

I never ceased to "put my spoke in the wheel", as my brother says. The truth, though, is that that was my way of hiding the fact that I was out of breath and needed to do something less demanding.

At the front of our house were two huge trees which, when October and November came round, were full of nuts. We all used to throw sticks and stones at them to knock down as many as we could. We peeled them very carefully, and the prize was that, between Sandra and me, we would make a nut cake for us and all the neighbors.

Summer was my favorite season, as I didn't get so sick then. Even though I wasn't getting enough oxygen, I found a way to be part of whatever was going on, as best I could. My dark-colored nails and lips were constantly on display, but I often didn't notice. Enrique Luis would occasionally give them a bit of an odd look, but he never said anything. Actually, I can't remember anyone having made comments, or, perhaps, I just didn't give them the chance, as, deep down, I didn't want to hear anything hurtful.

SANDRA

The child within you needs love and attention, just like any other. Don't neglect it.
SANDRA AND I

I've always wondered what my sister Sandra thought of being, so often, put on one side, because her little sister needed attention. Perhaps, she just accepted that that was how her life had to be. Thank God for my grandmothers, Chagüita and Abuela, who would so often step in and take over whilst my parents busied themselves with me.

Asking these questions has brought me some comfort, as regards myself. If this was how I had to live my life in order to stay alive, then, surely, that means it was the best way. And similarly, for Sandra, if she was called upon to live the life she did, then there must have been a purpose for that, too. My heart feels some comfort when I ask these questions, thinking about myself. If this was the only way I could live my life, then surely it has been the best. If she was given that life to live, there must have been a purpose to it. Sandra had her own struggles, fears and insecurities. I can't bear thinking that she ever suffered or felt alone, or was sometimes jealous for not receiving the same attention as I did. Whatever the case, she never let it show, and, for me, that is true love.

Still, when I was little, I couldn't understand why Sandra had to be so interfering, making it seem as if I had a second mother at home, who was always watching my every move.

"Mom. Ana Cecilia's climbing the tree and you told her not to."

"Get down from there immediately! Go to your room and stay there the rest of the afternoon for disobeying!" my mother would shout through the window.

I climbed down as best I could, and was so angry at my sister that I shouted to her that she was a tell-tale. I wanted to climb whatever I laid my eyes on: the tree, the roof, the walls. But there was always someone watching over me like a hawk.

What I didn't know, and much less understood, was that she, in fact, took very special care of me. She was always good to me, and simply wanted her sister to be well, all the time. Whatever I asked for, she gave it to me, very often without a second thought. That's why I would give the prize for patience and understanding to Sandra.

Years later, I found out that when we returned from Mexico City, Sandra started with anxiety attacks. She was taken to see the doctor, who said that there was nothing wrong with her, and it was probably due to the change of city and a new school.

"But, doctor, are you sure Sandra is OK? I have another daughter who has a very serious heart condition; she's very sick and I'm so afraid that Sandra might have something wrong with her, too. Are you sure she doesn't have a similar problem?"

"No, your daughter is perfectly healthy."

"Please do some more tests, doctor."

"Your daughter's heart sounds absolutely fine. No doubt she's a bit of a worrier and gets upset by changes."

Overhearing this conversation, Sandra could now realize the seriousness of my illness. She was probably better informed than I was at that time. This must have affected

MY MOTHER, SANDRA AND ME

65

her and led her to be so much more considerate towards me. Actually, we never touched on this subject when we were small, or even as teenagers, and it's only recently that she shared this with me, but I did realize that she took great care of me, loved me and admired me, all of which gave me so much strength.

She had to tolerate a sister who did not make her life at all easy. She used to let me take her place when we played; she gave me her popsicle, her seat, her doll, everything she could, just so that her sister would be happy. And what did I give her in return? Lots of headaches, no doubt!

I was born fighting, looking to make my mark, at whatever the cost. Throughout all this process, I did things which must have hurt her. It's not that I regret anything I've done, because it was thanks to my constant battling that I have found life. Still, I have tried to make amends for small wounds I have unconsciously caused along the way. My poor sister. I only hope that I will have enough years of life left in me to make up for so many troubled times in our childhood.

●FUN

*Waking up every day is
a miracle.
How I choose to begin
it is up to mei.*
SANDRA, ENRIQUE LUIS,
MARCELA AND ME

I shall be forever grateful to my parents for raising me in exactly the same way as my brother and sister, despite my fragile health, and for making the effort not to treat me any differently. All of us had to obey the same rules and received the same chastisements. My parents, however, have to go along to the school every year to explain my situation to the teachers. They didn't want me to be forced to do any physical activity, but asked that I should be allowed to participate in everything, until I decided that it was enough.

Neither my parents nor my teachers put any limits on my life or activities. It was up to me to decide how far I went. My rebelliousness and dogged will were what spurred me on to achieve whatever I proposed, which sometimes complicated my life somewhat. Whenever I was invited by friends to go on a trip outside the city, my parents always made sure to get to know my friends' parents and to send me well wrapped-up, in case the weather turned cold.

One day, when I was about ten, a friend invited me to a ranch in Montemorelos. It was winter and very cold. She invited me because they were going to be cooking a specialty of the region, barbecued goat, and we'd spend all day there.

Almost immediately after we arrived, we focused our attention on the horses. We wanted to ride them around the ranch. I loved horses and adored riding, so the day was devoted to this, but gradually, I started to feel my hands turningcolder and colder, to the point where they were hurting. My whole body was trembling, I was shivering, and I couldn't stop my teeth from chattering. The cold started to penetrate into my very bones, but I didn't say anything.

I felt *Ráfel*'s presence so closely, but I didn't want to turn around and see him, as that would be tantamount to giving up. I couldn't complain; I just had to bear it.

When we returned, still on horseback, I was in a very bad state, which alarmed my friend's mother. The cold and the exhaustion had practically paralyzed me, and my lips were completely dark, just like my skin. My friend's mother ran, terrified, to get me down off the horse any way she could. She took hold of me, and carried me, clutching me to her with all her might.

"Quick! Let's get her inside. Clear everything off that sofa that's in front of the fire. We've got to warm this girl up!" she shouted, absolutely desperate.

My friend, also scared by now, ran after her to see what was going on, and realized that I was completely purple. She sat me in front of the fire and rubbed my shoulders and legs. I could hardly move. Little by little, I started to get a bit of color back.

"Under no circumstances are you girls going to go out. You're staying here inside the house."

"Yes, Mom. We'll stay here until they bring us our dinner," answered my friend.

We looked at each other and burst out laughing, as if we'd done something naughty. My friend didn't question her mother's decision. We were a team, and we were both confined to the house, with no option of leaving. That didn't stop us from having great fun, however, and enjoying whatever we could. We told each other stories, laughed at all the adventures we'd had, and generally kept ourselves nicely entertained. I don't remember whether I ate any baby goat or not, nor how the day ended, just that I had lots of fun.

When she took me home that night, my friend's mother told my mother that I'd given her quite a scare, and she gave an account of what had happened, at which my mother thanked her for looking after me. And, as for me, there were no reprimands, no questions, just a goodnight kiss.

I went to the solitude of my bed and, lying there between the sheets,

I remembered how *Ráfel* had been with me all the time. Closing my eyes, I imagined him riding next to me on a black horse, holding my hand. Sometimes, his face had a kind look of someone who would take care of me and not abandon me, rather like a guardian angel; but other times, I didn't want to see him, as he felt like an intruder in my life. He interrupted my games, my fun. I didn't like it when I was feeling so cold and sensed that he wanted to take me away, to take over my life.

Sometimes, just when I wanted to forget all about him, I would overhear some comment that reminded me of how sick I was, and it was then that I realized that I was never alone. *Ráfel* wasn't planning to go anywhere.

I didn't tell any of my friends about all this; it was something I preferred to keep to myself. There was no point in mentioning something that might scare them. Besides, they never ostracized me for being different or for not being able to do the same things as them. I had a go at everything and never stopped trying, but at those times when I couldn't go on, then they would stay with me as far as my strength would take me, no explanations needed.

I tried so hard to keep up with them in the games we played, but, far too often, I became tired so very, very quickly. Once I had to be at home to breathe with an oxygen tank as my level of oxygenation was extremely low. Not to be put off by this "minor" detail, I invited my friends around, and we played and laughed all day long. My mother did what she could to tell us to take it easy, but it made no difference: I was in charge, and they fell in line.

One day, I played whiplash with my classmates of fifth grade. . We all held hands and the one in the center didn't need to run as much as the one on the outside. The game was to see how long the ones at the end of the line could keep running before they had to let go of their teammate's hands. I always tried to find a way to be on the end, knowing I would soon get tired,, have to let go, and we would lose. But, sometimes, my plan failed: no one knew the extent of my illness, nor the fact that I couldn't run and tired very quickly. I took my turn, just like everyone else.

That day, I was near to the end of the line, and I prayed to God that nobody would get mad at me, and that we wouldn't have to do too much running before someone else fell down before I did. I ran and ran until my energy was spent; I let go, which made the two classmates on the outside fall down, too. It wasn't long before the name-calling started. I could only run round once and, there I was, stretched out on the floor, breathless. I couldn't make a sound. Just managing to lift myself up, I headed off to the girls' bathroom to recuperate. I inhaled all the air I could, but it wasn't enough. I felt dizzy, numb, and my head was hurting. After a while, I re-emerged, as if nothing had happened, and I strolled nonchalantly off, so that they wouldn't invite me to play again.

Having anyone poking fun at me was something I hated, and I became very upset when it happened. Any cutting remarks made me feel stripped naked, exposed, hurt. I didn't want my heart problem to make the others feel sorry for me or to disregard me and not include me in their games.

I LEARNED THAT ONLY HE WHO STOPS HAVING FUN LIKE A CHILD STARTS TO GROW OLD ON THE INSIDE.
MY TRICYCLE

ADOLESCENCE

❶RESOURCES

The only way I found to know if I could achieve something was by making the attempt.
ME, SANDRA, MARCELA
AND ENRIQUE LUIS

There are many ways to overcome a physical or emotional catastrophe, but only one worked for me: a change of mentality.

I tried to create inside me a new way of thinking, different from the one which drew me away from health and life. I believe that people who are suffering in any situation, whatever it may be, have the choice as to whether to suffer or to make the most out of life, even amidst adversity. I don't believe being alive is just about the physical aspect. There are those who do survive and yet, on the inside, they are empty, inert, or spend all their time suffering and feeling sorry for themselves. On the other hand, there are those who make the decision to see beyond their circumstances and can survive joyfully. They live with intensity and choose to be happy. People who smile and are optimistic have decided to have a different way of thinking and acting.

My fear is not to die, but rather to live and not feel alive. None of us has tomorrow guaranteed, but I, even less than most.

After the ranch incident, when I had felt *Ráfel* riding beside me while my body was suffering from something very close to hypothermia, I made a decision: I didn't want to hear anything to do with bad news about my health or my future. I would not let those voices of defeat and sadness bring me down. I paid great attention, however, to those voices which spoke to me of hope, a bright future, and my happiness. I already had enough negative information stored some place inside my head. It was hard enough not to notice the fear and anguish of my parents. But I knew then, and I know now, that it was the way in which I faced whatever problems or happenings that should arise on a day-to-day basis that would determine the very dimension and importance of them. So, in my mind I fabricated the very thing that I wished for, and I enjoyed it even before actually having it.

I decided to be happy.

From being a small child, I had learned to stop time, on my imaginary visits with Chagüita. Growing up, I composed music, played the guitar, and would be transported by my lyrics and dreams. I played and sang with such intensity, as if I only had that one chance to do so. I learned to talk to myself, convince myself that everything was fine, that I was strong and healthy. I spent hours in a kind of inner meditation where I envisaged myself in this world for many years to come. I wasn't playing tricks with my mind; I believed it with all my heart.

Undeniably, many a time I would feel so tired, with an exhaustion so intense, that I could feel the doubts start to creep in as to whether those dreams I'd created would ever come true. That's when I would stop and take action. I would go by myself and dedicate some time to just listening to myself, being aware of myself. I would retreat to my room and lie down on my bed: that sacred place where no one would dare to disturb me or even make a noise if my eyes were closed. It was probably because they so rarely saw me lying down that, when I did, they respected my need for rest. I would breathe in deeply and visualize the air entering my lungs and carrying oxygen all through my body, which would slowly start to feel healthy and stronger again. In my mind, I drew sketches of myself running, dancing, walking along mountain paths and enjoying it all so much. I convinced myself that all was well. *Ráfel* was close by, as always in those moments, but he didn't bother me. I was at peace and not alone.

That gave me strength and I could get up from my bed, refreshed. While still tired physically, my spirit was fortified. I was not so weighed down by my tiredness. I think I learned to walk towards my heart and know it deeply, to recognize it again and again, until I knew that I had no reason to be afraid of anything, that miracles did exist. My heart was beating, was standing strong, behaving like a true hero. My heart was amazing. It was keeping me alive.

I understood that the best way to know myself was to accept and respect who I was. Knowing in a clinical way what my heart was suffering from, gave me a feeling of security and control, thanks to the information I had. But not accepting the prognosis gave me hope and confidence. I could not give up. I listened attentively to what my body needed, but I willed it forward and encouraged it to move onward through the information I chose to pour into it from my head and my spirit. All of my being responded to this display of confidence and the will to be alive.

I also learned to love each day as if it were the last, but I tried not to think about the possibility that this might well be true. I enjoyed each day intensely (and I still do). I took absolutely nothing for granted, and I valued everything, from a smile, a walk, a dinner, to my parents, my sisters and brother, and even a kiss. I treasured each new experience, not knowing if I would ever have the chance to live it again.

My philosophy has always been that, no matter how negative the circumstances may be, there will be a way to come through it, always. Visualizing things before they happen has been my specialty: to get engaged, to be married, to be a wife, a mother, a professional woman, independent and successful. If I had focused solely on the bare facts of my reality, I would never have envisioned my desired future.

MY FAVOURITE HOBBY

●DEFYING THE DIAGNOSIS

When someone's claws come out, remember they are nothing more that the reflex of a sensitive heart trying to protect itself.

As the years passed, I sometimes compensated for the insecurity I felt by becoming more and more rebellious. Whenever my mother intervened, asking me not to do something, I answered back, saying she knew nothing, that she couldn't possibly know what I could or couldn't do, because she wasn't me.

"Stop filling my head up with an illness I haven't got!" I shouted, when I could stand it no longer.

My retorts to her were hurtful and distanced me from her, but, in my heart, I was suffering, and what I really wanted was a hug and some recognition. Instead of asking for that, I withdrew and faced my battles alone.

In Secondary School, I wouldn't admit to being unable to do the same things as everyone else, as I couldn't bear to see myself as someone with limitations. In fact, I never truly believed that. As my parents went each year to talk to the teachers, I was allowed not have P.E. classes, but, even so, I used to go, and if it became too strenuous for me, I went back to my classroom. In summer, my classmates hurried back into the classroom, all hot and sweaty, in order to stand in front of the wall fans and cool down a little. They found me there, spotless and fresh. Some envied me, and others just couldn't understand why I was treated differently, especially as I had no intention of explaining.

Neither did I want pity from anyone, nor much less to be the center of conversation for something I hadn't done, for something that was beyond my control. For this and many other reasons, my character became strong, determined, assertive and with the firm conviction that I would achieve whatever I proposed to myself. I proposed to live life to the maximum.

Little by little, I acquired a better understanding of the medical terms of my malformation. Sometimes, I would lie back on my bed when I felt tired and imagine my heart functioning. A small quantity of blood came into my mind, which I called Lucy. It circulated through my body at great speed in search of oxygen. When Lucy entered through the vessels which would take her to the heart, she found herself in the area that was for oxygenated blood, not for her.

Taken aback, Lucy was pumped towards a new area, which would take her to the lungs. Instead of going into an empty space which was just for her, she immediately came collided with some oxygenated blood waiting to be pumped to the rest of the body; nothing separated them as it should have done. There was nothing to divide them, so both of them, Lucy and her new friend, now all mixed up, began their journey towards the lungs, which oxygenated them both equally and, with one heartbeat, both of them returned once more to the heart. Once they were back in the heart, they found themselves in the same space that they had abandoned a moment before, and they discovered it wasn't empty: there was more blood waiting to be oxygenated. So now Lucy, her friend and another non-oxygenated friend became thoroughly intermingled, and with one great push, the heart sent them off to start their journey to the rest of my body. They made a gigantic attempt to get the most out of the little oxygen they had between the three of them.

It was so complicated imagining how Lucy could possibly manage to supply me with oxygen whilst mixed up with friends who didn't have any, that it was simply better not to think about this, and sleep instead.

This dramatization in my mind helped me understand the reasons why I couldn't manage to do what my classmates did, why I tired so easily, and why I couldn't participate in the same physical activity. I understood that, not only was I different from my contemporaries, but I also viewed life in a very different way from them.

WHEN LIFE IS NOT FOREVER

● I LIED

Only the wise can learn to control the words which come out of their mouths.

In ninth grade, just as I was about to turn sixteen, I became ill and had to go to Houston to be treated for a bacterial endocarditis, affecting my heart. It was the first time I felt that my it was putting a brake on my activities, but I felt so bad that I had to miss the class trip, which we had all been looking forward to, and had to stay at home. I was devastated! When it was clear I was deteriorating, my parents decided to take me for a medical check up.

I stayed in the hospital for two weeks and moved myself around, pushing my drip and carrying my catheter in my hand. There were many children I met with similar problems to mine. It was nice to visit them and paint together in the hospital playrooms. They were all much younger than me, as nearly no one reached adolescence. A victim of my age, I forgot how bad I used to feel days before my medication. And so, I felt wonderful, healthy and strong, while seeing children who were so gravely ill they had little chance of pulling through. They told me of the death of one of the boys I had gotten to know over the past few days. That's when I started to question what it was that made the difference. Born with the same physical problems, they died and I stayed alive. It seemed as if God haphazardly decided who would live and who would die. That didn't seem fair, and it made me angry. Who lives? Who dies? Who decides? We should all have the same chance. My sense of justice was so important that when something was not fair, it created great conflict inside me.

I didn't feel any less fortunate than any of my teenage friends, I believed we all enjoyed the same opportunities. I began to think that God was invented by man to justify and give explanations for everything which could neither be justified nor explained. I very much doubted His existence and felt that if God were to exist, He would allow all sick children to feel like me. I asked myself why I was healthy and many others weren't; why so many children who suffered from the same sickness as me had died.

It was a painful time, I felt alone, without the protection of a superior being. For all my childhood, I had believed in a protective God, but now, seeing this situation, my confusion was great. It was easier for me to convince myself that there was no God, rather than believe that God was unfair and lacked compassion towards those who needed it the most.

Within this short period, I had two very important visits: one from my boyfriend and one from Chagüita, my grandmother, who had travelled together. I was happy, as this was my first boyfriend and I felt it was an important relationship.

In the hospital, I could wear my own clothes during the day, which cheered me up. In the three days that he visited, my boyfriend accompanied me to all my activities: the hospital library, visiting sick children, playing with them and helping them any way I could. My boyfriend would stroll out of my room with me, and this did not go unnoticed by the doctors and nurses.

It was during this time that maybe I took one of the hardest decisions of my life - I lied.

When my boyfriend had left, one of the doctors asked to speak to me in private. My father had gone back to Monterrey and my mother, at that time, didn't speak English as well as I did, so, for the first time, I felt in complete control of any information I received. My mother saw this as a good opportunity to ask a little bit about my future, what I could and couldn't do. I accepted to do it alone.

I chatted with the female doctor a little. Her first question chilled me to the bone.

"We can see you have a boyfriend and we have to ask you a question. Are you sexually active?"

I was well into adolescence, and many teenagers begin to have sex at this age. And yet, for a moment I was taken aback.

"I'm only just going to turn sixteen, and I'm not married," was my reply.

My boyfriend was all of seventeen.

"How could I have sexual relations?" I asked myself while I was giving her my answer. On the other hand, that question made me feel special, as if they were speaking to an adult. I imagined I was over twenty years old and could speak about these matters.

Only then did the doctor realize she was dealing with a young Mexican adolescent, with very different customs and upbringing from many youngsters living in the United States.

"I understand. Look, we doctors can only give advice, but in the end, you will make your own decisions."

It was the first time I had spoken of sex with anyone. I had never even broached the subject at home, not even in the sex education classes at school. These matters were simply not talked about with anyone. You listened, but you didn't ask.

"We recommend that, preferably, you don't get married. It isn't in your best interest to start an active sex life, as your body wouldn't stand it."

I just listened, but in my head I repeated the same phrase: I wanted to know what it was to love. What she was stating would put a stop to that dream for ever.

"But I have a boyfriend, and I want to marry him."

"Yes, I know you have a boyfriend, and that's what I would like us to talk about. Although you are young, it's important that you both know that your future is uncertain, and it would be better not to begin to have sex."

"I'll never be able to get married or have children?"

"Time will tell. Maybe one day, when we have found a surgical solution for your sickness, after which maybe your life will change so much that you'll be able to do a lot more things."

I didn't like what she said, even though she chose her words carefully. She wanted to make sure I understood the great risk I was running, because the doctors didn't know how my body was going to react. Now, I can understand that this was foreign territory for the doctors, too. They didn't have the slightest idea of what might happen if I over-exerted myself physically. All they could tell me were suppositions, as there was no other known case to refer to.

"Do you have any other questions?"

ANA CECILIA GONZÁLEZ

Many thoughts were racing through my mind: "I don't agree. You aren't God. You can't know what'll happen to me. You don't know what I feel and how I feel."

They had thrown a bucket of cold water over me, but my age allowed me to reject this information and to go out on a limb once again.

"No, none. I just ask that it be me who talks to my mother."

"Of course. That information is only for you."

The doctor withdrew, and my mother came into the room with a thousand questions.

"What did they say to you? Did she say whether you could get married and have children?"

This was the moment when I saw my chance. I could say whatever I wanted. I was in control of the information. Never before had I had this freedom, this sense of empowerment. My parents were always present when the doctors gave me any information. In Mexico, doctors would not have touched on this subject when they were alone with me, and much less would they have brought up the subject of my sexuality. It would be offensive. Only in the United States did they deal with these matters in such a direct and open fashion.

"The doctor said I could lead a normal life, Mom,, that my body would set the limit, but that I should try to go as far as I could. She said I could get married, and maybe have children, but time will tell," I said confidently.

"So, you're not in any danger?" asked my mother, naturally concerned.

For me, the only danger was not being allowed to live my life to the fullest. I felt strong, full of life. I couldn't accept what I had just been told.

"No, Mom. My body and I will feel it when I can't manage something, and I'll simply stop doing it. Maybe in a few years, there will be a surgery for me."

My mother was reassured. At least, that's what I thought. In fact, she would have accepted as normal anything negative I might have said, as she had doubted right from when I was born, that I could make it through to the next day. My parents never took my life for granted. Each new day that I lived was a miracle for them.

I don't know if I lied for her or for me. It wasn't planned, or even imagined. It was a survival mechanism. I lied about everything I had been told because it represented a death sentence. I was not prepared to accept it and neither would I put a label on myself which stated everything I couldn't do. Much less did I want my mother behind me, preventing me from doing anything I might feel like doing. I could see her telling me to break it off with my boyfriend immediately, to consider becoming a nun, and to put a stop to any further illusions of forming my own family.

All of these dreams were just in my head. I don't know what my mother would, in fact, have said, but I wasn't prepared to take any chances. I wanted to be happy, and I'd been taught that you grow up, get married, have children and live happily ever after. Only later did I know that this was too simplistic,, as life and happiness are much more than these stereotypes, blessings though they surely are.

I made a difficult decision, but it gave me the freedom to continue through my adolescence in the most normal way possible. My will far outweighed my limitations; my desire for achievements could not be kept down by any barriers, or imposed restrictions.

I returned to Monterrey and continued with my recuperation. A few weeks later, I was back at school and caught up with all my classes. I was determined to make up for lost time. I studied hard, looked to my friends for support with my exams, and was delighted when my average grade went up. I even thought I might get the prize for academic achievement. I didn't win any prize, and it was only recently that I found out through my mother that the teachers had, in fact, helped me not to fail the year. I would have rather not known that, but at least, at that moment, I felt proud of myself.

●MRS. WOLCOTT

*Give generously, as it will
always come back to you,
usually by way of other people.*
MRS. WOLCOTT

From a very early age, I was fond of writing of all sorts, particularly poetry, and I composed songs on my guitar. My first composition was for my music teacher Mrs. Wolcott, who had a great impact on my life. Writing and composing was my way of expressing what I couldn't shout out loud: "I want to live!"

Besides being one of my favorite teachers, Mrs. Wolcott also taught us literature, and it was fantastic. With her, I learned to enjoy stories, folktales, poem analysis and the deep exploration of the human mind. The final piece of work for completing the course was to create a poem. That was an easy task for me; indeed, I helped various classmates to write theirs. The poem I wrote held great significance for me.

In this poem, written only a few months after returning from Houston after my endocarditis, I felt at peace with God. I needed Him so much in my heart that my poem was directed to Him. In time, I understood how, through that poem, I was hoping to make a pact with God. That gave me the certainty, which I had craved, that I would live for longer. I needed to beg Him to keep that ghost out of my life, if its intention was to take me away, and that He would give me the opportunity to enjoy my life.

POEM:
For sure some day, I'll be there with You
For sure some day, I'll stay by your side
But I can't go now, there's too much to do
Even if I wanted to, I've got to live my life through

Life isn't easy as many may say
But there's for sure something I have to state
I just can't go anywhere, there is a determined place
I've got to choose first, to go the right way

You'll be waiting for me, I already know
There is just no way, you would say no
So I can't go now, there's too much to do
But for sure some day, I'll be there with You.

The poem must have told Mrs. Wolcott many things about me. We never spoke about it, but she knew that I was much more sensitive, compared with my classmates, where the theme of death was concerned. For me, it was simple to talk about that subject and *Ráfel* now accompanied me in a poetic and deep way, with no intention of abandoning me.

We finished Junior High and my friends didn't see anything different in me. For them, I'd been somebody absolutely normal, just like them. Very few of them paused to wonder, even, if my life was at risk because of my heart problem. It wasn't something I often talked about; perhaps there was the odd occasion when I spoke about it openly with two or three friends. I only did so to explain to them those occasions when I couldn't keep up with them walking or running or playing some sport.

They always told me that I showed a lot of confidence; I knew perfectly well what I wanted and what I felt. My values and convictions were unshakable. We would get together in one of their houses, and we invited the boys to come along, too. We used to have a lot of fun in our get-togethers, playing different games which I always took part in, except when we had to run.

When we were in High School, we used to walk to El Centrito, a meeting place for teenagers. If you went there, you had to be open to the possibility of flirting a bit and chatting one of the boys up. That walk must certainly have worked, as two of my friends met their present husbands there. We walked round a big square. It struck me as endless and ridiculous to have to walk, when we could just wait for the boys to parade in front of us, but no-I had to walk like everyone else. Sometimes, I'd pretend to buy something in a large drugstore which opened on to both streets on our circuit, and I'd just stroll around the store until I got my breath back, so I could go on.

I calculated, more or less, the time it took to reach the other side and run into my friends. Meanwhile, I'd flick through magazines, have some water and just while away the time.

I know I was reckless in some situations. I didn't always think about the consequences of living so intensely and with so much eagerness. Sometimes, I made wrong decisions, but I was always ready to put my heart and soul into everything I committed myself to. Perhaps Mrs. Wolcott was right when she told me, years later, that few people of my age had my internal strength and my will to live. I enjoyed life to the fullest. I had to grab the brass ring, as *Ráfel* was sometimes very close and, more often than not, would whisper: "Here I am. Don't forget: we're sticking together."

●ALWAYS DARING

*We all have doubts. I decide
if they hold me back or move
me forward.*
FIFTEEN YEARS

As adolescents, we fail to grasp
the gravity of certain things.
It may be due to naivety, or
we simply don't consider
our limitations. With time, everything changes: the innocence of
adolescence disappears and is replaced by the ephemeral idea of
immortality. I, however, knew all too well that I was mortal, and if
I took risks and was intrepid, it was because it was the only way to
live certain experiences before dying. My enormous advantage was
that my risks were quite modest.

My youth was magical. Like all adolescents, I enjoyed that age
where princes and princesses abound, where castles are fabricated in
the mind, and nothing is impossible.

I had various boyfriends, the first when I was fourteen. How lucky
I felt, like a grown woman. I was allowed to see him once or twice
a week and when he went to visit me, we sat on the veranda at the
front of the house. It was a sweet relationship, but we saw very little
of each other. Perhaps the most time we shared was when he came
to see me in Houston. We broke up when I was about to turn sixteen.

Several months after, I started going out with someone else. This
relationship was one of the most important ones of my youth, but
we both had strong characters and argued frequently. We were very
fond of each other, but broke up shortly before we'd been together
for two years.

One day, I drove to pick up Enrique Luis, my brother, from his
American football training, a few blocks away from my boyfriend's

house. I was barefoot, as I had taken my shoes off to feel fresher. Passing by his house, I turned to look at it, and then I heard a screech and a bang: a car had collided with me head-on.

My foot was broken from trying to brake and was in a cast for six weeks. Still, I went to classes every day, didn't stop going out with my friends and even taught one of my friends how to drive. Nothing could deter me from teaching her and going round and round the school parking lot. Beside that, it was a manual transmission, difficult to manoever: a Dodge Dart 1975, affectionately known amongst our friends as "The Coffee Machine".

I was on crutches. The effort to get from place to place was exhausting; now I had a good reason for going slowly and letting people help me. The most tiring thing was walking from the parking lot to the classrooms. At first it was a struggle to walk with the crutches. Getting up to class on the third floor was the cause for most concern, as it was practically impossible to go up the stairs. I had no strength and even less oxygen to stand the strain.

I fixed this situation by getting my friends to help me go up the stairs. I would sit on a chair and two or three of the boys would carry me. I felt like Queen Cleopatra, carried in my litter towards my final destination by my subjects, the pole-bearers, whilst my girlfriends took charge of my books and crutches. It was fun, and I tried to see the positive side of being so limited in my movements.

Around this time, I signed up to be on the softball team, alongside my school friends. I always liked sports, watching them, rather than playing them. My mother nearly collapsed when she found out that I'd be on the team. I was good at catching and throwing balls, so I convinced the trainer to let me have a go. He agreed, and many times I just walked around the pitch whilst the others ran. I spent my time catching and throwing the ball with my teammates. Besides, it was the perfect excuse to be with my boyfriend, as he used to go and watch me play.

I had a great time. No one asked me why I hardly ran during training sessions. I only remember having played on two occasions. The other team got me out immediately when I didn't make it to first base in time, but, at least, I tried. I never missed a training session or a match. I didn't mind being part of the supporters; to feel part of the team, and to be accepted as I was, was more than enough.

After that, there were two or three more boyfriends, one who lasted just a day. In the morning, I accepted to be his girlfriend, but by eight o'clock in the evening, I wished I hadn't, and we broke up. Many years later, we met up again, and even today, I consider him one of my best friends.

My friends laughed at me because I had one long-distance boyfriend: Alberto, who was already a lawyer law student like myself, a great friend with whom I shared some poems and a song I had written. He was my "long-distance-boyfriend" for some months, and with him I could share my greatest fears and longings. As we said everything in a letter without actually seeing each other, it was much easier to open up to him and reveal my fears unreservedly. It was a lovely experience and I felt very close to him. That relationship didn't last long, as he was never coming back to Monterrey and I had no plans to change cities, having only just started university.

Years later, I heard that Alberto had died of a heart attack. Yes, he died as a result of a heart condition. I was deeply upset when I found that out. How many times had I said to him that I might not get to enjoy many things that so many people take for granted? Neither of us would have dreamed that he would be the one to go first; further proof that no one, even those with healthy hearts, has life guaranteed.

Another boyfriend was on the scene for three weeks, and he was the best-looking of them all. By the third week, he said that his girlfriend had been looking for him and would I give him some time to think, at which I agreed, yes, of course, he should think about it, but he shouldn't come back to me. I knew that when a man says, "It's not you; it's me", that means that the relationship is over. Deep down, I always knew that he never liked the fact that I couldn't accompany him on bike rides and mountain-climbing, which his friends' girlfriends did. Many a time, I felt pressured to go along, but I didn't want to make a fool of myself, so I declined.

I made sure that none of these boys could see my anxiety when they took my hand and stared at my nails. My hands were long, like a pianist's, maybe beautiful, but my purple nails always put me on edge and I never let the boys look at them for long.

"You've got lovely hands. The only problem is your nails, they look weird," one of my boyfriends commented.

That comment pierced my soul, because there was nothing I could do about it. I wasn't interested in putting false nails on, and, besides, my nails were too knobbly and thick for them to fit on. My mother offered to paint them, which I didn't want either, as it would just make them more noticeable.

I tried not to let it get me down; my nails did not define me. I had other things to offer, and so I would cleverly divert a boy's attention whenever I felt uncomfortable by his stare. At least, I tried to convince myself that it worked. I'd smile and find a way to change the subject with my scintillating conversation, my skill with words being one of my best tools for getting out of these situations.

However, distracting them wasn't enough. Their comments hurt me and the looks on their faces made me angry, not with God, or life, or my parents, but with those people who were incapable of seeing beyond the physical, who would just point out anything that was different, without ever considering the harm they could do by their thoughtless comments. I wanted to shout at them to have a bit of empathy, to put themselves, for just one moment, in someone else's place.

That's what I would have done back in kindergarten, at the age of five, but as I couldn't behave like that now, , I would simply escape in my mind to my grandmother's. Not that it was always easy to use this escape mechanism in my teenage years, , as I was more aware of what was going on, but, even so, I needed a refuge to go to.

Doubtless, there were many occasions when I took my frustration out on my family, who were nearly always at the receiving end of my bouts of anger and desperation for whatever happened outside the home. Of course, this had everything to do with me: my sufferings, my limitations, and the family is very often the "soft place to fall" to mitigate the harshness of the blow.

My friends used to say I had a very unusual way of attracting men, that my sensuality was in my words and quick-thinking. They claimed I had the ability to look inside each of them and discover what I needed to. I could not only look into their eyes but, also, through and beyond their eyes.

I wish that had been true. It did happen that sometimes I could understand beyond what words expressed, and listen to silence. But I didn't always get it right and, naturally, with some people, I was way off the mark.

I had my last boyfriend at the age of twenty, and we married one year and four months after we'd started dating. I was twenty-one and he was twenty-six.

WHAT SHALL I DO WITH THE REST OF MY LIFE?

As I made my way through life, I understood that what is important is not to know what one has, but to accept what one is worth.

9TH GRADE GRADUATION

Shortly before finishing High School at the age of seventeen, I had to decide what to do with the rest of my life. Choosing a career is never easy for anyone, and I was no exception. My parents were concerned, as they didn't want me to put too much strain on myself while, at the same time, not wishing to limit my choices.

I had lived a life that neither my parents nor I could have imagined. I survived the first years and overcame sicknesses and hardships during my childhood. My body seemed to have found its own balance and I continued through puberty and adolescence.

I finished Junior High and High School, and was feeling more alive than ever. I was sure I would go to university, marry and even have children. I could visualize myself perfectly, briefcase in hand, getting ready to go to work; in the same way I envisaged my wedding day, wearing my white bridal gown. I could see myself taking care of my baby, changing diapers and enjoying every minute of it. Seeing this so clearly in my mind raised my spirits. On the other hand, however, I also had to acknowledge another reality; I was alive thanks to a pure miracle, and couldn't understand why I lived and others didn't.

And so I started once more to question Divine Justice. I was frustrated by not understanding God's motives. If He were just, He would give everyone the same opportunities, the same tools to survive. Each of us did what we wanted with what we had, but I didn't understand how a boy I had a photo taken with in Houston could, at such a young age, decide to give up. I failed to see what the difference was between someone like me and that boy who died. I wondered if I could do anything to help those children to live. I was alive, despite a damaged heart, and a child couldn't decide that.

I failed to find any answers to these questions. I was not God, and neither could I give health to those who didn't have it, but, at least, I wanted to try to do something. Were God to have stood before me in those moments, I would have made a well-argued case for demanding justice. I would have overwhelmed Him with evidence and appealed any sentence that I didn't consider logical and fair for those children. Somehow, I felt a duty to justify having a life in spite of my heart condition, unlike those who had been less fortunate.

I decided to study Law to try and understand human justice and see if, along the way, I could understand God more. And that is what happened: we read so many books on philosophy and ethics that it all began to make sense. We read Aristotle, Plato, and even Saint Augustus, amongst others.

They all dealt with the theme of justice, but it was only on reading the latter that I found inner peace, as I decided to incorporate this idea into my life: "When we are born, the natural law of justice is imprinted on our soul.

For Saint Augustus, justice is God. Eternal law and its reflection on the soul, just like natural law, is the moral and universal rule, and all human actions should be adjusted to that.

From the practice of justice is born the concept of human rights, which may be natural or based on custom.

The problem is not was not that God does not impart justice to all, in even measure, but, rather, it is man who stops acting as he should, according to nature. In our heart of hearts, we all know perfectly well when something isn't right and when we harm others, but we simply refuse to see it. But that does not mean that the circumstances in which each person is born and lives depends on who imparts justice.

Studying these concepts, I understood: it was one thing to impart justice and, quite another, that those to whom it was imparted were the same and lived in the same circumstances. I knew that was impossible. This made a lot of sense and coincided with my way of thinking.

So I concluded, finally, that life is lived and God is not responsible for each and every happening. The simple act of being born implies risk. God does not control everything that happens to the human race as if we were puppets, and, even though He created us in His likeness and image, the reality is that we live on a physical plane, where nature is governed by its own laws. There are mistakes in all species and throughout all nature. We must acknowledge these errors and learn to live with them as best we can, using to our advantage the very liberty which we, as human beings, have at our disposal. The circumstances are different for each one of us; some are born healthy and others are not.

I was one of those born with some kind of sickness. Why? Because on the physical plane, nature is imperfect. However, the actions that each of us takes, as well as deciding to feel sick or not, is a personal decision. At least, we humans can defend ourselves to some extent from nature through medicine. The only thing common to each human being is the possibility to love. Love for oneself and for others can achieve unimaginable things.

God was not an invention of man; rather, man was a design of God to manifest love and perfection. But that perfection dwells in the soul, not in the body. Justice is not found in what our senses can perceive; it goes far beyond what is visible. As the fox said in the book of The Little Prince: "Here is my secret. It's very simple: it is only with the heart that one can see well. The essential things are invisible to the eyes."

God and I became great friends when I understood that it was pointless to get angry over something that seemed unfair, and it was better to accept the circumstances. I matured and understood that I didn't possess the whole truth. Circumstances change, only love prevails.

I sometimes see this process through which I passed as a preparation for me to leave my mark and touch the life of someone in the future.

I stopped asking myself why I lived and others didn't. I accepted my good fortune and started to enjoy my life, and as my mother taught me, I began to give thanks for all. God was not guilty. The case against Him was dropped, and I found peace. Justice was to be found inside me and I started to love myself as never before.

Maybe I was alive because the circumstances were favorable towards me, because I had wonderful parents who never limited me and always encouraged me, because my body and spirit hadn't given up the fight and my soul was full of love for life. Maybe I was alive because I wanted to be. I accepted that God took care of me and didn't take any less care of others.

I started to enjoy my studies much more, now seeing that the application of Law was aligned to the natural way of all that came from God. Apart from this, I had the chance to spend a lot of time with my paternal grandfather, Enrique, a public notary, who invited me to do my social service with him. He was proud that his granddaughter had decided to follow in his footsteps.

During that period, I started to spend more and more time with many people with whom I could identify for the way we thought and looked at life. I made great friends with Carmen, who would turn out to be one of the greatest supports in my life. We would talk for ages about the values and principles we lived by, and we had fun organizing debates about different philosophies and ways of thinking.

Carmen couldn't go to my wedding, as she had moved to a different city for her job, which really upset me, but she took it upon herself to organize a hen party for me with lots of my old university friends.

"What a shame I won't see you at my wedding. I'm going to really miss you."

"Don't worry; we'll see each other again very soon. True friends always find the way back to each other when they most need it."

In 1986, we only had the telephone or the postal system for contacting someone in another city. Long-distance phone calls were costly and the post could take weeks to arrive. So, we did stay out of touch for some time. Her words, however, were true and full of significance. We found each other again many years later, when I needed her most.

MATURITY

THE WEDDING

*Each person you know is an opportunity, a gift which life gives
you so that you can learn, although, at times,
it doesn't appear to be so.*

I was twenty when I fell in love with a man who was a dreamer, full of plans and projects for the future. I liked how he treated me and won me over. He was twenty-five when we met. I always felt he kept some things to himself and didn't really let me see into his soul as I would have liked. Whenever I questioned something, he wouldn't go into many explanations, but he seemed to be a devout man, which was what I was looking for. He made me feel lucky, loved and unafraid to contemplate a future by his side.

I'd told him about my heart early on in our relationship. I explained that I was born with this physical defect and all that that implied. It was important that I could speak openly with him about what I was going through. I didn't want surprises or deceits, but, rather,, transparency.

Very soon, I got used to the fact that my boyfriend was a different kind of man. He was extremely skilled in convincing anyone of his ideas, regardless of how illogical they might seem. There was a joke in his family that I would only come to understand years later.

"It's incredible!," his sisters would say to him. "You end up getting your own way every time and still give the impression that you're behaving like a "perfect gentleman"."

And they would all laugh. They used the words "perfect gentleman" to refer to his reputation for being impeccable, well-mannered and very stylish. It didn't matter what they had all agreed to for, if he wanted to do something different, he would very politely and seriously say, "Yes", and then end up doing something totally different. He didn't pick a fight with anyone, didn't ruffle any feathers, and in the end he did precisely what he wanted, how he wanted.

I developed patience and learned to wait, as he always found a reason to arrive late anywhere we went. I'd been taught at home to be punctual at all times. Even on our first date, he was an hour late, but I didn't want to make an issue out of it. He gave a good reason, and I was more than happy with that.

However, this was an ongoing thorny subject while we were dating. He even arrived late for the pre-wedding photo shoot. The serious look on my face, captured in some of the photos where I was posing alone, reflects the doubts I was having. "Will he get here? What if he has had second thoughts and doesn't want to marry me?" But I kept hoping he would arrive because, sooner or later, he always did. When he finally appeared, he presented me with a bunch of red roses that did, at least, serve to quell my anguish. My face lit up, and all worries were instantly forgotten.

I always felt very grateful; he knew it and perhaps took advantage of it. I cherished the fact that he loved me and didn't mind me not going with him to all his sports activities, like his friends' girlfriends. I felt fortunate to have him by my side.

Before then, I'd had boyfriends of my own age, but he was five years older, seemingly mature and attractive. He told me I was very pretty, treated me well, was always a gentleman, just like my father, and assured me he wanted to take care of me and protect me. I forgot all about my nails, and I started to put aside all those fears that the man who loved me would consider them unsightly. With him, I felt I would be safe; I felt feminine, healthy and not like someone who was sick.

A few weeks before the wedding, we had an argument. We were eating pizza in a small restaurant. He voiced attitudes which made me feel very uncomfortable inside and made me doubt about him. He watched as I took the engagement ring and started to turn it round my finger.

"You always do what you want without taking me into account. Do you think this will change? Do you think we'll be able to actually agree on things?"

"Of course, there are ways we are different. You can't come out with me when I go cycling or climbing, and I don't say anything. I accept you like that. Don't make such a big thing of it!."

"Of course, it's important. How can I know if, when we're married, you'll just do things your way without considering my opinion. That is important, as far as I'm concerned."

"I'll take you into account when it's necessary. I love you very much, you're someone really special. No one will ever love you like I love you. We'll get used to our different ways of being. Don't worry."

His words reassured me.

I knew I was loved, but I felt there was something missing. That something that you can't always find, because it isn't the right person, or you're trying to find it in someone who will never have it. Maybe if I didn't take advantage of that opportunity to get married and enjoy married life a little, then I never would be able to. I loved my fiancé very much and wished to form a family with him, but deep down I knew I was trapped in gratitude. He knew it, too.

Sometimes, love gets confused with so many other sentiments: fear to be alone, desire or gratitude, amongst so many others. We are caught up in this utopic idea of a love that overcomes any obstacle, without taking into account all the elements which can lead to failure.

One day, I spoke to my father, saying that, at times, I got so desperate with my fiancé, I found it difficult to understand him. My father listened and then made me see that we all have things that make us desperate about others, but we must be patient and tolerant. The important thing was that he loved me and treated me well. Maybe he thought I was exaggerating, and he recommended I not give importance to his defects. Without realizing it, I placed a veil before my eyes and thereby stopped seeing what I didn't like, simply in order to keep going.

My parents spoke to him about my illness when we had been engaged a few days. They commented on the fact that I had a serious heart problem, and that they really had no idea how much time I could live a healthy life. They were completely clear and made sure he wasn't going to go into the marriage blind, and that he would know that his fiancée would probably be incapable of having children and that he might be widowed at an early age. This came as no surprise to him, as he was fully aware of everything. We were two young people in love and with all the illusion of living our lives together. I felt lucky and grateful because he didn't mind my sickness.

I felt he loved me enough to see a future with me by his side. And when he told my parents that my condition wouldn't affect his decision, he had them in the palm of his hand, just as he did with me.

Now I understand my parents' precaution, both of them being responsible people who didn't want him or his family to be deceived. In my heart, I couldn't help feeling hurt, but I knew they were right. The ghost of death didn't abandon me, even when life held out such promise to me. At every single important event in my life, the possibility of dying appeared. It wasn't simple, but I knew the best way to tackle it was by visualizing what I longed for in my life, and not to think about whether I might not be alive for it.

It was a beautiful wedding, full of my dearest friends and family. The ideal thing would have been that I finish my university studies beforehand, but for me, time was at a premium, and this was my chance to live life to the fullest, just in case my life became complicated or even came to an end.

We had a very busy start to married life. I'd get up very early to go to class in the morning, arrived home to fix lunch and returned to university in the afternoon. My husband worked all day. We saw each other at lunchtime and always dined together in the evening. We also joined a small Bible study group which met once a week. We kept the weekends for get-togethers with friends and relatives.

For the first two years, everything seemed to be going along just fine and my husband's business was thriving. We were able to travel and buy new things for the house. We did everything together. A couple of months into our marriage, we started talking about the possibility of having a child. I wanted more than anything in the world to bless my husband with the fruit of our love. I didn't know what was in store for me, but I knew that with love and God's blessing, we would manage to bring into the world a small being in whom we would leave our legacy; surely science would find a way to keep me alive. I had faith, and trusted that all would be well.

There were many visits to doctors, searching for a gynaecologist.

Uppermost in our minds was our desire to be parents and to find a doctor who would be willing to accompany us in the process. Some didn't want to be responsible for me, considering the difficulty of my case, arguing that the possibilities of my having great complications and dying were too high. At that time, I believed that they weren't worried about me, just about their own image, even though I now know that that was not the case. I simply agreed, but my heart only heard my own voice of faith and trust.

My mother was also very perturbed: to see her daughter, alive in spite of all the forecasts, risking everything to get pregnant, seemed like madness. My brother, sisters, grandparents and friends all thought I'd taken leave of my senses.

The only person who believed God would grant me a child was me. And, of course, my husband, who, for me, at that time, was the greatest blessing. Not only did he support me, he also encouraged me to believe in that dream and trust everything would be fine. Only he could have accompanied me on such an adventure. We trusted that God would allow us to see our love reflected in a child. We had some doubts, naturally, and talked about them at length. I told my husband that if my body couldn't manage to produce a pregnancy in spite of our efforts, then that would be the sign to stop, but that we should at least try. I didn't know if I would succeed, but it was clear that if I didn't even make the attempt, I would always have that doubt. All I cared about at that moment, the only thing I concentrated on, was that my husband supported me one hundred percent.

Whilst understanding the warnings of doctors and family members, there was something in my heart and soul which refused to believe it. Each night, I would imagine how my life would be with a baby taking his or her first steps around the house. I longed for a baby with all my heart. I conjured it up and sketched it out in my mind. I outlined its face and smile in my thoughts. It was so exciting to imagine having a little being in my belly, moving around and enjoying the start of its life inside me. I saw its fingers, nails, heels, legs, its tiny body, shoulders and arms. I could see its perfectly-formed rosy mouth, its smile, its closed eyes and long eyelashes. It was incredible how I could visualize so clearly that little beauty which was yet to exist.

I was hoping for a miracle. From the time I was a little girl, I had been accompanied by my dear ghost *Ráfel*, but my sense of survival was greater than any physical limitation. My desire to be a mother and form a family was stronger than any medical recommendation, and that made all the difference. I admit it could seem to indicate a small degree of irresponsibility, lack of maturity and common sense on my part. But, for me, it was about building a dream wherein no one could see the ending more clearly than myself. I felt it from the time I had held Dora, my doll, and the terrible pain I experienced that night when they tore her away from me. I knew it ever since I held my sister Marcela when I was barely six years old. Every cell of my body prepared itself to make a reality of what my mind and my faith had proposed. This time, I wouldn't let them tear my baby away from me, nor would I let it cry as much as Dora had done. I would take care of it and protect it.

At night-time, before sleeping, I would have long conversations with God. I asked Him to perform this miracle for me, but I also begged that my husband wouldn't be disappointed if there were complications. I felt I owed him so much, and this was one way in which I could return that love: by giving him a child.

Other doctors told me I should take into account the fact that, if my life was compromised by the pregnancy, it was important to know what to do in that moment; whether to opt for saving the baby's life or mine. It was explained that, normally, the doctors decide on the mother, as she could have more children, and the baby would have no chance of life. I just couldn't accept that this was right. The life of a baby, especially mine, was the priority. I was tormented by this dilemma all those months that we were visiting specialists in search of a child.

Finally we visited my cardiologist, Doctor José Luis Assad, to hear his opinion, as I trusted him so much. On this visit, he could see that the only recommendation I was determined not to follow was that of not trying to conceive. He didn't display much enthusiasm, which was to be expected, but we felt reassured by his professionalism. He then recommended a specialist in high-risk pregnancies, Dr. Humberto Espinosa. We decided to go with him, as it was essential for me to be in the hands of a doctor who could take care of such a risky pregnancy as mine was sure to be.

This gynaecologist was very practical. I told him how much I wanted to be a mother, fully aware of the enormous risk.

"You wish to have a child, and the diagnosis indicates that Ana Cecilia should not take this risk. But, we do have to take into account your desire to be a mother. We are going to give your body the opportunity to answer either "Yes", it's possible, or "No". We shall have your cardiologist close by. We trust that nature will guide us through," he concluded, looking straight into my eyes.

After hearing this, I became calm and happy that both my gynaecologist and my cardiologist trusted that out faith and our desire would be enough to make this highly risky dream come true. Today, I know I didn't thank them for journeying with me through the unknown; nobody with my characteristics had given birth, but, then again, nobody had lived as long as I had with these physical conditions. The way I looked at it, the possibilities of bringing a child into the world were enormous, in total contrast with science, which said it was impossible. All my senses, my body, my mind, heart and spirit shouted out that I was destined to be a mother.

But I had to wait a little: I got married one year before completing my studies, and at that time I was about to finish my last semester, so I promised myself I would not get pregnant before leaving university. That was not an easy task, as I couldn't use any form of birth control: my circulation and oxygenation deteriorated easily with any hormonal medicines.

I was in my very last final exams when I had my routine visit to the gynaecologist. The doctor checked me, saying everything was fine, with nothing to worry about, but he needed to do a few tests. He could notice some irregularity and needed to be sure what was involved. That same morning, I went to get some blood samples ordered by Doctor Espinosa.

I imagined many things. Even though the doctor didn't say precisely what the blood analyses were for and didn't give me any cause for concern, I had butterflies in my stomach. Over lunch, my husband and I discussed this. On the one hand, we didn't want to build up our hopes, but, on the other hand, we were overcome by impatience. We weren't looking for me to get pregnant yet, but we couldn't discard the possibility that that was what the doctor had observed. He had agreed to give me the results later over the phone.

The last thing on my mind was that it could be bad news. Next day, I would sit the last exams of my finals; I did everything but study: just the chance that the test might reflect my pregnancy was so exciting, and I couldn't get it out of my head.

I had spent weeks, months, years, probably my whole life, waiting for this moment. Not only did I have the opportunity to love, but also, far beyond that, I was also asking for the privilege to give life to another human being. It was one of the most important moments of my existence. That afternoon, I called the doctor to get the results. Such were my nerves that I could hardly speak. My tongue and lips were dryer than a desert, and I could hardly manage to swallow any saliva.

"Doctor Espinosa, it's me, Ana Cecilia González. I'm calling to see if you have the results of my analyses."

"Ana Cecilia, great news. Congratulations! You are pregnant! Everything seems to indicate you are three weeks along."

My legs started to shake and I went numb. I felt the blood rush to my feet. I sat down in the nearest chair and asked him to repeat the news. My face lit up totally. I smiled from ear to ear. My feet started to move uncontrollably and the heels of my shoes went "click", "click", "click" as I talked to him.

"So, there's absolutely no doubt, doctor? Can I tell my husband we're expecting a child?"

"Of course you can. Congratulations! You can tell all your family you're going to be parents," he said, sounding delighted.

"Thank you, doctor. I am so happy, so very happy!"

"I know. Now, take great care of yourself, because your baby depends on you."

He suggested I go to my cardiologist for very strict and careful monitoring.

I was pregnant; now I was embarking on a huge adventure, a project, a life. I had a tiny being inside my belly. I was swept away by an enormous emotion, and I wanted to shout out my news to the whole world. God granted me the miracle of conceiving a child. My thoughts tumbled helter-skelter inside my head; I just couldn't come to terms with it. Deep down, a fear I hadn't felt before suddenly surged up, one that my dreams and desires would come to nothing. But my confidence far outweighed that. This fragile, weak and limited body was harboring a life.

Nothing, absolutely nothing, could put a damper on my happiness. I would do everything in my power to bring her into the world, as from the moment I knew I was pregnant, my heart had told me this was going to be a girl.

As soon as I got the news, I phoned my mother. She only had to hear my voice to know something important was happening.

"Mom, you're going to be a granny. I'm expecting!"

She sighed deeply and congratulated me. I convinced myself she was as overjoyed as I was. She was very discreet and made an effort to feel happy and to sound happy, but I can still hear that sigh, even today. How much fear she must have felt at that moment. I know she must have experienced the thrill of excitement and happiness; she was going to be a grandmother for the first time, but, at what cost? I wasn't prepared to decipher that sigh. I just contented myself with her words of congratulations. The truth is, I wasn't worried about what she, my father, my brother and sisters or friends would think. I probably wouldn't have paid any attention to them even if they had made some kind of comment. Today, I know that I would have told myself what I unconsciously thought that day: don't listen, don't worry, she is happy, that's just her way of trying to survive.

Now, I know my mother felt an enormous sense of fear: more than ever, her daughter's life was, in danger. She, however, respected my decision and had no choice but to be by my side and rejoice with me during my pregnancy. In the end, this is what a mother does: stay by her children's side, whatever the circumstances, even though these could mean the risk of dying. In my heart of hearts, I felt the desire to give them moments of joy, to make up, in some small way, for all the hardships they had gone through during my childhood.

I never thought about my parents and their pain, their feelings of fear and anguish for what they would have to go through. It may well be that when you are young, you don't have that sensitivity, and that's why the young can achieve so much. It's only at this stage of our lives that we're capable of risking so much. Poor parents! I never imagined how I was snatching their sleep from them once again.

My husband didn't call as we had agreed, so I set about making the preparations to surprise the future father. I looked around for streamers, pieces of card and everything I could lay my hands on to give him the news. I stuck the message on the front entrance to our house so that, opening the door, he would find the surprise.

That day, he arrived late; the poster fell several times and I had to keep sticking it back up again. But it didn't matter. He jumped for joy when he finally did see it. We hugged and announced the news to all the family. I can't deny that I still had pangs of doubt, but I overcame my fears, thinking about the wonder of the final outcome: my baby.

I wanted to think that I had everyone's backing in my project, and yet, to support me in this venture was the most difficult thing a mother, father or an entire family could do, given the circumstances. I was thrilled by the idea of giving them their first grandchild which, I hoped, at least would make them forget a little how those first years of marriage had been with a very sick daughter. All I wanted was to be a mother and enjoy the delight of holding that baby in my arms.

I was convinced that I should live life to the fullest. I was responsible for my decisions, my actions and the consequences. But I refused to believe that my adventure of becoming a mother could end in tragedy. My thoughts were bold and unshakable. I always visualized my goals as being reached, I never stopped to consider the obstacles for, if I did, I would start to die, and it wasn't my time yet.

I applied the same principle I had done all my life, but now, it was about the life of someone else: my baby.

The following day, when I arrived at university, the look on my face left no one in any doubt that something incredible was happening. The teacher noticed, and asked me if something was going on. I told him about my pregnancy and my doubts as to whether I could go through with it.

At that, it was as if a party had ripped through the classroom.

Everyone congratulated and hugged me. Then the teacher checked my grades and decided I didn't have to take the exam, I could be exempt, as a gift for being pregnant.

Everyone clapped and cheered the teacher. I felt euphoric and, of course, accepted. I signed the teacher's grade book and attained a 98% final average in that subject.

And so I finished my classes, and all that was left was the thesis, which I was sure I could manage to do. My pregnancy was the best gift for having completed my university studies.

● PREGNANCY

There comes a point when taking care of myself is to protect you.

The doctors knew of the risks, but trusted that my faith and health would be enough for me to live and see my child born. The reality is that they could do no more than simply accompany me in the process in the best possible way, but all the medical knowledge and prognoses were hardly encouraging. Statistics were non-existent; there were no records of any woman with this heart disease who had been able to conceive or give birth to a child.

"The chances of you aborting are great. It will be a hard job. There are very strong possibilities of delayed intrauterine growth, and your physical condition could deteriorate seriously," Doctor Espinosa warned me in the early days of my pregnancy.

I knew this, but tried not to get scared, as each time I felt threatened in this way, *Ráfel* would show up even stronger. Sometimes, I felt I should show my claws and defend myself at all costs against anyone who wanted to take my baby. Now, more than ever, I would make sure there was no way that *Ráfel* would even dream of taking me with him. My only consolation was the knowledge that he wanted me, and not my baby, and maybe this would deter him, and he might even take care of us both. I didn't know. Sometimes, when I was sending up a prayer to God to safeguard my pregnancy, I remembered him.

"Keep far away, whatever you do. Let me enjoy my pregnancy, don't get too close," I would say to him, certain he was listening.

This concern was quickly forgotten and I concentrated on what was important. I had become a bearer of life and hope. Suddenly, I found myself in an almost celestial state. I had wanted so much to be a mother and now, that adventure had begun. My entire body was getting ready for that. "How great God is," I thought. "How wonderful Nature is."

The gynaecologist and I would have long talks, and I realized how he always went out of his way to encourage me. He told me many success stories of high-risk pregnancies. He asked me what I did during the day and how I filled my time when I was resting. I think he was trying to get an idea of my state of mind and my emotional strength.

I also had my monthly visit to the cardiologist, Dr. Assad, who would check my heart and blood pressure and encourage me by saying that everything looked good and my heart was behaving perfectly. He always made me feel that, yes, it was possible, even though he was, no doubt, very concerned. He supported me at all times and never revealed any concern he might have had.

In time, I realized that the doctors were my accomplices in this mad plan to bring a child into this world.

With so much support, I felt lucky, happy and full of life. I can't remember having lived such a richly satisfying time as those eight and a half months of my pregnancy. The gynaecologist insisted I be in semi-repose, which meant resting at home without much physical activity, but not necessarily lying down. I devoted my time to reading, writing and composing songs for my guitar. I listened to the music I enjoyed, such as Mocedades, Silvio Rodríguez and Pablo Milanés amongst others.

Occasionally, I would spend my time in prayer; I talked to God and to my baby. I had the advantage of being able to stay at home, and trusted that my husband was doing fine in the business.

I wrote reams about the significance of being pregnant and the great value represented by carrying a baby in the womb. I filled notebooks which, sadly, I lost when we first moved house. I live in hope that, some day, they will appear.

The first three months of pregnancy were calm, with nothing untoward happening. My husband and I went to our Bible groups once a week and tried to be close to the church. On Sunday, we would go to Mass, visit the family and be home early so I could lie down. Señora Fina helped me with the housecleaning, but in those days I cooked, purchased whatever was necessary and kept the household accounts.

In the third month, I heard the baby's heart beat for the first time.

On the day of my first fetal ultrasound, I arrived at the doctor's just as they had asked me to: with a full bladder. I had a sick heart, but I wasn't dying of it, but there, I felt I was dying of a bladder that was ready to burst. The pain was unbearable. The worst was the eternal wait to go through to the ultrasound room. I thought I would have to give up, put a stop to the waiting , say I wouldn't go into the consulting room and would come back when my baby was bigger and I didn't have to go in with a full bladder. Added to all that, it seemed that nobody was in the least bit bothered. But I persevered.

I would love to have had someone to complain to, to tell them how I felt, but I couldn't. I was on my own, as for some reason or other, on many occasions, my husband just couldn't arrive on time, not even to my medical appointments. That day, he had agreed to arrive on time without fail, but something held him up. This was hurtful, as it was the first time we would hear the beautiful sound of our child's little heart. I still hoped that he would, after all, arrive at any moment.

The appointment was for half past four. By now, it was twenty to five, and I still hadn't gone through to the consulting room. I so desperately wanted to hear my husband's voice announcing his arrival, but nothing. What could possibly make people miss moments like this?

I hadn't wanted to ask my mother to go with me, either. The last thing I wanted to do was to give explanations. Nothing should eclipse the pleasure of those beautiful moments I was living. I never spoke to my friends about these things, as it would make my husband look bad, which I didn't want. In any case, I was happy, and I wasn't going to let anything affect that.

So, that day, with my bladder full to bursting, I was finally shown through to the doctor's consulting room, and they lay me down on the bed. The doctor started to move slowly over my stomach with his fetal Doppler, and the discomfort of the pressure he applied was so great, I felt that at any moment, I would wet the sheets. One more slight push down and I would have emptied my bladder in front of the nurse and the doctor. But that didn't matter at all, I could stand any discomfort; all I wanted was to know if everything was all right. I could hear strange noises, but I couldn't make out the image on the screen. Suddenly, the doctor asked me to keep very quiet and listen carefully. There it was: a very fast boom, boom boom, which never stopped. The screen showed that the little heart was beating at 140 beats to the minute. I could only think of how beautiful that sound was. My baby was right there, and I could hear it. Besides that, the screen showed a little light that went on and off in a small shadowy mass: its heart.

Feeling a little concerned, I asked the doctor if the heartbeat wasn't too fast, at which he smiled and said that this was an excellent speed. Everything was going wonderfully. I could barely distinguish the image, but according to the doctor, everything was absolutely fine. It was impossible to deny the existence of God in my life. Only He could perform this miracle. I was so excited that my heart started pounding at about the same rate as my baby's. A huge smile lit up my face. It was hard to believe that this was real, that there was a tiny little body inside me and I was giving it life. I looked up to heaven and thanked God for this miracle. This was one of the most beautiful moments I shall treasure in my heart.

Just when we were about to finish, my husband appeared, and they showed him through straightaway. He heard the doctor tell me everything was fine, and he looked very happy. He was just in time to see the last images. He and the doctor talked for a moment, while I went to the bathroom, and they let him listen to a short recording of the baby's heartbeats.

I didn't want to criticize him for anything, as I wasn't prepared to waste any energy doing that. I felt complete. I forgot his lack of punctuality when I saw how happy he was and how he took care of me. None of it mattered, as I could imagine him being a very good father. I didn't complain and I accepted these aspects of my relationship just as they were.

I didn't put on much weight as my baby was so tiny, and my body was focused on keeping a healthy balance between coping with the pregnancy and, at the same time, my own illness.

From the fourth month onwards, I had to stay in bed most of the time, and I was close to the fifth month when I first felt the baby move. That was magical. The little being I was carrying inside me was alive and I could feel it. I could spend hours just waiting, keeping absolutely quiet and still, so as to perceive it once more. What a beautiful feeling!

In my case, the risk of death was very high, as everything was stacked against me. And yet, my body took it upon itself to make sure the baby was small enough not to represent an even greater risk due to its size.

The following months were spent with me watching television documentaries. I also read anything I could lay my hands on to prepare me for the arrival of my child, especially ones which were uplifting. We had our weekly Bible sessions in our house so that I wouldn't have to move. I also decided to read the Bible more, as I hadn't read all of it, and that was the best remedy to keep me healthy, strong and positive.

My time was spent between friends and doctors' appointments. When I was due to go the doctor's, my husband would pick me up, as I wasn't allowed to drive. In the seventh month, I came down with a stomach infection which put my health and physical stability at risk. By then, I had gained a total of five kilos in weight. After two days of diarrhea, I had lost one and a half kilos. I had bags under my eyes and looked so drawn that my husband became anxious and took me straight off to see the doctor.

They couldn't give me much medication for obvious reasons. No one could believe I was seven months pregnant as, judging from the size of my stomach, I looked as if I was only three or four months along.

I was hospitalized for a few hours whilst being put on an intravenous drip. Everyone was frightened there might be some complication, but I never doubted. I knew I would get out of there without any undue problem. Recently, I had been struck by something Henry Ford had said:

"The best automobile driver is the one with imagination: he imagines he has his family with him in the car."

I imagined arriving home perfectly safe. Many a time, I would see myself as one of those first 1919 Ford model T vehicles. For me, in my belly, I was driving my family, and it didn't matter how heavy the load was, or in what bad shape the engine was, I simply refused to stop. It could be throwing out smoke, rattling or having a burst tire: I just kept going. It was a matter of me pulling on the starting handle, giving it a few turns to get it going once again. My determination to keep my body and organism working, in order to make sure my baby found its way into my arms, was enough to keep the machine from stopping. I was the best driver of my vehicle. Giving up was not an option.

Shortly after, I had the second fetal echocardiogram done, and this time, thank God, I was not asked to go in with a full bladder. I almost cried, I was so grateful. My husband went with me and we could both enjoy the spectacle of our first child in action. It was small and perfectly formed. It had two legs and two arms, each one with its five fingers and toes. Its head was perfect and it opened and closed its eyes. It kicked and moved its hands at great speed, before calming down. Its heartbeats were strong and stable.

On being asked by the doctor if we wanted to know the sex of the baby, we said no. We wanted it to be a surprise.

My friends came round to see me on several occasions. When they arrived, since I couldn't go up or downstairs, I would throw the keys down through the window for them to let themselves in. They kept me company throughout this waiting period whilst I played the guitar, and we would all sing. It was an incredible joy for me to have them always at my side. They made me laugh and filled my days with their stories. They cooked and took the food to the bedroom. We always found something to talk about. Some were friends from the second grade of Primary, others joined the group over the years, and still others were my sister's friends who also became great friends of mine. With all the ups and downs, they have never left my side and have been my great Soul Mates.

Through them, I learned what it was to be unconditional, irrespective of the distance between us. They were, and still are, one of the greatest treasures God has given me, and they helped me through what would come after the baby's birth.

Many times, my husband would arrive home only to find my house full of friends, or my mother paying me a visit. Fortunately, he enjoyed their company and was glad to know I hadn't spent the whole day on my own.

By now, I was constantly aware of my baby moving inside me. We talked at length in the last weeks:

"Remember, my darling, you are a beautiful child, and very much wanted, and I love you, even without seeing you, and I know God has great plans for you. When you arrive, you will be an instrument to help many others, and God will grant you the gift of the word, to help raise up the fallen and console the suffering. You will be someone totally committed to their fellow man, and you will enjoy life intensely. You will know how to value and love each person for who he is and not what he possesses, and you will always give thanks for the privilege of living and being loved," I would say time and time again.

My mother helped me choose the coverlet and sheets for the crib. She would come and pick me up, I would go downstairs ever so carefully, and off we went to do some shopping. She chose the shops I could go to where I wouldn't have to walk too far, so I could simply choose and buy the things for the baby's room.

It was planned that I would have a Caesarean in the 38th. week. The actual delivery date came a week earlier. There was no threat of a miscarriage or any problems during the pregnancy, but any unexpected circumstances might cause a lot of trouble.

The previous night, I had been experiencing a lot of chills, and my mother was concerned when I told her about it the next morning. She called my husband instantly, asking him to get me to the doctor's without delay, and that if he couldn't, she would do it. She was afraid those chills were ominous.

I woke up with a strong urge to clean the house, tidy up and leave everything spick and span. I cleaned the bathroom and scrubbed the sink really hard. I went downstairs to the kitchen, got everything out for lunch, and asked my daily help to give me a hand to cook something different. I fancied a tuna and vegetable loaf. I explained how to make it, she wrote everything down in a notebook so as not to forget it. I went out to the washroom to make sure there was no dirty laundry left. I washed everything that was pending, and separated the clothes for ironing.

I filled my suitcase with my things and those of the baby, absolutely sure I knew what was happening. According to the calendar, there was still a week to go before the delivery, but that morning, I felt I had to have everything ready.

My husband arrived for me just after midday, which surprised me. He said my mother had asked him to call the doctor who, by now, was expecting me. We went to the appointment, but I left the suitcase, the food, the washing machine in progress and the cleaner at home. I was sure I would be back within the hour to enjoy my tuna loaf and to rest. That was not to be.

When I arrived at the gynaecologist's, he examined me, only to find that I was already dilated five centimetres. Because of my high pain threshold, I hadn't realized I was already in labor. My baby would be born at any moment. I felt no pain, just a little strange. My doctor couldn't believe it.

"Can't you really feel anything?"

Then I asked if all was well.

"Of course. Everything is fine. It's just that your baby wants to be born."

He instructed me to head straight to the hospital, where he would meet me twenty minutes later. I've never liked surprises, and as this change of plan was totally unexpected, I didn't take kindly to just leaving everything that I had prepared at home. At my insistence, we went back home, I picked up my suitcase and baby bag, and made sure the clothes had been ironed and put away correctly. I asked the cleaning lady to clean the stove really well and to leave everything nice and tidy before she left. She had to take home with her the food I had so painstakingly taught her how to prepare.

My husband, meanwhile, was getting desperate. I wouldn't stop giving out orders, but I still took the liberty to phone my mother and fill her in on all the details. I asked her to let all my friends know. My husband's parents were out of town just then, so he actually didn't

114

notify any of his family at that point.

Finally, we set off to the hospital, by which time it was almost two o'clock. I was starting to get nervous. I felt very well, really, strong and excited, but on the way there, I was overcome by the doubt as to whether the baby was all right. To take my mind off it, I started to think about if it would be Ana Paula or Andres Gerardo who was about to arrive, as these were the names we'd chosen.

We arrived ten minutes later than planned, and my gynaecologist, cardiologist and the operating room were all waiting for me. I lay back on the bed in preparation for the delivery. Doctor Assad said, jokingly:

"Just look at you! It looks as if you've just got a bit of a bloated stomach, that's all. What wouldn't many women give just to keep a figure like yours?"

We all laughed. I looked four months pregnant.

My parents, brother and sisters arrived a few moments later. They gave me their blessing, as did my husband, because the doctors were in a hurry to whisk me off to the operating room. I wasn't in a normal delivery room. My case was so important and so rare that they had summoned many doctors to witness this momentous event - the Caesarean of a mother with a severe heart condition.

The anesthetist arrived and asked me to roll over on one side to start the epidural sedation. When I turned, I saw a great number of doctors in the room. I started to tremble uncontrollably, out of fear or nerves, and the anesthetist couldn't proceed.

"Ana Cecilia, are you all right? Is something wrong?" asked Dr. Assad.

"I feel very awkward. Why are so many doctors here? What's happening? I don't see why they should be here looking at me."

I felt exposed, just like when I was being examined as a child, like a rare insect. I assumed something was wrong.

The doctor realized that so much interest from the medical staff was making me nervous, so he signalled for them to leave.

I was scared and excited, as I would soon get to meet my child. When Dr. Espinosa arrived to begin the Caesarean, my heart started to beat irregularly, which converted into an arrhythmia. This was the first time I had felt that in all my pregnancy. All the normal procedure of a Caesarean changed in that instant.

"Ana Cecilia, we're going to put you to sleep completely. We want to perform the Caesarean as quickly as possible so that Dr. Assad can take care of your heart."

I agreed. Suddenly, I felt fearful and cold. After years of absence, now *Ráfel*'s closeness to me was evident. I was in danger. They put an oxygen mask over my face, and I lost consciousness. When I woke up, they were still performing the surgery, but the doctors were chatting amongst themselves.

"You had a baby girl; she's tiny but very healthy." said Dr. Espinosa.

I could relax at that moment and I felt happy. Ana Paula was born.

"I want to see her. Where is she?"

"Your baby's fine. The doctor took her away to check her and put her in an incubator. You can see her when we've finished."

I was taken to Intensive Care to be put under observation. I had just given birth to a baby girl who weighed 1 kilo 650 grams and measured 41 centimetres; she was perfectly healthy and developed, but they wouldn't let me see her. She was in an incubator without her mother and I was in intensive care without my daughter. I was longing to see her, but had no choice, as my heart had to be monitored until it stabilized.

Everyone went to eat while I recuperated. Those in the waiting-room were told that one family member could see me. The first visitor I got in intensive care was my cousin Karen, who I had played with when we were little. She arrived smiling and happy and with very good news. She had seen Ana Paula who, she said, was beautiful, which made me really happy.

When I ask myself why life has given me so much, I cannot explain it, and can only give thanks.

A few minutes later, my husband arrived, followed by my parents and siblings. A thousand questions flashed through my mind, and I asked them all.

"How is Ana Paula? Is she all right?? Is she healthy? What does she look like? What's her hair like? Have you heard her cry yet?

How does she cry?"

"She's beautiful, very small, but reacting wonderfully. She's already done pee-pee and had a poop, so everything's functioning well. You'll be able to see her soon," said my husband.

Many friends came to visit me and they all said the same thing. The fact that they had seen her and repeated that my daughter was fine was a huge relief.

The next day, now recovered from my arrhythmia and feeling stronger, I was taken to my room, and then to see Ana Paula in the nursery, where she was still in an incubator. They wouldn't let me hold her, as she was under observation, but I was allowed to stroke her and to talk with her.

I wept. It was a miracle that I had managed to bring a little girl into this world. Ana Paula was alive, and so was I.

"You're just as I imagined my little daughter. Your face, your eyes and your mouth, your body, everything is perfect. Nothing is missing. You are a beautiful creation. Thank you for being here, thank you for entering my life," I said, caressing her.

She could sense it whenever I arrived to see her. She turned her face on hearing my voice and, if she was crying, she would stop. The nurses said our communication was incredible.

On my second day in the hospital, Dr. Espinosa came to check me. My ward was full of friends and family, which amazed and concerned him, seeing so many people, as I was fragile and could catch any virus, no matter how inoffensive it might seem.

"Good afternoon. I know Ana Cecilia is happy to see you here, but I would ask you not to use up my patient's oxygen. Only two people at a time, please, and no kisses, as I don't want to take any risks," he said, very gently but firmly.

They all drifted out, some embarrassed and others with big smiles on their faces, apologizing to the doctor. I just smiled and agreed. My gynaecologist was right: I had to take care.

Ana Paula was in the incubator for seventeen days. When I was discharged, my husband took me to the hospital, and I spent the entire day waiting to feed her and spend as long as possible with her. At first, I couldn't breast feed, but they fed her my milk through a syringe. They passed a very fine, soft tube through her mouth to her stomach, which is how I fed her the first five days.

She sucked on a pacifier and beame desperate because she wanted more food. So, the doctors decided to introduce her to the bottle, a little one with a very soft and thin nipple. She was so tiny in the beginning that they didn't want her to waste energy suckling on my breast. Three days before she left, I could breast feed her, and she accepted it very well.

When she was seven days old, they let me carry her. That was a wonderful feeling. She had gained a few grams of weight and her body, which weighed just 1 kilo 750 grams, was perfect. She opened her eyes and smiled at me.

"Darling, how lovely you are!" I said to her and she responded by making little expressions on her face which resembled a smile.

Then I could understand a little of what my mother had gone through with me, and how hard the waiting was: days and nights with no sleep, waiting for the moment to be with her daughter; just as I was doing now. The difference was that I had a daughter who was tiny but perfectly healthy.

The great day came when we could take her home. She weighed 1 kilo 900 grams. They told us how to take care of her. I felt I had my little porcelain doll in my arms. I held her, kissed her and couldn't take my eyes off her.

The pediatrician and gynaecologist were there that day and each one had his own recommendation.

"You must both take great care. If you start to feel bad, or tired, or with anything bothering you, stop breast feeding immediately and give her the bottle. There is some very good quality formula out there," said my gynaecologist, whereas the pediatrician advised:

"The longer you can breast feed, the better it will be for her, and her defences will build up."

Before going home, and with my daughter in my arms, I went to see Dr. Assad, to thank him for all his support.

"Thank you for everything, for believing in me, and for the enormous help you offered me."

"You've nothing to thank me for. None of us did any more than be by your side. You are the brave one here, the one with huge conviction. Thank you for allowing us to be close by. Your heart went through a difficult time. Don't hesitate to see me if you have arrhythmias or feel very tired," my cardiologist concluded.

Each one of the doctors was right. I was the one who had to pace myself and be guided by my common sense, as a woman and as a mother.

Miraculously, I was able to breast feed for four months, only stopping when I caught a cold and had to take antibiotics. It was a shame, but I felt pleased with what I had achieved. Not only that, but I managed to produce so much milk in those months that it seemed like an eternal fountain. Every day, I went to the hospital where Ana Paula had been born, to donate nearly a liter of milk to some newborn babies.

When she was in hospital, I learned of some cases of children who were premature and very sick, whose mothers didn't produce any milk for them. The mothers were in good health and their babies were hospitalized, whereas I, who was supposedly the "sick" mother, had enough milk for their babies and my own.

In the hospital, the nurses taught me how to empty the milk into little sterilized bottles in order to avoid any contamination. They said there was nothing better for a child than breast milk. It was lovely to feel that I was helping to give life to another life that was just starting.

I dedicated myself to looking after my daughter and enjoying her. We took advantage of any occasion to dress her up prettily and take her out. We had to watch over her more carefully than a normal child, as she was so tiny.

When she was three months old, I took Ana Paula to the pediatrician and, on finding that she weighed the same as in the previous month, he became concerned and suggested switching back to formula rather than breast milk. I could continue to breast feed, but, for her, it was

COMING HOME

simpler to feed from a bottle as it wouldn't entail using up so much energy, so that is what I did.

She started to gain weight little by little, and by the eighth month, she had recovered completely.

Years later, my gynaecologist, Humberto Espinosa, sent me a lovely letter:

First of all, I want to tell you that, perhaps, you are one of the most special patients, if not the most special patient I have had during my twenty-five-year professional career. Needless to say, all patients are special, but some are even more so, given their medical problem, in this case obstetrics.

This pregnancy was successful thanks to your will and your determination to be a mother. At one point, I mentioned to you that your chances of having a miscarriage were great. It was very difficult to see how your pregnancy could go to full term. There were high probabilities of intrauterine growth delay, and, once the pregnancy was over, you ran a high risk of suffering deterioration in your physical condition. Well, nearly everything was stacked against you, except your faith in God that everything was going to be fine. And it was.

ANA PAULA TREE MONTHS OLD.

●I WAS SEPARATED FROM ANA PAULA

When I have lived through dark nights, I am upheld by the certainty that, sooner or later, the sun will always come out.

ANA PAULA TWO MONTHS OLD.

As the months went by, Ana Paula was growing in strength and vitality. At first, it was simply a case of carrying her, caring for her and feeding her. She was a healthy child, happy, tiny, and didn't make great physical demands on me. At the crawling stage, she wanted to be up and down the stairs, and I would have to go after her. She was a healthy eater and played all day long, but she demanded a lot of my attention.

I was so excited that I forgot about my heart, which held up throughout all the pregnancy and birth like a true champion, but now, with the extra physical demands being made on me by Ana Paula, it started to fail. My spirit would follow her around, but my body just couldn't do it anymore. It was difficult to keep up with her when she was nine months old. In the end, she didn't need me any more in order for her to survive; she was healthy, strong and full of life.

When she was about to turn ten months, we went to see my cardiologist. My husband had noticed that something was not quite right with me, but he put it down to the normal exhaustion of a mother looking after her child, and he even began to suspect I was simply getting too lazy to attend to his needs. I explained to the doctor that it was really hard for me to go up and down stairs, and going after Ana Paula was tiring me out.

He did some tests, checked over a few things, then got in touch with a colleague. After a while, he called us back again into his office and said that the time had come.

"What's happening to you now is what we've been expecting since you were born; a cardiac decompensation. Thank God it didn't happen before, but now you need to take action."

"What does that mean, doctor? Do I need surgery?"

"Absolutely. Your heart is struggling hard to get oxygen, which is why you're so tired. It's not that you're getting lazy or that the baby is taking it out of you. It's your heart that needs attention."

At this point, my husband and I looked at each other. I could see from his expression his concern for my wellbeing, but also for the economic aspect. I didn't have any medical insurance that would cover anything related to my heart. When I was born, it was not very common to take out that kind of insurance, and when my parents did, the pre-existing conditions were not covered. Having an operation would represent a huge expense, especially if it were done abroad, as the doctors suggested.

"Your condition is not common, and in Mexico, we don't have much experience in your type of heart disease. The ideal thing would be for you to see the experts. In Houston, they've got your medical records and have followed up your case, and I know that they will be able to help you."

Dr. Assad arranged for an appointment in Houston, and we were under the impression that it would just be a medical check-up and maybe I would be given some kind of treatment. Never would we have imagined what was to come!

We went to see my parents and told them that Dr. Assad had recommended we go to Houston.

This came as no surprise to my mother. She had been worried about me for weeks: one day, she called me, and, even though I was just a few steps away from the phone, when I answered I was panting as if I had just climbed a mountain.

We made preparations to leave Ana Paula in good hands.

The first time I left her was when she was five months old. She stayed with my mother because my husband and I had gone off with some friends to go skiing for a week. I can't think how I imagined I would be able to ski, but I would be going with some of my good friends, and my husband had accepted, so I couldn't miss this opportunity of spending time with them. Not only could I not do any of the activities, but I was also badly affected by the altitude. I spent my time in the hotel lobby, just relaxing, with another friend who wasn't much interested in skiing, either.

Now, though, I was going to leave my daughter, but under very different circumstances. I imagined that, in any case, it would be just for a few days. I prepared her bag with clothes, bottles, milk, blankets and toys. Deep down, I was grateful that I would get the chance to rest a little. Any activity, no matter how small, implied a lot of effort for me. I supposed I would take advantage and rest while my mother looked after Ana Paula.

"I'll take good care of her, don't you worry. As soon as you get news, call us to see if we should go there to keep you company."

"Yes, Mom. I hope we'll be back soon with some good medicine to sort out the problem. Thanks for looking after Ana Paula."

We hugged, and I felt a lump in my throat as my little girl waved goodbye and blew me a kiss. She was as happy as could be with her granny. Neither of us could ever have imagined how long it would be before we saw each other again.

My husband and I went to Houston. I was calm, as Ana Paula couldn't have been in better hands than my mother's. I knew my husband was very worried about the financial aspect, and he was right: if I needed surgery, it would cost thousands of dollars. My parents would be there to support me, as always, even though they themselves were going through tough times, economically, just then.

At the airport, I had to have a wheelchair, as I couldn't walk any more. Luckily for us, a good family friend, Gustavo, was on the same flight, so he pushed my wheelchair everywhere, whilst my husband took care of the luggage.

The next day, we arrived early at our appointment. The doctors were very surprised to see me. There didn't seem to be any logic in what I was telling them. When Doctor Nihill examined me, he saw the scar from the Caesarean.

"Did no doctor tell you that you couldn't have children?"

"Yes, of course, they told me I was running a great risk, but we trusted that God would watch over us, and He did."

After having analyzed my case, he suggested doing a cardiac catheterization in preparation for surgery.

"Am I that bad, doctor?"

"We can't waste any more time. Your heart is very weak and demands urgent attention. We are doing a new surgery which we are certain will help you."

"But I have to let my parents know. You can't operate on me without my mother being by my side. When do you propose to do this?"

"We'll do the catheterization the day after tomorrow, and, unless this indicates that we need to follow another course of action, your surgery will be in four or five days."

The very same heart I had been born with, completely damaged from the start, had been able to withstand my childhood, adolescence, a pregnancy, and now, it had to withstand a surgery. There was no other way. That was when I knew I wouldn't be going home as soon as I had thought, and I called my parents.

"Mom, the doctors are telling me my heart is very weak, and they have to do a test which will tell them what to do next. The most likely thing is that I need an operation, otherwise I won't get through this. Can you come tomorrow?"

"Good heavens! We'll come right over! Who should we leave Ana Paula with? How shall we do it?"

As my husband's parents were out of town, I had thought my baby could stay with her godparents, Moises and Pilar, who were delighted to take her in.

"Mom, Pili will go to pick Ana Paula up at your house. Please give her everything: nappy bag, push-chair, car seat, toys, clothes and shoes. She'll take care of her till my parents-in-law comeback."

The next day, my parents set off to Houston after following all my instructions. They went by car, so they could move around more easily. My brother and sisters were still studying and Sandra was working. They couldn't join me immediately.

●THE NEXT FOUR DAYS

I learned that the best way to overcome any difficulty is always to keep a good sense of humor.

The next four days were different for each one of us. One the one hand, the doctors had to go over my case and be sure that an operation was the best thing for me. On the other hand, my family and I had to prepare ourselves mentally and emotionally for what was to come.

I was operated on in Texas Children's Hospital, which specialized in children and adults with very complex congenital diseases like mine. They all remembered me really well, even after all this time, or so I was told by Dr. Roma Ilkiw, a pediatric cardiologist, who was later to become a great friend of mine. It wasn't so much my name they remembered, which is quite common, but they remembered this young mother on whom they performed the Fontan surgical procedure. The doctors were surprised the first time I appeared for surgery. It was as if I had come from another world. They asked many questions, especially Dr. Roma, who immediately felt a strong empathy with me. I was completely different from what she had seen, studied and worked on before. No cardiologist on her team had attended an adult with a congenital problem in such extraordinary conditions.

When they went to see me the following day, Dr. Roma and her medical team asked many questions. Where have you been all these years? Why haven't they operated on you before? Why did no one advise you not to have children, given your heart condition? My case went against everything they had been taught: a child with a heart condition must be operated on between three and four years old, or there is no way he will live much longer. It was unheard of to have a pregnancy under these circumstances, the risk was too high both for the mother and the child. They were all surprised at how healthy I looked and at what a normal life I seemed to have led.

The doctors commented on the fact that nobody had forbidden me from doing any activities, no one had put limits on me. I devoted myself to living a practically normal life and it just didn't seem to relate to the reality of my medical condition, according to medical statistics.

Following this first interview with some of the leading cardiologists in Houston, it seemed very likely that they would perform surgery on me. The normal procedure is to have a series of meetings and discussions with all 20 of the pediatric cardiologists on staff at Texas Children's Hospital, before making the final decision on how to proceed with the patients. Dr. Roma reached a conclusion, and her team agreed: I demonstrated that there is more than one way to look at the same problem, which meant that all the medical staff in the area of pediatric cardiology should question very thoroughly what they had been taught up till then. There were various hours of lengthy discussions about the case of Ana Cecilia.

Dr. Roma commented to me that the older cardiologists had the best perspective on such matters, as they had been attending patients since before the days when cardiac surgery was possible, and they knew the nature of many of these heart defects. They had a more common sense approach towards the patients. The questions that arose amongst them were: "Can we do this procedure?" and "Should we do it?", which are two very different topics. In fact, not all patients are appropriate for surgery.

Deciding whether or not to operate on a patient depends to a large extent on the malformation that he or she has. Very often, in the case of very complex cardiac malformations, the patient is not being offered a definitive cure, as it is impossible to redesign the heart or faithfully replace vital parts which are missing. At best, one must exchange one series of problems for others which will be, hopefully, less serious, and less of a threat to the patient's wellbeing. The doctors would have to decide what would happen in my case.

Emotions were running high as it was most unusual to have a patient who was married and also a mother. A pediatric cardiologist normally deals only with the issues between parents and their child, whilst they prepare the child for surgery. In my case, they had to take into account the added relationship between husband and wife, and their small child. There is always a possibility that the patient will not survive the procedure, and, in my case, the loss of this particular patient had such far-reaching implications that none of the doctors involved felt comfortable talking about the subject. But they also knew that they had to attend to me, since no adult hospital had ever had to deal previously with cases such as mine.

The catheterization which had been performed two days after my first visit had shown a very low oxygen saturation, as well as a heart that was large and worn out, due to the way in which I had lived for twenty-four years, and also because I had given birth to a child. There was no doubt; they must go ahead.

The doctors knew that performing good surgery almost guaranteed that the child was going to improve, as that is his nature. A child recovers much more quickly because his body is strong and has much less wear-and-tear. But it is also evident that, not only is the physiological factor in a surgery of vital importance, but also the psychological one.

The pediatric cardiologists attending me were used to the kind of psychology seen in a child who doesn't give up until he reaches his objective. However, it was a very different matter to have to deal with an adult, and they wondered how I would bear up mentally and emotionally.

Adults stop trying or, usually, don't make as much effort as a child, for various reasons, one being that sometimes they have too much information which keeps them stubbornly rooted in the prejudices.

Although Dr. Roma and I had many opportunities to chat in the various appointments I had with her, she was still doubtful as to how prepared I really was for the surgery. No one was sure as to my mental state at that time.

Years later, I saw one of Dr. Roma's medical reports: "She seems happy and confident, displays a lot of empathy and skill for communicating and connecting with any doctor who visits and talks to her."

When I commented to her recently on this, she said, "You had a magical smile which seemed to entrap them all."

I might have had a big smile then, but when I showed the photograph of Ana Paula at nine months, they knew that I would be a mighty warrior, unrelenting and willing to go to hell and back if necessary, just to see my baby again. There is no stronger bond than that between a mother and her child. I had the psychological element that I needed: I wanted to live, and I was ready.

After the catheterization, we were all summoned: my parents, my husband and I. When it was confirmed that surgery was necessary, my parents were left speechless. This news was like a sword piercing the defenceless and unprepared bodies of my family. I tried to explain the procedure to them, but it was difficult for them to take it all in. Their pain was greater than their capacity to understand the news.

My mother was surprised at how I was dealing with the information. For her, I was talking as if they were going to do all this to another person, and not me. Even today, she always remembers that I was strong and tried not to worry them, which is true, as I felt responsible for that. But, more than anything, I could see a solution, so for me, it was so simple. My mother, on the other hand, could only see pain and suffering at that point. But as Dr. Roma once said, in a quote from the American writer Mark Twain: "One needs the ignorance to know that the impossible is possible, and enough confidence to convert the impossible into a reality."

I can only imagine how hard this must have been for my mother, whose heart was torn apart for me. All those years of looking after her daughter so that nothing and nobody would harm her, only to have her now in the hands of some doctors who were saying they had a solution to avoid the end, which would inevitably come, if nothing were done.

Some friends of my parents called to offer them their house in Houston, where they could stay as long as necessary without the need to spend on a hotel. Their financial situation was not very good at that time. Not that they went short for anything, but even so, going to Houston, for an unknown length of time, implied a huge expense. Other friends went to visit them and some offered financial help, which was gratefully received.

●THE NIGHT BEFORE SURGERY

Sometimes it's necessary to move away somewhat,
in order to see where we are standing.

We duly settled into the house we had been lent, and this would be my mother's home for the next two months. Meanwhile, Ana Paula would be in different homes, as we never imagined how long I would be staying.

My surgery would be performed by Dr. George Ruel, Sr. and my head cardiologist would be Dr. David Fisher. Dr. Roma would accompany me throughout all my recovery process. I trusted that they knew what they were doing. I put myself in their hands, and just wanted to see my daughter again.

I couldn't sleep the night before the surgery. I had to be hospitalized early in the morning so they could insert an intravenous line and do some pre-op tests. The surgery was scheduled for 8:00 a.m.

My parents tried to rest in the next bedroom. I could hear their voices, but not what they were saying. They would suddenly become silent for long spells, before they started talking again. It was natural for them to feel afraid, anxious and even sad. I suppose they asked each other many things. Would I survive the surgery? What would they do with the little girl if I died?

That night, I wrote a letter to Ana Paula's godparents, with whom she spent a few days. I wrote to my grandparents, my parents and my brother and sisters. My feelings overflowed and my heart was totally with Ana Paula. There was simply no way to explain to her what was happening: she was only 10 months old. And there were no video cameras in those days for me to, at least, be able to see her on tape. I wanted to feel her, know where she was, what clothes she was wearing, if she was happy, if she had enough toys to play with. I wanted to smell her, stroke her and put her to bed. All I had were two photographs which were with me all the time I spent in hospital.

My thoughts and those photographs were the only way I could feel close to her.

My husband would get up, lie down, go to the bathroom, and come back. He helped himself to some water and offered me some. But I didn't stop writing at all. He just asked me if I had nearly finished.

"Did you bring all that paper so you could write to anyone and everyone?" he asked me, reproachingly.

I couldn't sleep. How could I sleep if I had no idea how much longer I would live? How could I know if my hours were numbered? How was I to know if I'd left everything in order, just in case I died? I had made no will, but, then again, I had nothing to leave. The most valuable possession I had was my daughter, and she couldn't be left without her Mom. How could I sleep when I had so many things to sort out in my head before the surgery? Just thinking about them wasn't going to solve anything, but what else could I do?

I reflected deeply on my twenty-four years of life, as I wrote. I put my letters in envelopes for my husband to post the next day. I thanked people again and again for their friendship, their love, their generosity of spirit, their time. Truth be told, I was just deceiving myself, and years later I saw that I was really saying goodbye to all these people.

Thank you for all the care you have given to my little girl. Rest assured I shall remember everything you have done for her. You have been the best godparents we could have chosen. I know you don't have any experience with children, but God will guide you as you watch over her, as she is in His care. Thank you, Moi and Pili.

"Have you nearly finished? Leave that and come to bed."

"I'm just finishing these last ones, and I'll be right there," I answered my husband.

Granny and Grandpa: we'll see one another again soon. Take great care of my parents and give them the support they need. I'll soon be with you, so you can enjoy your favorite grandchild…Ana Paula.

Mum and Dad: thank you for taking care of me all these years. You have been the greatest support I ever could have had. I know Ana Paula has the best grandparents in the world, and her aunts and uncle are amazing. Sandra, Enrique Luis and Marcela are the best brother and sisters I could ever have wished for. Thank you for giving me life and for accompanying me along this difficult road, health-wise, which I have been destined to live. Thank you! I love you very much.

Many thoughts lingered in my head and, up to this point, I didn't allow the ink to express on paper anything but my gratitude. It was too risky to give vent to my fears and the awful possibility of leaving an orphaned daughter. That was not an option. But in each letter I wrote, between the lines, you could sense the fear behind my words.

Chagüita and Papa Grande: you have always been concerned about my health. Thank you for taking care of me. I love you very much. Chagüita...

"Twenty minutes have gone. How much longer are you going to be?" my husband's voice interrupted my thoughts.

"Nearly done."

Chagüita; thank you for always taking care of me when I felt at my most alone, even though you didn't even know it. You were always with me in my imaginary trips to your house so I wouldn't have to deal with the pain I felt when people stared at my nails. Thank you for consoling me whenever I needed you.

I assured them all that, soon, I would see them to thank them personally for what they were doing for my daughter. I especially thanked those would be taking care of Ana Paula, such as my Aunt Martha, my mother's sister, who looked after her and to whom I also dedicated a letter.

Aunt Martha, it's a blessing to have you as my aunt. Thank you for taking care of Ana Paula and making me feel she is in the best hands. The ways in which you care for her are like gentle caresses of affection for me. It's a gift to have you as an aunt and a blessing that you are the great-aunt of my daughter. I'll see you soon so I can hug you to say thank you. I love you.

"It's getting very late and you're not in bed yet!"

I realized I didn't want to stop writing. I got up and went to the bathroom. I knew what he needed, what he wanted of me, but my mind was far away from that. I looked in the mirror at my haggard, thin face, the bags under my eyes and the purple lips. My oxygenation was very low and my state of health extremely precarious, but I knew he wanted me close: that would help calm him down and would give at least one of us the chance to sleep.

"Is he scared?" I thought. "Is this his way of making me feel protected? I don't think I'm all that attractive just now, to say the least!" It was difficult to understand that my husband was actually expecting more than just a hug. What I needed was affection, tenderness. He wanted something else.

I got up close to him and embraced him slowly, looking into his eyes For me, this would have been enough, but he kept insisting on something more, and so, in spite of my body having nothing to give, I complied. My mind was not with him, his caresses or his kisses; it was with my little daughter sleeping far away in her bed. I could only express myself in gentle caresses, void of any passion. I took care not to exert myself so as not to be left short of breath. Maybe this would be our last time together, no one knew. My farewell letter to him was exactly that, the message I wrote on his skin that night, as was his to me; a letter that was to come back and haunt me later in Intensive Care.

Most of the night for me was spent writing away, eyes full of unshed tears, while my husband slept soundly by my side. The pen wobbled between my fingers. I breathed in and out slowly and deeply so as not to burst out crying. I knew this was not the time to weaken: the emotional stability of my family rested on my shoulders. If I broke down now, all that we had built, up to that moment, would collapse. I had spent years telling myself and the others that I was fine and that my physical and internal strength would allow me to deal with any difficulty I might encounter, such as the one I was facing right now.

I stopped for a moment, when I could go on no further. My head was bursting with so many ideas flying around, I had to get up. I needed to breathe. I opened the door very softly and went out on to the balcony without waking anyone, as if anyone could actually be asleep at that time. I felt the cool breeze, and the pajamas clung to my thin, frail body. My hair was tousled by the soft wind, and I breathed deeply. I rested my hands on the railing and started to speak to myself very quietly.

"Ana Cecilia: do you realize what you've achieved? You came this far: you've gone beyond the age when any other human being with your illness would have died; you have enjoyed your youth; you were the first of your friends to have a boyfriend. Lots of boyfriends! You were the first to be kissed on the mouth, you got married, you lived as a married woman, which, at the age of sixteen, you were warned you shouldn't do; you got pregnant and had a beautiful healthy baby girl. And now you have your daughter and a whole life ahead of you. Today, more than ever, you've got to keep going. Ana Cecilia, you've lived life to the fullest, you can't give up now. Please!"

Tears started to roll down my cheeks. I felt the wind refresh my face. I looked upward to heaven and smiled.

"You must squeeze the strength out of the very weakest cell of your whole being. Think. Concentrate. You cannot weaken now. God is with you, as He has always been. You're only twenty-four and you've got a wonderful life to look forward to. Dear God, give me strength, please, and help me beat this. Breathe deeply, Ana Cecilia, and calm down. Fill your body with peace. Breathe again. You have a daughter who needs you. Be at peace."

But, finally, the sobbing began. I couldn't do any more. I wiped my nose with my hands and on my pajama sleeve and I was inconsolable. I breathed deeply again and then I was speaking to Ana Paula. I got hold of my pen once more and wrote what was to be my last letter that night.

My darling daughter, the love of my life: you are the greatest treasure that life could ever have given me. God has been so good to us in letting us get to know each other. The day you were born, I thanked him for allowing my body to give life to your tiny being. The day I held you in my arms, I gave thanks for your warmth and for the wonder of knowing that I could feed you from my breast, and that you needed me. The day you pressed one of my fingers with your little hand, I thanked God for creating such a perfect creature, and I slowly perused every bit of your body, one by one: your eyes, your eyebrows, eyelashes, your nose and mouth, your arms, legs, fingers and toes. Your body was so fragile at just 1 kilo 600 grams, but it was perfect, simply perfect. That was when I realized that God is able to manifest Himself through perfection, even though the circumstances are not. Only He knows what I felt the day you smiled at me for the first time, looking right into my eyes and saying "Goo".

I know darling, that your life will be extraordinary, because you are a being whom God loved even before the moment of birth. He planned for you to arrive in these circumstances because only someone like you would have been capable of surviving the lack of oxygen coming to you from my body. Only someone like you will be able to make the most of life, because you have done just that ever since you were in the womb. You will have the humility to know that you are loved, desired and privileged, and you will not give in to feelings of arrogance. You are someone who will always be accompanied by angels who will watch over you, but you also have a great mission. Your life is extraordinary, as are your circumstances; it's up to you to see that all of this bears fruit in yourself and in others. Trust in your talents and in your values: they will always guide you wisely.

I send you all my love. And if, when you read this, I am no longer there, just remember that on this night, it has been you and you alone who have given me the strength not to crumble, and to fight even to my last breath for the chance to see you again. Remember: you made me the happiest woman in the world and I will always, alwaysbe by your side. I love you.

– Mommy

●DOCTOR ROMA

I understand that anything can be achieved when the desire is there, no matter how impossible that may seem.
DR. ROMA AND ME

Doctors are always reminded not to have favorites amongst their patients, as it is unprofessional. They are required to treat all patients equally. They say, however, that it was practically impossible not to be drawn to my particular case. The whole medical body became very interested in me, due to my age, and my baby. This was especially true for Dr. Roma Ilkiw and Pamela Lombana, the practicing nurse who took care of me during many of the nights in Intensive Care.

Years later, Dr. Roma confided in me some of her experiences: the night before my surgery, she couldn't fall asleep. She tried reading some fashion articles just to take her mind off the big event of the next day. A surgery like mine could last for hours and be totally draining.

Her mind kept coming back to one thought: "Tomorrow is the most important day in the life of Ana Cecilia. For most women, that would be their wedding day. Yes, a lot of emotions and happiness abound at the start of a new and better future, with the promise of a better life from that day on, but there is also a very real touch of apprehension, maybe even regret. Just as on her wedding day, she might well be asking herself: "Am I doing the right thing? Is this the best moment to be doing this? Do I really know these doctors who are going to change my life for ever? Can I trust them?" the doctor reflected.

She was certain the operation would go well, for Dr. Reul was an excellent surgeon, a calm person with ample experience and sound judgment.

She knew that the Fontan procedure was technically simple in itself, and yet, she also knew the chance of complications was very high, even in the best hands, as there was still so much about this technique that was not fully understood. Ana Cecilia's heart beat the same way for 25 years, and, after surgery, it would be asked to beat another way. In fact, the blood flow was actually going to be reversed in one part of the heart. How would her heart react to all these changes? This was the unknown variable.

"It's not as simple as closing a hole in the heart. We cannot give Ana Cecilia what she needs, which is another ventricle, no one can, but we can separate the circulations so that she will no longer be blue and her body organs will receive more oxygen. Tomorrow, we shall be reorganizing all the circulation through her heart so that the non-oxygenated blood no longer arrives at the heart, but rather only at the lungs, so that the lungs send it to the heart which will then distribute it to the rest of the body. All of this cardiovascular surgery depends so much on technology, and on the skill and judgment of the surgeon," she thought, whilst trying to get to sleep.

Sleep was hard to come by, knowing that, no matter how much they checked the equipment and surgical material, things could go wrong. She was terrified at the thought of losing the mother of a little girl very much the same age as her own son. What reassured her was the knowledge that Dr. Fisher, the cardiologist in charge of my post-operational care, was the best.

She knew that he was someone with a substantial background in physiology and laboratory science, and was particularly experienced in the management of patients undergoing the Fontan procedure. She attended to other details as well, like which nurse would look after me. The success of a surgery depends on the details. Suddenly, her son cried, so she got up to attend to him. "Will Ana Cecilia see her daughter again, stroke her, embrace her, and console her? Would she still be willing to go through with the surgery, if she knew all the difficulties awaiting her?" she wondered.

The following morning, the doctor wanted very much to see me in the pre-operative room. But she stopped herself. She knew it was better to leave the patient alone, with herself, her God, and her own thoughts. She even thought that it was inappropriate and irresponsible to visit just to promise, "Everything will be all right." For one cannot make such a promise, there are no guarantees in life, and those words are empty, too informal, too trivial, inadequate and almost cruel. After all, she said, I'm not the one who is facing the risk, the uncertainty, the one who is bearing all the burden. I cannot be the one to say that.

I said goodbye to my parents and husband, who tearfully put me in God's care, and went off to the waiting room. My parents were informed that I would be very swollen and almost unrecognizable after the operation, whilst I, on the other hand, was obliged to sign my agreement to accept the long list of risks and complications which could occur. I knew I had no choice and that there was no way around this, as it was certain that I needed this surgery in order to survive. In any case, the words I read were nothing more than black and white marks on a page. Can you really understand what is meant by these complications in terms of personal suffering, anguish, and how one's life will be affected? I think not. So, I trusted, and, as always, didn't let negative thoughts get the upper hand.

It was only when my parents were told of the possibility of my surgery lasting for around eight hours, and about the state I would be in for a few days, afterwards that my mother started to see the magnitude of the whole proceedings.

As the hours of the surgery advanced, my parents and husband grew more and more agitated, passing the time telling stories and memories of me, retracing my life from when I was little, and my parents recalling the naughty little tricks I used to get up to, and the headaches I caused them through my childish pranks. They all concluded that, in spite of my illness, I was full of life as a child, always wanting to devour the world. My husband learned of my little adventures and seemed to be listening attentively, although no one knew what was going on in his head at that moment. They kept me alive through sharing these memories and through their desire to go on seeing me there, with them.

During the operation, Dr. Reul, thanks to his great skill and knowledge, realized that they could make changes that they hadn't anticipated and which had never been performed before. He connected a vein which passed behind the heart, using it as a bridge to transport the non-oxygenated blood to the lungs. This was a very bold decision, as a mature heart makes it all the more difficult for any changes to be incorporated naturally, especially as this type of procedure had never been embarked on before. The surgery lasted the expected amount of time. My body seemed to respond to the new circulation, but I depended completely on the artificial respiratory machine.

And so began my first night in the hospital.

The very detailed pre-op explanation given to my parents didn't prepare them psychologically for seeing me for the first time in the recovery room. What had the greatest impact on them was not the quantity of bandages or the appliances filling the room, or the blood in the tubes coming out of my chest. For my family, the greatest shock was finding me so sedated that there was no way for my personality to come through, the one thing that made me real and alive in their eyes. The realization that I could not communicate nor respond in my usual way was the hardest blow, as if I had suddenly become a stranger to them. Nobody could reach me in that place where I was. I was resting just like "Sleeping Beauty", patiently biding my time until I was eventually awoken by a magic spell.

Dr. Roma also shared with me later that my family would simply my hands and stare at my eyes, like when you see a dying person, hoping for the slightest movement to indicate that I was there and could hear them. My parents hugged each other and stroked my hair, which by now didn't bear any resemblance to my usual hairstyle, and they smiled at me with great love. They were at a loss as to where to put their hands with so many things on top of me: the artificial respirator through my mouth, tubes emerging from my chest and connected to some bags which measured the quantity of fluid leaving the body, tubes underneath my gown, intravenous tubing through my veins, bandages tying my hands to the bed rails so they wouldn't pull out the tube when I woke up, and bandages around my feet to help circulation. I would spend my first night alone, there, without parents or husband by my side and far from my beloved baby.

The feeling of having to leave their daughter alone in a hospital ward was not new for my parents; just the opposite, it reminded them of when they left their 3-month-old baby or 4-year-old child, weeping and shouting at them desperately, as well as the many other occasions during my childhood. But for my husband, this was all new. He, unlike my parents, had never experienced leaving me before. For him, this night was different: I didn't shout, didn't talk, just stayed there alone, without them. This time, I was sedated, so that my heart would undergo less stress, would have time to heal and the stitches would have time to take. They all just hoped against hope that I would make it through the first night, that being the most critical time after such a grueling operation.

When you have to choose between two paths, always choose the one which will bring you peace.

Doctors are always tempted to call and ask about a patient's progress, but even they know it's a mistake. The patient might be reported as fine, but then, as soon as they hang up the phone, the whole situation could suddenly change and take a turn for the worse. Besides, the nurse would be too busy to be answering the telephone, so they nearly always refrain from doing this, knowing full well that they will be located if the need should arise. The day after surgery, the doctors make their usual rounds and find out who has survived the night. Even so, it is such an upsetting question to ask that they take it stage by stage, eventually finding out the facts.

All doctors have their routines, and the first thing that Dr. Roma did upon entering the recovery room was to wash her hands and, only then, she raised her head and looked into the small mirror over the sink to look at the patients in their beds, indirectly through the mirror. She could see reflected the two beds closest, with their patients still there. One had had his tubes removed. She steeled herself and moved her head so as to see a little further on, to where the inflated beds were for the patients in the most critical state.

I was in the first row of patients, 3 or 4 beds down from the entrance. Dr. Roma couldn't see me, as the curtain was drawn around my bed. A drawn curtain could mean that the nurses or doctors were carrying out a procedure which required privacy, or that the patient had died. She noticed that the nurses were moving in and out of the curtain quickly and knew that I was alive. She got closer; saw that my blood pressure was very low, though my hands and feet were warm, the first sign that my heart was beating well. I was still in an induced coma, a very deep sleep the doctors wouldn't let me wake up from. That meant they had detected a serious problem, or were deciding whether they needed more tests, or if I should go back to the operating theatre.

The doctor checked my color and saw that I was extremely blue, and I was very sick. Although receiving the maximum supply of mechanical ventilation, my body was not responding. She immediately called Dr. Fisher, and it was decided I would remain in an induced coma and be intubated for some more time. By then, I should have been more alert and communicative, but they couldn't allow that, given the condition I was in. The induced coma would mean that I felt no pain or suffering. My mother and father had initially thought that, once I had had the operation, I would be feeling much better in a few days, but it wasn't like that.

"Good afternoon. I have to speak with you," Dr. Fisher addressed my parents and husband.

"Ana Cecilia is in a very delicate state. She doesn't seem to be responding and her body is not getting enough oxygen. Her skin has become blue, which indicates to us that she's suffering from a lack of oxygen, and some organs may start to fail."

"But she always gets like that when she's cold. Could it not be the air conditioning that's set too strong, and she's freezing cold?" asked my mother in a moment of desperation.

My husband and father listened, scared.

"Is there something that can be done? What happens next?" asked my husband.

"We're waiting for her body to get used to the new circulation and, meanwhile, we shall keep her sedated and she will be oblivious to what's going on."

Nobody could have foreseen the next days. For my husband and parents, the world crashed down on top of them; all that had kept them strong and hopeful came hurtling down and was smashed to smithereens. In one instant, what had been solid ground became quicksand, and they had no way of being sure that the next step would return them safely to firm ground.

They hardly slept at all for the following nights. There were many moments when my parents simply thought that I wouldn't survive. So great was their pain at seeing me in such bad shape, that no consolation was to be found.

My stay in Intensive Care was so tough that my mother came out utterly destroyed. The spectacle was devastating for any mother: my body restrained and dependent, tubes coming out of my mouth and chest, countless draining tubes, the veins of my hands damaged after many unsuccessful attempts to insert the intravenous drip, the oxygen mask over my face and there I lay, surrounded by an endless array of contraptions, all going "beep beep". The hardest thing was my not being able to communicate with them. I was sedated, or very tired, and stayed with my eyes closed for long periods. The doctors did all they could to keep me stable and oxygenated.

My blood pressure was low. The specialized nurses who, very much like accountants, love numbers, urged the doctors to do something to raise my pressure. They suggested giving me more liquids, or start on some drugs intravenously. But Doctors Fisher and Roma knew that this would not solve the problem because, when all was said and done, a balance in my body was being achieved. My organs were receiving enough blood flow, which was why they weren't failing in spite of my bad condition. They trusted that I would get better.

And I did. A few days later, my blood pressure started to go up gradually and I stayed awake for longer periods.

Dr. Roma remembers very well my parents and husband during my stay. She says my parents were like two well-rooted trees: sure, solid, the kind that don't bend or break under the strong wind of a storm. They were always together, perfectly balanced. My husband, on the other hand, was an enigma. He often kept himself apart, at some distance away, with his hands in his pockets. He was nervous, which was understandable, bearing in mind the fact that he could lose his wife, but he didn't appear tense. He didn't display the usual exhaustion or weariness which was common after spending three or four days sitting in cold waiting rooms, staring at the television or reading magazines. He looked as fresh as a daisy every day. The doctor said my husband reminded her of a jackrabbit, in the way they are constantly zig-zagging from side to side and changing directions.

I'm sure he was scared to death, and that was his way of reacting.

At some point, my parents started to feel that recovery was almost impossible, and they didn't want to see me like that any longer. "Why keep trying? Why have her clinging on to life but suffering every day?" they asked. It must have been one of the most difficult times for both of them.

There were endless phone calls from all their friends. My mother cried with each one, and while she told friends and family that my situation was extremely grave, my husband, on the other hand, said I was fine. The truth was that he always had a different way of confronting things. He was a very optimistic man, or maybe he refused to see things as they were and preferred to tell them as he wanted to see them.

This created quite a rift between him and my parents, as some friends thought my mother was exaggerating. It was easier and much nicer to hear news that appeared to be good, rather than facing such tragedy. The truth was that everyone was coming to grips with the situation as best he or she knew how, using the tools at their disposition to manage the pain. Some people face up to it and others evade it.

After five days in the recovery room, my oxygenation improved enough for them to take my breathing tube out. I could be awake and conscious. It was unlikely that I would need to return to the operating room, so I could now be transferred to the Intensive Care Unit. I don't remember much from those days, but I do remember waking up and seeing the faces of my mother, father and husband. When they spoke, I answered with short phrases. I heard afterwards that part of the procedure for those patients who have been in a coma and intubated for a long period, is to ask them questions to see if the brain is functioning correctly. When I could communicate in English by writing in a notebook, this not being my native tongue, they realized my brain had suffered no damage whatsoever. My system was functioning and my thought processes were intact.

I had no notion of time, but I did know when someone was with me, and that cheered me up enormously. My husband sometimes sat with me for hours reading Bible passages. I could hear him, and it calmed me down. He was allowed to stay longer than the permitted time because they dared not interrupt him while he was reading.

I remember my mother asking if I wanted to see my brother and sisters. The easiest way for them to move quickly was by plane, but my parents' financial situation at that time was not easy.

"Mom, if it's possible, of course, I want to see them. I need to see them," I said, smiling.

That was reason enough for them to make a huge effort and find a way to travel from Monterrey to Houston to be at my side. In reality, I felt very weak, but I knew that my mother needed them more than I did. That she feared for my life was obvious from her words. The idea of dying didn't occur to me, but this time, *Ráfel* was closer to me than ever.

●THE INFECTION

*You choose to remember what causes you anguish and pain,
or that which gives you peace and happiness.*

Dr. Roma visited me every day. I knew that once they moved me to
another ward, I might stop seeing her, so I asked her to keep visiting
me if possible, as talking to her helped me a lot. She smiled and
assured me she would.

Ten days after the surgery, I left Intensive Care. They took me to
intermediary care which was in a private room, with more comforts
and where I could have company. That's where I would wait until
I was fully recovered and able to go home. At least, that's what I
thought.

At the beginning, everything went well. Having my family close
cheered me up, and my parents could go and rest whilst I stayed
alone with my husband. Now, the nurses made their regular rounds,
just like with any other patients. It seemed the worst was over. The
reality, however, was that, as the hours passed, I was feeling worse
and had great difficulty breathing. Each time I uttered a word, I
needed to take a short breath in order to pronounce the next one. At
first, I didn't get alarmed, thinking it must be normal. Each time I
breathed, I felt a small pain, but little by little, this pain grew until
it was very uncomfortable to breathe. I tried staying still, hoping it
was a muscular problem, but no - there came a point where the pain
in my chest was so intense that every time I attempted to speak, it
only got worse.

My pain threshold had always been high since I was a little girl,
and I was used to waiting and tolerating the pain until I could stand
it no longer. This time was no exception. I tried sleeping, moving the
position of the bed a little, but nothing worked.

I was supposed to have dinner, watch a bit of TV, take it all very
calmly, and then rest. However, the fact was that with each tiny

breath, I felt an enormous pain in my chest. Eating took great effort and, if I chewed, I consumed oxygen and felt I was choking. I could barely utter a word, as each attempt pierced me like a dagger. No matter how much I tried not to think about the pain, I was in total agony and tears were filling my eyes. I really fought against the idea that something was terribly wrong, as my only wish was to get out of there and go home.

My husband's attention was on a TV program, so I used grunting noises and hand signals to tell him I couldn't stand it anymore.

"Well, it's logical that it hurts, they've just taken away the morphine for the pain, you're still recovering. How much does it hurt, so I can tell them?" he said, not knowing what to do, as he couldn't understand me.

"Hurry, I'm choking!" I could barely whisper.

I pressed the button at the side of the bed to call the nurse. I couldn't speak, so it was up to my husband to explain to her how I felt over the intercom. The pain was more intense and each breath took a huge effort. The nurse didn't come immediately. My husband couldn't see that my plea for help was utter agony.

"You go. They're not coming!" I begged him.

At that, he rushed out looking for any nurse, yelling at them that I felt very bad and they needed to come right away. His voice was hoarse, he felt so desperate and helpless.

Various doctors and nurses hurried to my room. They asked me questions to which I couldn't reply. The doctor wasn't happy with that, and said I had to make the effort to tell them exactly how I felt, so he could evaluate the seriousness of the situation.

"I need you to say in your own words what you're feeling. Otherwise, we can't help you."

"It (breath) hurts (another breath) to breathe." I just managed to make the words audible.

They saw how I needed to inhale air each time I pronounced a word and, realizing the situation was serious, summoned other doctors. X-ray machines and emergency ECG equipment were produced. Everybody scurried around. I was exhausted and felt the blood drain out of my face. My husband could only look on from a distance, not knowing what to do, just waiting. As they connected the wires for the ECG, I fixed my eyes on him. When our eyes met, I smiled softly and mouthed the words, "Thank you".

For him, this was a titanic ordeal. He had been thinking that the worst had passed and never imagined what was round the corner. Dealing with sickness was foreign to him, as he and his family had always enjoyed the best of health. And now, here he was, ensconced in a hospital, and his wife in a critical state, her life hanging by a thread. I can't imagine what was going through his head at those moments. No doubt, at that moment of signing the marriage certificate, when my illness didn't seem to be such an issue, he could never have dreamed what he was going to have to face. Neither of us could.

They took an X-ray and immediately detected that the cavity around the heart and close to the lungs was completely filled with fluid. I couldn't breathe because there wasn't enough room for the lungs to expand. There was only one thing to do. I had to go back into Intensive Care.

It was then that my husband came up close to me and, without saying a word, hugged me, his eyes brimming over with tears. That was it, then; we had to separate once more, and for how long this time, no one knew. He had to leave the room, go back to my uncle and aunt's house, where he and my parents were staying, and try and get some sleep. Little did he know that I would have to stay in the place they were taking me to for all of one month, and much less that my life would be turned around for ever.

I spent that night alone in Intensive Care, wishing that Dr. Roma would pay me a visit, but knowing that doctors have their schedules and rounds assigned to certain areas. I wasn't sure if she knew I was there, and when I asked, they couldn't tell me whether she'd go to see me, but, they did say she had been informed. It was at those moments that I truly missed her. I wanted to connect to someone who cared about me, and didn't just see me as one more patient to deal with.

The noise in the ward was endless: machines were beeping constantly, nurses forever going in and out. I couldn't sleep. At my side were two doctors who talked non-stop. It was on the tip of my tongue to tell them to stop, but, for one thing, I couldn't muster up enough strength to do so, and for another, I needed their help, and it wouldn't be in my interests to get on the wrong side of them. Who knows what they were talking about? Football? Women? Well, it certainly wasn't about me! And the perpetual noise just wouldn't let me sleep.

The following day, more X-rays and scans of my chest were carried out, and it was seen that there was a further accumulation of fluid. More medicine for the pain was injected into my veins, which helped reduce the pain somewhat. During the day, they carried out various procedures, which included moving the drainage tubes and putting me in different positions. Nothing worked. They would have to insert a large needle to aspirate the fluid from around the lungs.

At around 4 p.m., some doctors arrived, just when a storm was raging outside, and the rain was pouring down incessantly. I was lying on my side, next to a window, and had a good view of the city and the neighboring parks. They raised my head a little to put me in a better position, and I could see what they were doing. They injected a local anesthetic directly into the area where they would be carrying out the procedure and then inserted a long needle into the lower part of my ribs, beneath the sternum, through which small amounts of fluid were extracted. With the first attempt, I immediately felt some relief, even though only a little fluid had actually been removed. Again, the doctors suctioned to extract a little more, but this time without much success. I saw a jet of very dark blood shoot into the syringe.

"Oh, we've punctured the heart! We have a problem!" the doctor carrying out the procedure said to his colleague nearby.

They immediately removed that needle and covered the area up with a piece of gauze.

The heart was perforated and started to bleed. It would have been so easy to go right then to my grandmother's house, but that escape route didn't work anymore. I just kept looking out the window at the marvelous scene outside. The intense rain transported me immediately to the sea. In my mind's eye, I could see myself walking along the beach, free, healthy, and happy, with a long dress of white chiffon; and when I stretched out my arms, the wind lifted up the delicate material of the long sleeves, and it seemed as though I were about to take flight.

"Quick! We've got to move! Get Dr. Reul. He should still be in the hospital," a doctor's voice interrupted my thoughts.

I preferred not to think about what was really going on. The nervousness of the doctors present was catching. I had no choice but to pray in silence, saying the first prayer that came into my head: "Guardian angel, sweet companion, do not abandon me by night or by day…"

The doctors were in a state of alarm, calling others of the medical staff, talking earnestly amongst one another, whilst I didn't even want to see them. I purposely resisted the temptation to see how things were, and didn't want to be pulled along by their words, much less by the negative comments that were flying around.

"Guardian angel," I said, and then forgot the rest of the prayer, so I started again. "Guardian angel, sweet companion, does not abandon me….by night or by day." I couldn't think properly, but I knew I had to concentrate on my prayer and on the beach where I had imagined myself so light and free. My prayer was to express my thanks and to ask for my life to be spared.

One of the doctors in charge came up.

"We think we've perforated the heart and it would be best to take you to the operating room."

I couldn't respond and just looked at him, and continued in silence; "Guardian angel, sweet companion, do not abandon me by night or by day." I said it over and over in my mind. It was like a mantra that I had to say again and again. Each time, it was that bit harder to focus my mind on the white dress and the beach, as now I could feel how my whole body was put on alert - my life was in serious danger.

"Guardian angel," I repeated as I breathed in and out deeply. "Calm down," I told myself, smiling inwardly, "and have faith."

The torrential rain that day turned out to be a stroke of luck. The city was flooded and, as a result, many doctors hadn't left the hospital yet. The doctors who had performed my first surgery were still there, thankfully, and came immediately when called.

My parents and husband had only just gone to rest in the waiting room, so the doctors went to look for them and inform them of the latest events, saying that they had no choice but to perform another surgery, to extract all the fluid and to repair the perforated heart.

Ten minutes later, I was hurried off to the operating room, so my family had no choice but to bid me a hasty farewell. My parents took me by the hand, and the look on my father's face touched me deeply: his smile was full of hope and trust, but he couldn't hide the fear in his eyes. My mother shed some tears, and I smiled at her, and pressed her hand to say we would see each other soon. Then followed my husband, and I held tightly on to one of his hands while he signed an endless stream of papers with the other. A smile, a kiss, and the hope of seeing each other later were the last things we shared before we were separated, and I was whisked away.

The corridor leading to the operating room seemed eternal, but in reality, it took just two or three minutes to get there. By this point, I could only speak to God, as my voice was too weak to speak to anyone else, which is what I would have liked to do. I had a strong sense that the end had come: I didn't need to be a genius to know that things were taking a turn for the worse. I still remember my conversation with God that day.

"I'm coming to join You, aren't I? Everything's got complicated. I know I'll be fine because I feel at peace. Please take care of Ana Paula. I hope her father can give her everything she needs. Guide him so that he can look after her and keep her close to my family. I don't want any of them to suffer. Please help them." I implored God as I delivered myself into His custody.

"I know I said to You one day that it wasn't fair that children with the same problem as me should die, while I keep on living. I also told You that I didn't understand Your idea of justice. Well, I still can't, but I want to ask You, please, if my moment has indeed come, to reconsider Your decision. You blessed me with a beautiful baby girl, healthy and perfect, for which I'll always be grateful. But if there is the slightest possibility, please let me be the one to take care of her."

"Forgive me if I was rebellious and gave You lots of headaches. All I want at this point is to live. If I did anything wrong, please forgive me, and let me make up for it by bringing up my little girl to be a good, upstanding woman. Give me a chance to love her and take care of her."

Suddenly, I was aware that my heart was beating differently. The doctors confirmed it was a tachycardia. I breathed deeply various times, and felt a white light entering my body and cleansing it throughout, allowing me to experience again that feeling of peace and inner calm.

"Guardian angel, my guardian angel," I said, to the rhythm of the tachycardia. More than ever now, I wanted *Ráfel*, my companion of former days, to become this guardian angel. I could feel him near me now and spoke to him.

"Where have you been? I haven't heard from you in years. I thought you were just a part of my childish games, but now I see that you never left. Help me, will you?" *Ráfel* looked at me at that moment with an expression of love and tenderness. "I don't know who you are, whether you are a ghost or a guardian angel," I thought to myself

"But I can see you are always with me, and I thank you for that."

"Now, please don't take me with you yet. My daughter is waiting for me." I perceived a great surge of heat throughout my body, and an immense love within my heart. I felt accompanied, not alone. *Ráfel* became my guardian angel and my healer at that very moment.

Could it be that I was starting to hallucinate? All I can say is that, for me, it was the most lucid conversation I had had in a long time.

I placed myself in God's hands once more.

My will to live never deserted me. I remember feeling very calm entering the operating room, and even managed to say hello to the doctors, nurses and assistants. I gave the impression that I wasn't aware of how grave things really were. Perhaps I wasn't, or I was just putting on a good face to give those around me more confidence. I told them I had a little daughter, and all I wanted was to see her again. I don't know if I was reminding them or myself.

I do know that I didn't want to be bombarded by hearing so much medical terminology or think about anything at all besides getting out of there alive. The doctors made as if they were listening to me, but all the while they were talking and hurrying backwards and forwards, as the surgery could not wait.

They cut open the hospital gown I had on, and pulled it off me. For a moment, it occurred to me that I would die having lost all dignity, my nakedness in full view of all those doctors. I couldn't cover myself up as my hands and feet were being held down. Just then, someone covered me with a white sheet which left my chest exposed for that area to be cleaned. My veins were so damaged they had to connect me to an IV not only in the arm but also in the top part of my foot. They took my arms and fastened them to a couple of boards placed on the side of my body. A doctor came up to me, smiling, and put a mask on my face which I could see through. This was the anesthetic, but it must have taken some time to have any effect because I can still remember a lot of the thoughts that were going through my head in those moments.

"I am like Christ, delivering myself up," I thought. If I had to go, I was ready. But I asked God, "If you can, please let me see my baby." Even though my body felt under attack, I never lost that inner peace and the certainty that everything would be fine. I was willing to surrender completely and, absolutely aware of my situation, I never stopped smiling and trusting that God was in control. "Guardian angel, guardian angel... Ana Paula." was the last image I had before losing consciousness.

The surgery, which lasted a couple of hours, involved opening up and working on the very recent operation performed barely a few days before, besides extending a little way below the previous one. Maybe it was due to the pressure of time, but on this occasion, they weren't concerned about the esthetical aspect of the operation. The amount of fluid accumulated was much greater than they had originally estimated from the results of the most recent tests. They sewed up the heart, which was bleeding profusely, and managed to re-establish the cardiac rhythm and regulate the tachycardia.

Some patients, like myself, are able to hear and feel quite a time before the anesthetic wears off completely. When it was over, I realized I was still alive, but what I was hearing was not encouraging at all. The nurses and doctors who were in charge of cleaning me up and getting me ready to return to Intensive Care talked non-stop, and

I heard them say how sad it all was and how I might never get to see my family or my ten-month-old daughter.

"Why are they talking like that about me and my family when I'm still alive? All of you, stop talking like that, I'm here and I'm listening to you!" I shouted desperately inside my head.

The situation was very delicate. The tests made on the fluid they had extracted were not at all encouraging: my whole body was invaded by the bacteria called staphylococcus aureus. The task of eradicating these bacteria was difficult because of my particular circumstances. The area might have been contaminated during the first operation. It was hard to say.

I woke up in Intensive Care in a private ward surrounded by walls of glass. On opening my eyes, I could see all my family around me and their pain-wracked faces told me that what I had heard was real and not a figment of my imagination. I was on the brink of death, and yet, deep inside me, in my soul, my spirit was stronger than ever. There was no way I could convey that trust and strength, as I was connected to the artificial respirator again and could only communicate by way of hand signals.

The doctors asked me how I felt, and I lifted my arms up in a triumphant gesture like the boxers of the Rocky movies. This didn't go down well, and they immediately fastened my hands to the bedrails, afraid I was trying to pull my breathing tubes out. I saw the doctors withdraw to speak to my parents and husband outside the Intensive Care Unit.

"It's very likely that Ana Cecilia is delirious or suffering from brain damage. We are checking which antibiotics to use to treat the bacteria she has."

"But, what's wrong with her, doctor? What are we going to do now?" asked my mother.

"She has been infected by staphylococcus aureus. It's only just starting, but it's extremely dangerous."

My parents withdrew a little while my husband continued talking to the doctor.

"How serious is it, doctor?"

"It's very serious. What I'm about to say might seem harsh, but I suggest you sort out the papers in Admission. She is registered under her maiden names. If she were to die, you would have a lot of trouble in obtaining the release of her body."

"Die?"

"There are two options open to us for medicating her and eradicating the staphylococcus. As we still don't have the final test results, we shall have to take the risk and begin treatment with one of the medications. If we don't start today, trusting that it is the right one, we'll definitely lose her in a few days."

"So, what do we do?"

"Go and rest. There's not much you can do tonight."

Heartbroken, they trailed back to the house where they were lodging. These days, hospitals have comfortable sofas, and the wards have been adapted so that a relative can stay all night close by a critically ill patient, but in those days, there was nowhere comfortable for my family to spend the night.

Hope is like a ray of light which reaches you in the most unlikely way and illuminates everything.

Meanwhile, inside my cubicle, I tried many ways to let them know that the tube in my throat was bothering me: I moved my hands and head as much as I could, but what with my hands being tied, the breathing tube and the after-effects of the anesthetic, I wasn't making myself understood.

Finally, I managed to get one of the nurses to give me a pen and paper so I could write down what I wanted to say. All I could write was: "Throat hurts." One of the two nurses who were permanently with me patted me on the head and said it was natural for me to feel uncomfortable, but they had to leave the tube there. It was impossible. Nobody was taking any notice of me, and the pain I felt was not normal. I had had a tube put down my throat before without any discomfort, but now it seemed pointless to try to tell them the tube was not put in right.

That afternoon, my father called my siblings to give them the news but only managed to find Sandra, which was lucky as there were no mobile phones then,

"Sweetheart, I'm phoning you to say that Ana Cecilia is very sick."

We will know in 48 hours if the medicine the doctors gave her was the right antibiotic. If it wasn't, we are going to lose her."

"But how, Daddy? Why don't they just give her the right antibiotic now and be done with it?"

"Because they're not sure which one will work best until they get the test results back. All we can do is pray. Please tell your brother and sister to do the same. Let's ask God to save her."

This news was a bombshell for Sandra. She left for work in floods of tears, not knowing whether she would ever see me alive again.

Sometime later, in the early hours of the morning, there began what is probably the most memorable experience of my life. One of the nurses told the other that she was going to see her boyfriend in McDonald's, on the first floor of the hospital. The second nurse told me that she was just going to fetch some water, as everything seemed to be under control. The water was a few steps away from my room. Both of these actions, of themselves, were totally natural and would be of no consequence. Except that I had been trying to tell them that the breathing tube was incorrectly placed. Now, some phlegm which had been secreted blocked the tube and I started to asphyxiate.

With no one to turn to, my first reaction was to try to pull the tube out, so I could breathe, but this was impossible, as both of my arms were tied. I tugged and pulled with all my might, ending up bruising and hurting my arms in the attempt. I kicked my feet so fiercely that the bed actually moved, but no matter how much I twisted and turned, it was to no avail. There was no relief. The seconds seemed like hours.

Almost simultaneously, the alarm of the respiratory machine started sounding again and again; with such a piercing fury that I felt there was an ambulance right inside my cubicle. At this point, what seemed like a whole army of doctors and nurses came charging in: I could hear them shouting.

"Respiratory, respiratory". They called out to the team of specialists.

Everyone was yelling like mad and the scene was pure pandemonium. I could hear all this, but I couldn't breathe. While some nurses held my legs down, trying to immobilize me, the doctors took out the upper part of the tube that went down into the throat, trying to correct the problem. They put a small amount of liquid in the tube that came out of my mouth and tried to suction the phlegm. I was still fighting to find any position I could in order to take a breath. My desperation to take in even the slightest amount of air, together with the adrenaline pumping through me, produced in me such an almighty strength that not even four people could keep my body still.

The body clings on to life, in spite of being weak, infected, newly operated and with no life-giving oxygen. It doesn't give up easily and will fight, until the bitter end, to survive.

They tried again and again to release the tube, but couldn't, probably because it was not put in correctly. I became overcome by a feeling of dizziness, and I lost consciousness and my body started to give up. I entered into respiratory failure, and, practically immediately, cardiac arrest. And then I was gone.

●PALE YELLOW

At the end, you will only take with you the memory of the road you have traveled along. Empty-handed and, with your soul full to overflowing, you will be richer than ever.

I suddenly opened my eyes and felt totally free. I saw myself in my gown, and the doctors all around my body, trying to resuscitate me. I could see how they were all frantically moving around from one side to the other. And all the time, they were looking smaller and further away. It was a strange sensation because I felt completely whole, and yet, I could see my motionless body before me. I just floated and nobody was trying to hold down my sore arms. The relief was tremendous. I had no control over what was happening and I let myself be taken on a wonderful journey.

I floated inside what seemed like a tree. I was a spectator.

Firstly, I saw something resembling a layer of branches full of small animals: squirrels, rabbits, birds, dogs amongst others. It was all harmonious and exuded peace and wellbeing. They all radiated a sense of love the like of which I had never felt before, least of all from an animal. The sounds penetrated my soul, and anything I might have left behind now lost all importance. I felt completely submerged in what was happening.

I continued to float. My body relaxed and the muscles no longer hurt. I breathed freely, feeling no tiredness whatsoever. The relief was not only external but internal, also. I immediately saw a second layer of wide-stretching branches: an incredibly beautiful spectacle. Here, larger creatures were to be seen: horses, giraffes, elephants, lions and many more. The color of skin of each species was breathtaking, and, for the first time, I perceived these wild animals as harmless and friendly. It was as if we knew one another and were part of the same family. My love for them was palpable, and I could sense that they, in turn, loved me.

Up and up I continued, until I arrived at the third layer of branches, and here the scene was full of children of all ages and races: each one different and beautiful in its way. I can't say if they were bodies, like we are used to seeing, but I knew they were children who were all living happily together, and the only sound to be heard was laughter and singing from the sweetest of young voices. Their faces beamed as they played, ran across the grass, and splashed themselves happily in the water of a fountain which stood in the middle of the garden. I couldn't speak to anyone, and made no attempt to do so, content solely to contemplate and enjoy this beautiful view. No words were exchanged during all this time, but I felt immersed in a love that said it all. It was a spectacle to behold, and I would have happily stayed there if given the choice. I was like a balloon that has escaped from the hands of a child, unconcerned about what I was leaving behind, merely floating contentedly wherever the breeze might take me.

Ana Paula came into my mind, but the image didn't cause me concern, as I knew she would be fine. I found myself looking at her sleeping in her crib with such a blissful expression on her face that I could also be at peace and feel close to her. I moved nearer and nearer to where she lay until I was gazing down at her and watching over her.

I realized I had the ability to see everything in front, behind, above and below or on both sides, all at the same time. No matter where I turned, and without even having the need to turn my head, my eyes could see at an angle of 360 degrees. This was not a bad thing and it didn't make me afraid. It was a lot of information arriving from all sides, but I could assimilate it all and be fascinated by it. There was magic in that place.

A little bit higher up, I found what appeared to be another layer of large branches and this time, there were people of different ages, all together in an atmosphere of harmony, serenity and joy. People smiled, which made me feel stronger. Their voices were clear, melodious and eloquent, and communication flowed very naturally. It was remarkable. No sounds were emitted when they spoke; it was as if only their minds were saying things, and I could definitely hear them. The atmosphere was of peace and absolute love. Here, as well, there was a large garden with a fountain in the center, surrounded by flowers of many colors. The water fell in varying rhythms which formed images, and the sound was wonderful. People were sitting all around, chatting and smiling. Some people were lying on the grass, reading a book or simply soaking up the moment. It was a splendid scene.

I continued on my journey upwards, reveling in it all, within this tree that seemed like a tunnel full of life, and I felt complete, and I felt free. I could breathe deeply and take in plenty of oxygen. There was no weakness in me, and nothing hurt any more. I remembered my husband and my parents and knew they were suffering but, also, that they would be fine, too. I wanted to console them by loving them more and more. Nothing, absolutely nothing was a cause for sadness, as if I knew that, sooner or later, they would enjoy the same feeling of wellbeing as myself. And so, I stopped worrying.

I moved on up a little towards another layer of far-reaching branches, but this time, there was a large group of smiling and lively older people, many of whom were sitting and talking, and enjoying the view. They were in the midst of gardens full of flowers, trees of various species, and rivers flowing with clean, fresh water, strolling along the pathways and telling stories to one another. Most noticeably, no one needed a walking stick or a wheelchair, and they all moved around easily.

At this moment, I looked up to see what followed, delighted with the amazing spectacles and sensations I had never before experienced. It was then I saw a small, pale yellow light which attracted me like a magnet. My natural curiosity urged me on to investigate what was behind it.

Much as I was keen to enter there, there was no way to move quickly. With some anxiety, I just let myself go, and I started entering that tiny space, which seemed as soft and delicate as silk. But, as my head and shoulders went through, and I finally thought I could experience that celestial light from within, somehow, when I was halfway through, something prevented me from advancing. It was as if I had got stuck. And yet, I felt the light flood into all of my senses and into every pore of my body. Blinded, and in complete ecstasy, I breathed in and filled myself with that marvelous sensation. I neither wanted nor needed anything more. There I was, at the final destination, and there could be no greater love than this; I felt it, I knew it, and was enraptured by the sheer thrill of it all.

There are no words to express the sensation of being embraced by that all-pervading light. Without moving an inch, I could perceive anything. The feeling of unity abounded. I felt loved, accepted, without conflict or confusion. It was just like being at home with all the family of Creation.

Still unable to see, I almost immediately felt the gentle touch of a hand above my head and, just then, an unimaginable love poured into me. I was in ecstasy. I was whole. Just when the hand touched my head, I heard a soft, beautiful, almost mystical voice say:

"Stay calm, and go in peace. Do everything I have asked you to."

I wanted to ask, understand, find out more, but immediately, my journey back began. Again, I saw the layers of branches, but this time, at top speed. I would have liked to stop and enjoy them at my leisure, but there was no way, and I was unwillingly thrust upon a violent return and separated from this most beautiful experience I had been going through.

"Why do I have to go back when I was finally able to rest? Why are they waking me up? What are they bothering me, keeping me here?" I asked myself.

Once again, I saw myself, from a distance, in the hospital bed with the doctors still surrounding my body, attempting to resuscitate me. In an instant, I was back. My head was spinning, and I felt pain, anguish and a lot of anger. I felt so dizzy, I couldn't get my bearings of time and space. I opened my eyes and saw myself in the midst of many doctors. Then, I felt an intense heat in my chest, brought on by the electric shock to try and restore my heartbeat. Someone shouted:

"She's back!"

"No! I don't want to be back! Leave me alone!" I shouted to myself, unheard by anyone there.

I was desperate, as I didn't want to be there. Why, I asked myself, did they wake me up, after I had finally managed to sleep after battling so hard to breathe? Nobody seemed to care about what I wanted. They just wanted to bring me back to that place of suffering. It felt as if hours had passed, and yet it was only a matter of minutes. My body resisted, and once more, my heart stopped, throwing the doctors into general panic, screaming out uncontrollably.

"She's going! She's going! Try again!"

I struggled to go back to where I had been a few seconds before. Why should I stay here, where I was in so much pain and suffering? All I wanted was to be back in that light, that very instant, to feel once more the immense love and joy which had pervaded me. Nobody heard my shouts emanating from the very depths of my being. Incredibly, for me, just then, nothing else mattered: not my daughter, my husband, parents or family. They all paled in significance, compared to my brief encounter with paradise, where I had found such a glorious relief. I knew they would be fine, and I needn't worry about them.

"Leave me alone! I don't want to be here! I want to go back! Please, let me go!" I silently begged them.

After what must have been an hour of battling with cardio-pulmonary resuscitation (CPR), they finally managed to restore my heart rate. I regained consciousness, and was back in the hospital, full of wires, breathing tubes and an array of people all around me who gradually left, except for the two nurses on permanent duty and a cardiologist who stayed with me all through the night.

At first, I was dumbfounded, confused. It's impossible to go through something like that and then come back, expecting to understand it all. I was angry with everyone, but there were other things I couldn't get my head around. Who had said those words to me? Why did he say that? Could it have been a doctor whispering into my ear? Or, was it, indeed, God pointing me in a direction that I had to figure out for myself?

The doctors and I couldn't have been in more different worlds in those moments: me, delighting in what appeared to be paradise, and the doctors, very much of this world, battling to keep me alive.

Hours went by before I could get my mind adjusted to the fact that, indeed, something significant had happened. I had been in another place in another dimension, or maybe it was the same place but I could see what had previously been out of view. Something had happened, and I wanted to understand why I had left my body. I was desperate to communicate, and the only way was by writing. They put a pen in my left hand, as my right one had an IV inserted into it. At first, no one understood what I had written, and even if they did, I was given no explanations, no answers. Despite all my attempts to write in my little notebook, I got no further in grasping what had happened.

I felt disconcerted, and yet strengthened, not knowing where I had been, yet understanding that it was not of this world, as we know it.

I had been given a glimpse of the marvelous universe that awaits us after death. Everyone was acting as if I was at death's door, but I wanted to let them know that I was healthier, in fact, than ever. They should stop behaving like that. Even though I looked in a bad way to them, I wasn't. The pain was much less, and I knew I would live. The trouble was, I couldn't communicate any of this. But now, the strength which had been building up inside me helped me to stand my ground when faced with all the bad news that was about to come.

No one wanted to tell me why I was in such a delicate state; my body was infected and I could only be kept alive by a miracle. But I knew that the miracle had already happened, and, at that point, no one else could know of my glorious journey that night. I had known death, and it took some time before I could see that I was blessed to experience something only a few people can. It didn't matter where I was or what I was going through; it was up to me to decide how to view my life. The great physical pain, which was still present, was no longer a source of grief. I had to find a way to put into words all of this information I had been a party to.

I had lived through something so amazing that, now, the only thing that remained was to make it a part of my present reality. From that day on, I contemplated in my mind the sheer beauty of what I had seen and lived through, and I tried to assimilate it into my life each instant and thank God for it.

The next morning, my family arrived early, only to be told that it was touch and go as to whether I would live past that day, as I had had a very bad night and was seriously ill. My husband didn't want to fix the issue of my name as it appeared on the registration papers, preferring to avoid what would be a very painful procedure. So, he stayed outside with my parents, waiting for further news.

I wondered what would have happened if I had died alone that night. In Mexico, the first thing a family does is "set up camp" in the hospital where their family member is very sick. It was hard for everyone to be separated, but that wasn't uppermost in my mind. All I could think of was, "I want to live!"

It was only a year later when I was given access to the medical information regarding what happened that night. Thanks to the friendship which had flourished between myself and Pamela, and with the help of her husband, Fernando Lombana, I learned that I had respiratory failure and cardiac arrest. They were newlyweds, Fernando was a doctor, and both of them worked at Texas Children's Hospital. They both said that none of the medical staff understood how I was still alive after such a dramatic episode. I don't know whether the nurses' behavior was due to a breakdown in protocol or observation. Nobody can explain that, and we are left with pure speculation. What is absolutely for sure is that the experience would change the rest of my life, even though it would be years before I finally came to understand it.

● INTENSIVE CARE

My soul speaks through my actions, not through my words.

My stay in the hospital was very long, borne out by the fact that I witnessed the arrival and departure of over twenty patients during my time there, most of which was spent in Intensive Care. My family had to obey strict visiting hours when they came to see me. Memories of those early days are vague, as I was completely sedated to help my heart and circulation get back to normal after the great "crisis", which, for me, was the "great dream".

My father and husband traveled back and forth between Houston and Monterrey in order to hold their jobs down, so they had to deal with household matters as well as their own personal activities. My mother was the only one who didn't leave my side, not even for one day. That was truly a gift as, once more, she was with me, in the waiting room, far from all those she loved most.

I was connected to a respiratory machine for so long that there was a moment when it was thought I might need a tracheotomy. My health was delicate and my body responded very slowly, but, at least, I was alive. My mother, in the brief moments she could be with me, would stroke my hands and refresh my face with damp towels which alleviated, to some extent, the discomfort of being so swollen. I would make signs to her to do the same on my legs. Besides enjoying the presence of any family member, these were the few things that offered me any degree of pleasure.

Friends traveled to be with us, and it was thanks to their visits and help and, of course, that of my family, that my mother was able to be relieved and find time to rest a little. Eating outside the hospital, enjoying a shower and just having a break were a blessing to her, so she would go and spend some time at the apartment, knowing I was not on my own. We shall forever be in the debt of all those friends for their visits and support.

It was Dr. Roma who received me in the ICU once the breathing tubes had been removed. She would visit me every day and stay longer than the other doctors normally did, and we would chat for ages about this and that. I didn't dare ask her what had happened during my recent crisis, as I suspected that it would be very easy for the doctors to disregard my experience, putting it down to the medicine or to me being in a state of shock. So, I kept silent, meditating and analysing.

One good thing was that, by now, I was breathing on my own, and feeling slightly more comfortable. I did, however, have to endure a series of quite serious infections, which complicated my recovery, although the main concern was to eradicate the staphylococcus aureus. I, meanwhile, was calm and at peace; I was alive, which was all that mattered, and I would do whatever it took to stay that way. With that in mind, whatever the doctors decided was fine by me, and I wouldn't challenge or question it.

When I was discharged from the hospital, Dr. Roma handed me a report which said: "Ana has the strongest willpower I have ever seen. She faced her recuperation with a focused clarity of mind, always ready to do whatever was needed or asked of her. She was the ideal patient."

And how was I not going to try to be a good patient when my close encounter with death gave me another perspective on things? Now, I was in no hurry; on the contrary, my stay in the hospital allowed me more time to meditate and analyze carefully what I should do and say: "Stay calm and go in peace, and do everything I have asked you to." I was at peace, and I was calm; I just needed to decipher what it was that I was being asked to do. Maybe I had to share this experience with others, but how? I didn't know, and even I was struggling to find words to talk about it.

As Dr. Roma once told me, a patient's state of mind is of great importance for his or her recovery. My state of mind was not the problem, but keeping my body alive was.

My health was not good, and I required the constant care of a nurse. I tried to make personal contact with anyone who came to my room, and I felt a great need to share this love I had inside for each one of them. Of course, in their eyes, I was just another patient, but I needed to feel that I was a person who actually mattered to them. I needed to connect. I depended on them for everything.

A few days later, I received a call from my sister, Sandra, who was worried and needed to hear my voice and feel close to me.

"Ana Cecilia, I was told you could only talk for a couple of minutes, but I just wanted to hear you speak and find out how you are."

"I have been through one of the most incredible experiences imaginable."

I tried to describe to her a little of what had happened, but I was still full of doubts, and confused about those parts I didn't understand. She was excited just to feel close to me. Then, I spoke to Enrique Luis and Marcela who were obviously concerned, but chatting with them brightened me up so much and made me feel stronger. I realized how much I missed the three of them.

One night, Pamela arrived. She was a trained nurse who had just begun her specialty. It seemed that no one wanted to be with me as I was an adult patient, not so easy to manage, and they all felt happier looking after the little children who didn't challenge them and with whom they basically got on better. Besides that, they would rather not have to deal with so many variables, as in my case.

I was a twenty-four-year old woman with a daughter and a husband, who was a frequent visitor, and I had an opinion about everything. A child's way of seeing things is so different from an adult's, but still, as patients go, I was, indeed, very patient, and understood that my sole concern was to get better, and do what the doctors and nurses told me.

Pamela and I hit it off immediately. She looked me in the eyes and enjoyed talking to me. It was very easy to strike up a friendship with her and that was the beginning of a wonderful relationship which I hold dear even today.

In Intensive Care, you never knew for sure if it was day or night, as the lights were always on and the medical staff were constantly attending patients in the different cubicles. I was in an isolation room again, as my infection was very serious, and the last thing they wanted was for me to pass it on to someone else. So, when Pamela arrived, she would close the door and, even though the walls were windows which anyone could look through, I felt a certain amount of privacy.

Those first nights were exciting. We always had so much to talk about. With her being Colombian, her conversation was rich and colorful, and I felt as if I was chatting with an old friend. She kept an eagle eye on my monitors, but I gradually felt she did it more out of her concern as a friend rather than out of duty.

Even though I felt I could trust her, I couldn't quite pluck up enough courage to share with her openly what I had lived through, so I didn't mention it. Would she believe me? Would she understand that I wasn't going crazy or being affected by the medication? In any case, I couldn't find quite the right words to describe it all, and I was paralyzed by fear.

However, I saw that I could still laugh in the midst of the pain, and people in the hospital were amazed by that. I joked a lot about the state I was in physically and not being able to move, depending on everyone for everything. I felt such love for those around me that I now treated them differently. I was calm, trusting and happy to wait for things to happen in their own good time.

I did get frightened whenever another nurse appeared instead of Pamela. Other nurses were sometimes brusque and, without realizing it, hurt me by just lightly touching my skin. I had spent so much time lying down that the bedsores were getting bigger and bothering me more than the actual surgery.

Once, I got a nurse who helped me know myself much better. I realized I was prepared to do anything it took to get this nurse's attention and strike up a connection, simply so that I could let her know that I trusted her. I knew I should share some kind of message with her, but, so far, I didn't have a clue as to how to do it.

Her name was Sara. I remember that because, as soon as she entered, I remarked on how I admired Sara from the Bible. She paid no attention, or, at least made me feel she wasn't even listening. I tried a little smile, just to make that connection I needed, but nothing worked. She just wanted to do her job and make sure I was fine and in a stable condition.

The time came for me to be bathed, which was a ritual in itself. Bath-time was a perfect opportunity to change the sheets and turn over the protective covering on the bed. So, the nurses would roll me over to the left, first of all, and remove the sheets beneath me as far as she could. Then, my back would be uncovered and they would soap me down. If they wet the sheets, it didn't matter, as they would be taken off, anyway.

On this occasion, Sara rolled me over, and I immediately felt a sharp pain in my back and hip. I winced and asked if she could be a bit more careful.

"I'm doing it as carefully as I can. I do know my job," she said.

"I'm sorry. I didn't mean to tell you how to do your job. It's just that it hurts."

"OK," she replied, abruptly.

When she rolled me over the other way, I said jokingly;

"One, two, three; help me or I won't make it!"

"That's my job, to roll you over."

I felt sad, besides which, I felt very exposed, being almost naked with my back and the rest of my body completely uncovered so I could be washed. I needed to feel that Sara was aware of this and not just bothered about getting me bathed and having done with me. Whatever privacy there was, in all truth, I was in a place full of windows and in full view of anyone who cared to look.

She put the usual gown on me and finished adjusting the sheets, the wires and draining tubes, before sitting me up in a comfortable position. I thanked her, to which she replied, absent-mindedly, "You're welcome."

Shortly afterwards, I decided to pray. I had gotten into the habit of talking a lot to myself and to God. I would do it, on this occasion, by moving my lips and speaking very softly, knowing full well that Sara would be watching me from outside the cubicle, a job she performed very efficiently. And so I knew that, at some point, she would be coming in to ask me if I was all right. A nice little plan to get her attention!

I began by thanking God for being alive, and moved on to give thanks for the life of Sara and all those who attended me, doing all they could to keep me alive. Just when I was giving thanks for my family, my plan worked!

Sara suddenly appeared in the room.

"Are you all right?" she asked, looking worried.

"Yes, I'm very well, thank you, Sara. Actually, I was praying to God and giving thanks for being alive and for having you to take care of me so that I can be out of here before long."

She stopped in her tracks, not knowing what to say. Approaching my bed, she adjusted the tubes, plumped my pillow to make me more comfortable and, for the first time, looked me straight in the eyes and smiled.

"That's so great that you're feeling well. If you need anything, you'll let me know, won't you, Ana?"

"Of course, Sara, thank you."

There it was. The connection! I felt really proud of myself, getting a smile from her and having her show interest in my wellbeing. At least, that little victory made me feel good that night. But I still missed Pam.

I know Pamela asked to be with me during her shift. We got on so well, and she was so caring in whatever she did, that I felt only a true friend with a great love for me could be so giving. What I didn't know, of course, was that she was like this with all of her patients. But, still, Pam made me feel special. The way we communicated helped to keep me cheerful and hopeful. With her, I could talk about my daughter, in my own Spanish language, and could open up my heart to her.

One day, she told me she admired me. She trusted me enough to say that she couldn't understand how I could be so cheerful and inspire a spirit of calm and peace in all those around me. It was only as the days passed that I knew the reason why. My experience had given me so much strength that I was only barely beginning to understand it myself.

●NO PAIN, NO GAIN

*Sometimes pain is the best indicator that
I have something to learn.*

At the foot of my bed was the photo of Ana Paula. Always. Wherever I went, that picture went with me, and everyone knew that. It was my strength and my motivation and was a constant reminder of my sole objective, which was to see her again.

During the next three weeks, my health worsened. I was so weak that the simple task of speaking was practically beyond me. But Pamela took care of me, and like the true guardian angel that she was, she did not abandon me. To keep my eyes open demanded too much effort, and so, most of the time, I preferred to keep them closed. I know now that she often thought there was no way I could leave that place alive, but that didn't stop her encouraging me and caring for me.

I was now incredibly weary. The physical struggle was becoming overbearing, and even I was beginning to have my doubts about the outcome. *Ráfel* was nearby and constantly roaming around my room. I could feel it. The doctors, meanwhile, were doing absolutely everything they could, now with the challenge of another serious infection which left me weaker and hardly able to breathe.

Anyone gets worn out eventually with the tension of a prolonged period in hospital, but, for me, it was the isolation which made it so much worse. You feel you are imprisoned, cut off from the real world, but it was the not knowing which was excruciating. At least a prisoner knows how long his sentence will be, and can count the days until he is free at last. I didn't have that luxury. How many more days? What does the future hold? Will there be any more obstacles that appear from nowhere? What else can happen to me? I was adrift, like a boat in the middle of the ocean, no wind to move me one way or another. The waves would suddenly lift me up, only to break and send me crashing down again, each wave carrying me further away from the shore. Life was getting harder and harder, and I just couldn't seem to stabilize my health. Each day, I was weighed on scales where my whole body was lifted up in a sling, as they couldn't move me. I lost more than fifteen kilos, weighing now 44 kilos, far too little for my height of 1 meter 70.

My lungs continued to fill up with fluid and it was hard for me to breathe. Twice a day, I had to do breathing exercises, and it was a nightmare. Each time my dear Lorna, the physiotherapist, came to see me, I grimaced, as I knew how much it was going to hurt. In fact, as soon as she entered the room, the pain started. Of course, I knew that the exercises were vital to my survival, but even so, I came up with all the excuses in the book to put off the moment of truth. I joked with her, and tried to persuade her not to make me go through with the torture just then.

"Can't you see I'm asleep, Lorna? How about coming back later?"

"Now, Ana, we've got to do this right now, which you very well know. Come on, let's get started."

"Honestly, nothing will happen if we don't do it today. I'm too weak right now!"

"You're not weak. In fact, every day you're that bit better because of these exercises. Let's get started!" she said, adjusting the bed so that I could lie flat on it. Then she began tapping me lightly on the back to loosen the phlegm and help me expel it.

I had undeniably lived through a marvelous experience which changed something in me forever, but, even so, I knew now that my body was suffering just too much. In those moments of pain, I remembered my grandmother Nena. When we were little, my cousins would run off and play, and I complained to my grandmother that my Mom was telling me not to run so much, as I would get tired and my lips would turn blue. With that, she hugged me and whispered in my ear:

"Sweetheart, if you want to run, go ahead and run. Then, when you get tired, you just stop running. You can do that, so go ahead."

"Really, granny? Can I?"

"Sure you can. And if your Mom says anything, I'll tell her I gave you permission."

I don't know if my granny understood the implications of what she was telling me, but she definitely helped me to have the strength and confidence to start running and to be a little girl who could overcome her fears.

Now was not the time to stop. I had to keep going and come through this difficult patch.

"It's so painful to breathe, Lorna. Do you think one day it will stop hurting?" I asked her.

"It'll stop hurting sooner than you think."

Tap, tap, tap, she went, on the other side now of my back. Sometimes, the pain brought tears to my eyes, and Lorna stopped when she saw this. She offered me some water, and said:

"We've got less to go than when we started. Just a bit more, Ana. Let me do a few more taps."

I gave her a very forced smile and got into the right position again. Being able to look at the photo of Ana Paula gave me the willpower to hang in there a little bit longer.

Next came the job of breathing into the spirometer, a plastic device that measured the efficiency of my lungs. I had to inhale slowly, as deeply as I could, to make a tiny ball move up and touch

GRANDPARENTS NENA AND ENRIQUE

a certain point. It was a struggle to even manage half of what I was expected to do, but I moved that little ball a tiny bit more each time, even though the pain involved was horrendous.

It seemed that the only way I could make any sort of progress was at the cost of intense and exhausting pain. Lorna tried to get me to talk, to make the therapy session slightly more bearable. One day, I told her that if I had to go through all this pain and repeat the whole experience, I would gladly do it, just to see

171

my little girl again. Lorna just looked at me and kept on with her work.

When we had finished, she asked me how I felt and I always gave the same reply:

"In pain!"

And she would always say the same thing to me:

"No pain, no gain. Remember!" with a big smile on her face.

PHOTO OF GRANDMOTHER NENA

●MY PENULTIMATE LETTER

On the inside, I am much stronger than what I appear on the outside. Only I know what it has cost me to be who I am.

I was vomiting every day, several times a day, for some reason, and I always had my little bowl at the ready. It was a mystery, and worrying, as I couldn't keep my food down. One afternoon, my sister Marcela was with me when there was a changeover of doctors on duty. I was feeling particularly bad and started throwing up what I had eaten only a moment before. Marcela helped me, sat down again, and, just at that moment, an assistant nurse arrived and said it wasn't normal that I was vomiting so much, and there had to be a reason.

A doctor, who was new to me, came up and asked:

"Is there any chance you might be pregnant?"

As they didn't treat many adult patients in the children's hospital, this was new territory for them. The possibility of this simply hadn't occurred to them, and it certainly wasn't normal procedure to even ask. I immediately smiled and said, jokingly:

"How can I be pregnant when I've been in here for the last month?"

And at that very moment, my face changed and I went deadly pale. I remembered the special kind of "letter" I had written to my husband. Of course, I might be pregnant! I was with my husband the night before my surgery. It had never crossed my mind at that moment that it could be risky. I just wanted to say goodbye to him and give him peace of mind. It was madness, but, yes, it was possible! I started to cry, which was really difficult to do, as I could hardly take in enough air to breathe, let alone cry. I sobbed, and was in such a state that my sister came up close to try to calm me down. Two more nurses arrived and saw that I was inconsolable. The pain in my chest was immense, not only physically, but with the impact of all that this could imply.

I told them that, yes, there was a chance I might be pregnant, knowing full well that, in spite of taking precautions, anything could happen, as it often did. My heart was not healthy, but my uterus was perfectly healthy and ready to receive yet another baby. I thought about what could happen. On the one hand, I was panic-stricken, but part of me couldn't help but be excited at having been able to conceive once more. But then, common sense returned. If my baby did survive, how could it possibly be healthy with all the torment it had had to withstand while inside my womb?

I had just undergone an extremely difficult surgery, followed by a second one less so, but both under complete anesthetic. I had been given endless medications, antibiotics, even electric shocks. No baby could survive all that! For a moment, I went just crazy thinking about what would happen if, after all, I had indeed conceived.

The nurses sent out an emergency call to Dr. Roma, who arrived a few minutes later.

"Ana, stay calm. I've just been informed what's going on. We'll do a couple of blood tests and get the results back within the hour. Please don't distress yourself anymore. It's not doing you any good to be upset."

She was annoyed that I had ever been asked that question. My health was so fragile that a piece of news like that, in my state, was simply catastrophic. The hospital could easily have ordered a simple blood test, without me even knowing about it.

I cried and cried, until I almost choked. Now, my pain was coming from the depths of my soul. Marcela, who was only eighteen at the time, could only sit and watch me cry. She had no idea as to how she could help me. But she knew that I loved listening to her sing. When I had calmed down and was sobbing less, she came up to my bed and started to sing. It was the song by Pablo Milanés: "The Brief Space". Listening to the lyrics, I thought about my daughter and remembered that I had to share her with others at that moment, but, even though she was far away, I didn't mind, just as long as I did have her. Marcela knew that, and her song comforted me.

I leaned my head against the pillow, looked up, and then lived another of the most beautiful experiences of my life. I started to pray and ask God to calm me down. Looking at the ceiling, and trying to take in deep, regular breaths, while I listened to Marcela, I focused on my prayer. Suddenly, I felt pins and needles all through my body. With my eyes wide open, and fully in control of my senses, I saw two angelic beings descend and settle themselves, one on my right and the other on my left. They radiated light, and I could perceive the movement of their clothes, which resembled silk tunics. They seemed to be floating all the time. I don't recall having seen large wings or haloes, just transparent bodies which emitted an immense brilliance and radiated love, at its most pure and complete. They began to bathe me; firstly, my head, oh so gently, and then my torso, arms, stomach and legs. I could feel my body freeing itself from all pressure and, relieved of pain and lovingly embraced by these beings, I could revel in the scene, a wonderful spectacle before my eyes.

Marcela just kept looking at me, not understanding what was happening, but noting that at each moment, I became more at peace as I looked at my body from left to right.

I slept deeply for several hours, and rested as I hadn't done for days. My breathing showed a remarkable improvement. Crying was the best exercise I could have done, managing to achieve in a few moments what Lorna hadn't succeeded in doing over days! With all the effort of the sobbing, air entered my lungs, which released a good amount of the fluid and phlegm.

No matter how dark certain events may seem, they sometimes bring with them a light, which gives sense to the pain. It's what I call, "growing in the pain".

When I awoke, Marcela was no longer with me, and it wasn't till just a few years ago that we actually referred to this incident. My blood tests were ready. I wasn't pregnant and had no need to be worried. That was such a relief, and I felt an even greater peace than what I had experienced before falling asleep. My body was very weak and battle-weary; my spirit, on the other hand, felt stronger than ever. That night, I couldn't help thinking about what I had experienced: the sight of angels around me. I thought, maybe, I had imagined it all in dreams brought on by sleeping pills. Doubts entered my head, and I simply decided not to mention it to anyone.

The next day, I got a call from Martha, a friend I hadn't seen in ages. She had asked for my extension and told the nurses it was urgent she talk to me. They put her through. It was a call that made me reflect deeply and realize that God had always accompanied me.

"Ana Cecy ,how great to talk to you. I just had to call, as I had a very vivid dream and I had to share it with you. I dreamed that you were lying in bed and two angels came down from high to be with you. They watched over you, caressed you and healed you while you slept. My dear friend, you are not alone; God is with you and His angels are at your side."

I was in shock. I couldn't move, but, if I had been able to, I would have leapt into the air and shouted out loud. It wasn't a dream, it wasn't my imagination, it really did happen. The pain and suffering in my soul were so great that God sent the help I needed to console and strengthen me.

My body was still very weak, but I felt that every part of my being found a balance and a great sense of peace. No matter how much pain and discomfort I endured, I was in a state of absolute serenity.

By then, I had lived through two life-changing events: my out-of-body experience and the soothing visit of two angels. I never considered myself to be the kind of person who is a strict observer of religious rites; rather, I thought of myself as very spiritual and a strong believer. What I had experienced was not merely a beautiful dream, but actually something very real and wonderful. I could feel a peace that went beyond my own thoughts and understanding.

It was then that I started to comprehend that phrase that was constantly going round in my head: "Stay calm and go in peace, and do everything I have asked you to."

Irrespective of what I might have to go through, my job was to live life to the fullest, just as I had been doing up to that point, without consciously thinking about it. I was still alive, and I loved life. More proof was not needed. I was not alone and I should trust.

Later on, I learned that the doctors couldn't understand how I stayed so peaceful, in spite of my poor physical and emotional state. The pressure was growing: on the one hand was the financial situation, with the hospital expenses going up and up. I couldn't help thinking that each day there meant more expense, and I knew that it would be impossible for my husband to pay the hospital fees if they kept on growing. On the other hand, my health wasn't improving. I had a series of infections because my immune system was so weak, which meant my life was in constant danger.

Despite all this, I felt at peace. The doctors could see I had a different look on my face, was smiling more, and generally being more positive. I was convinced that God was with me, and I hadn't the slightest doubt that I would leave that place in good health.

The vomiting gradually disappeared with no special explanation, in much the same way it had started. But I still had ahead of me a long month to go before being discharged. All I wanted was to see my daughter, as she would soon be turning one year old.

I couldn't speak to Ana Paula, and I felt as if I was missing out on some very important moments. I had to content myself with what my husband told me and with phone calls from my family and Ana Paula's godparents. They all tried to keep me up-to-date, whilst I, in my turn, would do my best to give out instructions as to how to dress her, tuck her into bed and give her baby food.

I didn't want her godparents preparing food for her, so I asked my husband to buy lots of baby food to take to Monterrey and make sure she had more than enough to eat. I thought it would be cheaper to buy it in the United States, and it would be better quality. Nobody dared go against me. He bought the food and an extra bag to take to Monterrey.

I wanted to feel that Ana Paula needed me, and that only I knew what was best for her, when, in reality, I had been away from her for almost five weeks. At her age, routines change quickly, and the needs of a baby can alter from one month to the next with no warning. I so longed to see her take her first steps, hold her hand and teach her how to walk.

Things were not looking good. I seemed to be going two steps forward and one step back. My strength for giving out instructions and just keeping awake and aware of everything around me was failing more and more. My appetite for food had almost gone. What sustained me was a great internal strength. My body was weak, but it was kept alive by my spirit.

The family fed me like a little child. At first, my mother would spoon-feed me. I didn't have the strength to hold a knife and fork. At other times, my grandmother Chagüita would take over, or my siblings, or my father. Anyone who arrived would try to feed me: uncles, aunts, even the nurses. Every mouthful took me ages to chew. I wasn't interested, but I opened my mouth to make them all feel as if they were helping me, which made them feel better. This was all they could do; my body was skin and bones, so any kind of gentle stroking of my skin, full as it was of bedsores, was too painful.

●I NEED TO WRITE

Enjoy your own company.
You will talk to yourself more than to anyone else in your life.

Around that time, my husband and father were approached by some lawyers, those who go round hospitals seeing if they can be of use to any patient who feels he or she has been neglected and wishes to sue the hospital for financial gain. The lawyers insinuated that they had grounds for blaming the hospital for my state of health, and that they should go ahead and sue. They pointed out that we had nothing to lose and a lot to gain. The expenses would continue to rise, and before too long it would be impossible to pay off the debt. They were touching a very sensitive point, as both my father and husband knew it was true: the debt was soon going to be enormous.

My husband couldn't resist the temptation to tell me about this and to hear my opinion. As I listened, I looked him straight in the eye and spoke very calmly. This was still no easy task, as my throat was very sore from having the tube down it for so many days, and I had no choice but to speak slowly and in short bursts.

"I am alive. The doctors are doing everything they can to keep me that way and to help my health improve. I'm not interested in making enemies. I want them on my side. Please, don't even consider this."

"But, just look at the hospital bill. It's hundreds of thousands of dollars. Do you realize I'll soon have to sell the cars, the house and everything we have just to pay off this debt?"

"That won't happen. You'll see, we'll find a solution and we'll be fine. Trust me, I feel well, and I know I will leave here alive. Over my dead body will you sue them. As long as I'm alive, I do not accept it."

He took my hand and assured me they wouldn't do anything, but deep, deep down, I doubted whether he would actually heed my words.

When I saw the bill later that day, I understood that things were at

179

a critical stage. My father and my husband could see that the financial aspect would be more serious as each day went by, and my father knew that he should intervene. They weren't sure whether to initiate legal proceedings or not. I knew I had to make a big effort to find a way to ensure that under no circumstances were they going to sue. I felt grateful to the hospital and the doctors, and I had to find a way to make this clear beyond a doubt.

It may be that there were times when, unconsciously, I wasn't sure whether I would ever get out of there alive. It was two o' clock in the morning and I couldn't sleep. And so it was that, after going through so much hardship and being able to do no more than send up my prayers, asking for help, one night of insomnia I decided to start writing.

That night, Pamela wasn't with me, so I called the nurse on duty.

"Thank you for coming. Please, I need a notebook and a blue pen."

At first, she was not too willing to go along with that.

"Yes, of course, but I shall have to go and get it; I don't know if we'll have to charge it on your bill or not."

"That's fine. Could you also bring me a tray and help me put my legs right, so I can rest the tray on them? I need to write."

"Do you feel OK? Is something wrong, Ana?" she asked.

"No, nothing. There are some things I don't want to forget and I'd rather write them down."

A little later, she brought what I'd asked for and, that night, I began to write. The nurse was rather surprised and perhaps a little scared. She didn't know why I felt the need to write and feared it might be a complaint or, even worse, the start of a legal action.

I felt a great need to start recounting my experience and not forget a single detail. In one way, I was writing my last will and testament and, at the same time, I was healing my inner self. Writing was liberating. It was like releasing everything that had built up inside me. I wrote about the pain, the anguish, my sadness and longings, but above all, each and every one of the blessings which had accompanied me through my life up to that point. I wanted my husband, parents, brother, sisters and Ana Paula to understand what I had lived through and what my expectations were.

Years later, I read an article on how writing can heal a person on the inside. Now, I can see it was my medicine and my sustenance. It was how I killed all the bacteria and all the doubts, I'm sure of that. After a few days of writing, of having this cathartic experience, I knew more than ever that, yes, I would leave there alive. I could feel it.

●THE OUTSIDE WORLD

Sometimes, the only thing
which will keep you alive is to
follow your dream.
PAMELA AND I

Pamela and Dr. Roma were alarmed by my starting to write, and were desperate to help. What, for me, was relief, for them was a sign of depression, something to cause concern. Above and beyond medicine, they knew that what I needed was to connect with the outside world, the normal world, to be able to speak about the little things that make up a regular day, that make up the rhythm of our lives. Pamela, on the one hand, was always an excellent companion during the nights. She was like a friend dropping in to see me every day, and we used to chat for hours on end. I became very fond of her during our times together.

And then there was Dr. Roma, who wanted to create a thread of continuity with me, a conversation which could be picked up and developed every day. Without any concrete date for my discharge, I needed something else to look forward to. But what?

It was then that she began not only to speak to me about my condition but also about her son, and so we started to share wonderful stories about our children. She told me about her problems with her hair and her search for the perfect haircut, which is always an entertaining subject for women, but something that men, sporting the same haircut all their lives, will never understand.

She said she had a "bad hair day" five out of every seven days of the week, on average. Her hair didn't look good, she said, and she didn't mind wearing the cap that's worn in the operating room so she didn't have to worry about styling her hair in the mornings.

"The more I fuss about my hair, the worse it looks. Ever since I was a little girl, in every photo of me, my hair looks uncontrollable, either because it sticks out everywhere or because my mother twisted my unruly hair into a curl on top of my head, and it looked like a pile of dog poop!" she would say.

And I, lying, inert, in the bed like a sack of potatoes, had such fun conjuring up that image in my mind that I roared with laughter for a good long while. It felt so good!

That was all I needed. I started to laugh, and so did she. I felt electricity coursing through my body, and that wonderful feeling of release which caused my worries to fade away. There's nothing more therapeutic than laughing until the tears roll down your cheeks.

Again, this was one of my best breathing exercises. Neither Lorna nor any breathing contraption had ever had such a good effect on my lungs. Dr. Roma took it upon herself to have a good new story to tell me each day, so that laughter would become a part of my day.

By now, I was writing non-stop. The more I laughed, the more the ink flew out of my pen. I was starting to eat, the bacteria were disappearing, and I was getting better. It was working: live and laugh to the maximum, and health will return to your body.

One day, Dr. Roma suggested to my mother that we call the hospital beauty salon, who offered special services to patients, like myself, who had had a lengthy hospitalization. I liked the idea, and the next day they paid me a visit.

They arranged the bed so that they could put a kind of bowl behind it where they could wash my hair, which they did, giving me a delicious massage, as well. This was so different from the other times, when they merely washed my hair with foam and I couldn't enjoy the marvelous sensation of water falling on my head.

Everything was done slowly, calmly, as nobody, least of all me, was in any hurry. I could feel them massaging my scalp, round and round in circles. I won't go so far as to say it was like being in heaven, but it really was the most glorious feeling I had enjoyed in weeks. They put a treatment on my hair, and while that was taking effect, they gave me a face massage. I felt renewed, refreshed, caressed. That human contact that we crave for was there for me to enjoy for the first time in a very long time. Finally, they cut my hair and shaped it nicely, as by that time it was in quite a mess. Then, my hair was blow-dried and styled.

By the end, I was exhausted, but relaxed, happy and much prettier. I needed that. I was never one to spend hours in the beauty salon, getting my nails painted or having a pedicure while they styled my hair, but that day, it was wonderful and I could understand why women did it. Dr. Roma was right: these small things made me feel different, fresh and alive.

Years on, I could understand that my friendship with Pamela and Dr. Roma were an enormous help in keeping me alive. They gave me a reason to keep going.

They made me want to be out there, enjoying life and friends, and they reminded me of my longing to be reunited with my daughter. We got on well as we were more or less the same age, and I could talk to them openly about anything. I'm sure they were an essential factor in my total recovery.

● A VISIT BY ANA PAULA

What really limits you are your thoughts.

After a little more than two weeks in ICU, I improved enough to be allowed to leave there. My body was finally managing to combat so many infections. I started to take a few steps, and, little by little, I was regaining some strength. I was moved to a room where I would be staying for two more weeks, if all went well.

The first days were fun. Unlike Intensive Care, where only a priest entered to give the sacrament on occasions, in this new room, I was visited by many ministers of various religions. They knocked on the door and asked if they might come in and say a prayer for me. Perhaps in those days the forms we filled in didn't include one stating my religion.

I let them all in. I listened to them, accepted their prayers for me and thanked them for their interest. It was amazing to me how all these religious people, dressed in various styles and with different customs and traditions, all of them, simply wanted to pray for me and my family. They all had the same end in view: to help me get better. None of them spoke to me of religion or rules; they just gave me their blessings, each in their own way. I would have loved to talk for hours to each of them. I'm sure I would have learned a lot, and it would have helped me with what today is one of my main resolutions: not to judge, but to respect and to love.

My grandmother Chagüita visited me during those days and offered to stay the night with me, so that my mother could go and rest. Visitors were allowed in this new room, but sometimes I wanted to be alone. However, my grandmother wanted to be there, at my side, in case I needed anything. I didn't want her to feel offended, but I said that she really didn't need to stay as I would be fine on my own, which meant that sometimes, I'm afraid, I didn't let her stay. What I wanted was to write, and I could write much better during the nights as I'd become used to being alone. Writing was what kept me motivated, and I couldn't concentrate the same if she or anyone else was there.

I knew that Pamela only worked in ICU and that, at any moment, she would go and pay me a visit, as a friend. I wouldn't see her at night. We exchanged telephone numbers and email addresses so we could stay in touch. I was very happy there, but not even Dr. Roma, who used to visit me every day before, was dropping in to see me. I missed her and felt alone, as if something was missing when she didn't show up. One day, I decided to tell her this in a letter.

The nurses were rather reluctant to deliver the letter to her. I later found out they all had their reservations about me since they knew I was a lawyer, and a sealed letter to a doctor could mean anything. I would never have imagined that.

When Dr. Roma received the letter, she was quite taken aback, as she confided to me not too long ago.

"That was when I realized I was your friend, Ana. I cannot remember the exact moment when we became friends, but I can remember, with stark and chilling precision, the moment when it suddenly hit me that our friendship was vital for your survival."

Friendship is so important for all of us, and maybe we don't appreciate enough how greatly it can affect our lives. As C.S. Lewis said: "Why do we need friends? Friendship is unnecessary, like philosophy, like art ..It has no survival value; rather it is one of those things that give value to survival."

I knew nothing about rules or protocol. I was just sincere and told her what I felt. She opened the door and invited me to step inside her life; so, I did the same. Now, I needed to feel we were not only friends because of the circumstances, but that we would continue the friendship in my new surroundings.

She went to see me that afternoon. She apologized, saying that she simply didn't want to invade the other doctors' territory, but she was still there for me. She recommended that I establish a routine whereby I imagined myself out of hospital, which, in any case, was nearly true.

"All I want is to see my daughter. I need that so much."

"I know, and we need to do something about that," she said.

I was tired, a little discouraged, and desperate to return to normal life. Ana Paula would be one year old within a few days but I wanted to see her, cuddle her, and feel her before then. She had already become used to a certain routine. She spent nearly the whole time at the house of her paternal grandmother, where my husband would spend the night, when he wasn't with me and in Monterrey, so he could see her every day.

Dr. Roma suddenly got a great idea.

"What about if we asked her daddy to bring her this weekend?"

My face lit up.

"Can we do that? That would be incredible! Will they let us do that?" I asked.

She promised to look into how it could come about.

The hospital administration opposed the idea immediately. In those days, children who were not patients were not allowed to pay visits, for fear of possible infection. These days, things are much more relaxed, and even dogs can visit their owners in hospital.

We formed a great plan worthy of the most sophisticated spies, and started to put it all in place. My husband would arrive with our daughter, and Dr. Roma would admit her, as if she were a patient. She would disguise her in a hospital gown and receive her on Sunday, which is when many new patients arrive, and, consequently, the nurses would be busy and, hopefully, not notice. If, by any chance, they stopped her, Dr. Roma would say Ana Paula was a new patient who was about to be admitted. Dr. Roma would be carrying a bag full of her own child's toys, which she promised to sterilize twice in the dishwasher.

My mother was very nervous about Ana Paula's upcoming visit, as she was concerned about what she would do with a baby in her apartment, in case I refused to let her leave. I knew she couldn't say "no" to me. We had to clear this up before the baby arrived, so that my mother wouldn't feel pressured. I promised her that Ana Paula would only come for three days and would return, as planned, to Monterrey with her daddy.

Roma (who, by this time, was no longer just the doctor so I called by her first name) knew that there was a chance that Ana Paula would not recognize me or could be scared by seeing me, as I was still weak and tired. I needed my daughter, and she knew it would be devastating for me if my daughter rejected me; however, she knew it was worth the risk and insisted on bringing toys to my hospital room, which could serve as a distraction to keep Ana Paula occupied for a while, until we were used to each other again.

The day of Ana Paula's visit arrived. It was early July. Nothing went according to plan. My husband had to endure a long ordeal at the airport. It was suspicious to see a father, alone, carrying his almost one-year-old daughter in his arms. They feared it was a case of child abduction, like on so many occasions when children are taken, never to be seen again by their mothers. In immigration, he was required to give convincing explanations of why he was travelling alone with his child. I shall always be grateful to him for making this journey and blessing me with seeing Ana Paula again.

My husband arrived with the baby in his arms and found Dr. Roma waiting for him with a small backpack of toys. Unobserved, they entered the elevator and made their way towards the unit where I was, and they didn't stop walking until they arrived at my room. Absolutely no one stopped them or questioned them. Roma remarked later that it was as if they were both invisible.

As was normally the case, I was lying down and my mother was in the room with me. Seeing Ana Paula come in, I immediately stretched out my arms, as much as I could manage, got out of the bed and walked over towards her. I was beside myself with emotion. The first thing I could utter was her name.

"Ana Paula, my beautiful daughter. How's my little darling?"

Ana Paula promptly hid, clutching tightly to her father, but my mother wasn't going to have any of that. She took hold of her, thinking that the longer we let her hide, the more we would be battling with her to come to me. She and I hadn't seen Ana Paula for over a month which, at this age, was a long time. I had lost 15 kilos and my hairstyle was different. Ana Paula didn't recognize my face or my smell; everything was different. My voice had also changed after so many days of having a tube in my throat, so this was not the voice she recognized from when she was inside me: a voice which made her feel safe and which belonged unmistakably to her mother. I listened to myself. My voice sounded like broken glass, like a badly tuned exhaust pipe on a car. That is when I realized that, for her, nothing was the same.

Slowly, I walked up to her and caressed her. I tried to play with her without speaking, making no sound. All that mattered was seeing her, feeling her, hearing her. There she was before me, so healthy, and her usual happy self. The emotion was so intense that, after only a short time of seeing her, without actually touching her, I was exhausted. I lay down on the bed and just stared at her in amazement whilst my mother played with her. Finally, when she had fallen asleep, my mother laid her gently at my side. Ana Paula turned and snuggled into my chest and the crook of my right arm. It was the closest I could have her. It was a beautiful sensation.

"Doesn't it hurt you? Are you all right?" my mother asked.

"I'm fine, Mom. It doesn't hurt at all."

That moment was magical. I felt her warmth, her gentleness, her innocence, the fragile nature of her body and the strength of her spirit. I came back to life, my strength returned and my soul was overcome with joy. Nothing could ever spoil that precious moment. I surrendered to sleep, with her next to me, and the two of us slept for several hours.

My mother must have enjoyed that moment: her daughter and her granddaughter finally together. It would have been wonderful if she had taken a photo of us, like we do today, taking photos of anything and everything, but maybe the fact that I was in bed, in my pajamas, stopped her, out of respect for my privacy. I don't know. How many things do we do or not do based on ideas that, when years have passed, seem so unimportant?

Later, when we both woke up, Dr. Roma was there. She thought it would be a good idea if Ana Paula and I went for a little walk together⌐⌐, as it would help her feel comfortable with me and would keep her occupied. I needed to walk, and she was barely at the stage of putting one foot in front of the other, so we would both greatly benefit from it. We were joined by my mother, as I shouldn't be walking on my own, either.

We went out into the corridor, and nobody put up any objection at seeing Ana Paula. They were all amazed that I was walking hand in hand with a little girl. I suppose they all knew she was my daughter, but no one dared ask, as they didn't want to be the ones to put an end to the visit. Dr. Nihill suddenly appeared, the first doctor I had come into contact with there and who was astounded that I had dared to have a child.

"Hello, Doctor, how are you?" I asked, really emotional and very proud.

"Very well, but not as well as you, I think. Who have we here?"

"Look, doctor, she's my daughter, my little miracle," bursting with pride.

He picked her up.

"No, my dear Ana. You are both miracles," and, looking at us both, he gave me a big, warm hug.

I've come to the conclusion that all of this planning by Dr. Roma was part of her way of motivating me to think about life outside the hospital. She made me feel we could work magic, that nobody saw us, and it all worked out perfectly. Thinking about it now, I suppose everyone wanted me out of there and knew that my daughter's visit could be crucial in achieving that, but only Dr. Roma was willing to make it happen. Later, she told me that she knew she would be in trouble for ignoring the rules, but she felt certain that when everyone saw the results of Ana Paula's visit, they would understand and forgive all.

Ana Paula's visit worked wonders for me, so much so that in two days, I was sent home. My husband decided to stay on two more days, which meant that, once we had arrived at the apartment, I could enjoy my baby for a bit longer in another kind of environment. Waiting for me there was my beloved Chagüita, who happily helped me with Ana Paula. It was my chance to spend more time with my daughter and let her get used to my voice and my presence, little by little.

Later that day, a very dear aunt and uncle of mine arrived, bringing with them a priest, a friend of the family's, who gave a service of thanksgiving there in the apartment. It was the best present I could have been given, and I cherish it in my heart today.

Ana Paula had to leave the next day. It was so difficult to let her go with her daddy, but I was revitalized and filled with the energy I needed to finish my recovery. I had to stay on almost two weeks more before going home, as I needed to be checked in the hospital every 3 or 4 days. I was so weak, the doctors had to be very cautious before finally agreeing to let me return to my country so far away.

Some days before my discharge from hospital, my husband had had to finish sorting out the hospital bill which, by this time, had risen to tens of thousands of dollars. He spent hours in the administration office, convincing them to offer us a discount. Just as the hospital handed him a bill, he handed them his own calculation. He reminded them of the many setbacks we had had to go through: the staphylococcus, the heart which had been punctured by mistake, the badly inserted tube and the crisis I endured as a result, and I don't know how many other incidents. They arrived at an agreement: the hospital condoned a large part of the debt and gave us several years to pay it off. We knew that would mean a long road for us.

Both my parents and my husband's helped us out financially. Some doctors didn't charge for their services: the surgeon, the anesthetist, and the doctors in charge of my case. They didn't need to go without being paid, as they had done a good job every step of the way. I knew that any mistakes that there might have been were not of their doing, but they wanted to help me and my family recover, not only physically, but financially, by not charging. They knew it was a miracle that I was still alive and I know they did it to show me that they were on my side, and it was a great blessing. Once again, I felt how God was at my side. I had been right. It would have been wrong for us to sue, much less create a bad relationship with the hospital staff.

Ana Paula turned one when I was still in Houston and all the family went to my parents-in-laws' house to celebrate and enjoy her first birthday cake together.

VISIT OF ANA PAULA THE DAY I LEFT THE HOSPITAL

WHAT THE HEART MUST ENDURE

●RETURN HOME

I learned that, to fly high, will power is enough;
the wings will come later.

The doctors said that, in spite of all the problems, the surgery was a success. I would have to be on medication for the rest of my life to regulate tachycardias and fluids. It was likely that, in ten years, I would need another operation, as this was not a permanent solution. I would go on with my life, taking certain precautions, and the new circulation could start to cause problems after some years. We would worry about that later: for now, I was alive and full of plans.

When I could finally return to Monterrey, my husband and I were exhausted. I was still weak, and living with sickness for so long was hard-going and it crippled us emotionally. We returned, but our expenses were enormous, and my recuperation would take some time.

I stayed at my parents-in-laws' house for three or four days. Ana Paula felt totally at home with her granny and, as I couldn't look after her, I relied on my mother-in-law to take charge while my daughter and I got used to each other again. She slept in the crib by my bed, so I could enjoy her and play with her.

I was so weak that I couldn't stay on my feet for long. My muscles were atrophied, and I could hardly keep awake. My body demanded sleep for most of the day and I needed help with anything that required a special effort. I sat on a chair to have a shower so as not to get tired and found the simple act of soaping myself challenging.

My mother took advantage of this time to put her house in order and to get back into her old routine. She helped hire a lady to stay with me all the time and take care of Ana Paula. I wanted to be in my own home and rest in my old familiar bed.

When I finally did get home, I went up the stairs and didn't come down again for weeks, although I was visited regularly by family and friends. They helped with the food, with Ana Paula and made the

194

days go by more easily. My mother visited me every day and nearly always brought me some prepared food so everyone could eat. She never failed to be there for me.

The return back home was hard on everyone, not least myself, for many reasons, apart from my physical weakness. No one goes through what I went through without some sort of transformation. Many memories flooded into my mind, and I challenged everything I had experienced. Now that I wasn't being constantly visited doctors and nurses, I had more time to write and to think. I felt as if an incredible sensitivity had been stirred within me; I was much more perceptive and felt more alive than ever. I needed to understand myself and see everything clearly.

I remembered some events that didn't make sense; my husband needed to talk to everyone, but hardly ever to me. I don't remember him feeding me, and he constantly disappeared without telling me where he was. Besides that, when my friends came round, he insisted on talking about himself and what he was going through, hardly leaving me any time to go into detail about my experiences, which, actually, I rarely did. Probably, talking about how he felt helped him relieve his stress.

The staphylococcus which had me on the brink of death had also destroyed a little the veil over my eyes from when we were first married, the veil which allowed me to keep going without really seeing. That suddenly was gone, and I started to notice things I hadn't seen before.

Those first weeks were challenging for Ana Paula, as well. I wasn't allowed to carry her, as my chest shouldn't exert itself more than necessary. So, between my mother, my daily help, some friends who stopped by and my husband, they took turns in looking after her.

Ana Paula couldn't understand why I couldn't carry her and she cried and asked me to pick her up constantly. Now, she needed more of my attention and care than anyone else's. She demanded that I be the one who attended her, carried her and spoilt her, but even when I did, it was never enough.

One day, my mother was with Ana Paula and me in the bedroom. When my mother had to leave, she took Ana Paula to her bedroom and put her in her crib, much against her will. I needed to rest. Ana Paula was so furious that she leaned against one side of the crib and then flew against the opposite side with such force that she was propelled out of the crib and fell head first on to the floor. My mother ran to see to her, picked her up and tried to calm her down. I got up and followed her, moving as fast as I could. Ana Paula just held out her arms, pushed her grandmother away and looked at me. When she was angry and had a tantrum, she would hold her breath, go bright red, almost blue, and finally burst out crying. But this time, she kept going longer than normal, which scared me.

I had to do something, so I picked her up, sat her in front of me and blew hard into her face to make her react. I took her in my arms, rocked her gently, put arnica on the bump on her head and calmed her down as much as I could. I called the doctor, who gave instructions not to let her sleep for at least an hour, so I played with her, gave her some biscuits and things to distract her. Finally, I went to my room, lay down in bed with her in my arms, and the two of us fell into a deep sleep. We needed each other. Mercifully, the bang on the head wasn't serious.

A few weeks later, one of my uncles and his wife went to offer me a considerable amount of money. At least, it was a lot for me in those days. He told me never to mention his name, but he wanted me to use that money for me, for whatever I needed: buy some clothes, go out to dinner, buy something for my daughter, give myself a little treat, as well as pay off some of the debts. He just wanted to give me a break amidst all the many expenses we had. It was a relief and a huge gift for which I shall always be grateful.

I used part of the money to go to therapy. I needed it.

My great Soul Mates made a similar gesture. They collected a sum of money from all our old friends from Secondary School and handed it to us some weeks after my return. Help was coming in from all directions.

I know my return home wasn't easy for my husband. I was still lacking in strength and energy. Despite many attempts to make our life as a couple as normal as possible, it took me a long time to fully recover. My body reacted like that of a much older woman. The physical and hormonal damage was significant.

He waited and tried to understand, but I realized that he found it hard to cope. On many occasions over a period of months, my body just didn't react as it should have done, under normal circumstances. Far from feeling attracted, I felt used and manipulated, which made me feel sad. I didn't blame him; instead, I wrongly blamed myself.

The most important thing, and what was ever-present in my mind, was that I was alive, I had a daughter and she needed me. Sometimes I felt guilty, too, because the little energy I did have was used up looking after Ana Paula. Anyhow, I made a great effort to please my husband, so that he wouldn't get desperate.

His daughter and I would wait patiently for his return every day. I tried to have the dinner ready, cooking his favorite dishes. He constantly arrived late, and if Ana Paula had dropped off to sleep, chances were I had, too.

He nearly always announced his arrival as he opened the door, at which I would do my best to get up, shake off my drowsiness, and go down to be with him. For years, even after recovering from my surgery, I tried to be happy. When I married, it was to be for as long as I lived, and I intended to keep my promise. With my operation, there was a great chance of me living much longer. At least, that was my hope. We looked for ways to share more time together, although our conversations were fairly shallow. Sometimes, I missed that veil that prevented me from seeing and which made me blindly believe that all would be well in our relationship. In time, we stopped looking at each other, admiring each other, reading to each other. Or, I should say, I stopped doing that.

However, I realized that what made me really happy was sharing my experience with others. The more I did that, the greater value I discovered in what I had witnessed. I now saw life differently, how our life transcends unimaginably after death, but I found it difficult to understand. I needed to rediscover what had kept me alive in Houston. I became very interested in studying the Bible more, and during the next months, my friend Lilia from the Catholic group of Propagators of the Word helped me to start teaching Bible study. I prepared days and nights on end, and started to discover my voice, and I realized that words of wisdom were coming out of my mouth, which I never would have imagined, words which were not biblical but which came out of my inspiration. I was finally teaching two groups a week and felt very strong spiritually, which boosted my confidence.

My sister, Sandra, got married six months after my surgery. I bought a dress which, a few days before the wedding, didn't fit me, which, far from being bad news, meant that I was gaining weight, so I sent it to be let out. I felt better, but still didn't have enough energy to do many activities. It took me about a year to feel well and strong enough to do whatever I wanted.

A year after surgery, I decided to resume my university studies. I had finished my degree, but still didn't have my professional qualification. The university gave me the opportunity to do three Master's subjects with a view to getting my qualifications. After talking to my husband at length about it and assuring him that my parents could pay for it, he agreed. From 7:00 to 10:00 at night, I studied for two semesters, twice a week. Ana Paula stayed with my daily help and when her daddy arrived, he took care of her. It took a lot of effort, what with the studying and the late nights, but I couldn't be without my professional certificate. It was an achievement that I wanted to present to my parents and to myself.

I completed one year of study with a good average. Now, I was a Law graduate. Today, I can applaud my decision as, even though I didn't know it then, the degree would provide me with economic stability and independence in the future. I would really have liked to work with my grandfather Enrique in his public notary, as was his dream, ever since I started to study Law. But the emotional and physical demands it would make on me made it impossible. I preferred to dedicate myself to looking after my daughter and devote some quality time to our marriage.

When I graduated, Pamela and Fernando Lombana visited us. We were very happy to receive them in our home, as we had become good friends, and they used to put us up in their home whenever we went to Houston for my medical check-ups. I remained in close contact with Pamela and Roma in the first years after my surgery.

We sent each other emails to stay in touch, which Roma and I would read together again many years later.

MY FATHER AND ME A FEW WEEKS AFTER THE SURGERY.

●DANIEL

*Each of the battles in my life
has made me learn a lot,
especially the ones that I
have lost.*

Once I had recovered, our wish
was to have another child, but
that was no longer possible, as
I was operated on one year after
the heart surgery, to avoid any chance of pregnancy, which would
present too great a risk. So, adoption seemed to be the best course to
follow. I was convinced that all children come from the body when
they are conceived, but all will be children of the heart and will be
carried in the soul throughout one's lifetime.

My parents and some doctors were against the idea as, in spite of
my reasonably satisfactory recovery, my heart was always going to
be prone to complications. Even so, we trusted that, if this was what
was best for us, then we would find a way to make a success of it.

Ana Paula was about three years old when we decided to adopt
Daniel. My husband wanted a boy; as for me, I didn't mind one way
or the other, I just wanted Ana Paula not to be alone and to have
a little playmate. Our search began. At night-time, we would pray
alongside Ana Paula that, if it was the will of God, He would allow
us to have a brother for her. She was very excited with the idea.

Daniel arrived in our home when he was one year old.

On the day we adopted him, there was scant information available
regarding his origins. We would spend the next years trying to find
out what was the matter with him, as his behavior was totally unlike
that of any other children. He seemed to be in his own world, and
it was hard to communicate with him. My days and nights were
dedicated solely to him. He lost his temper easily, and I couldn't

take him anywhere, as he would burst into fits of anger and, in his desperation, he would hit out at anything that crossed his path. I stopped going to many get-togethers so that I could devote myself solely to him. Maybe I also neglected Ana Paula, as I was focused entirely on his insatiable needs. Fortunately, she was a patient and understanding little girl, and she adored her brother. He was her playmate, and they had great fun playing together.

As with any child, over the following days, months and years, I loved him more and more. My maternal instinct came to the fore, and I was the same protective and devoted mother as I was with Ana Paula. For me, nothing was more important than helping my child to get on, and I believed that, if he was entrusted to our care, then there must be a good reason for it.

I tried to interest Daniel in swimming, football and music as he grew older, but nothing seemed to work. He hit the other players when he got desperate and reacted aggressively to any problem. So much so, that it always ended up in the same way, with him being excluded from the classes.

I wanted him to find something that made him happy, something he was good at. We didn't have the money to pay for all those classes, so I sold my university course books to the daughter of the director in order to pay for the swimming classes. Daniel was really good at swimming, due mainly to his strong constitution, and by the time he turned five, he was an excellent swimmer. The problem was that if something didn't turn out the way he had expected it to, he would get frustrated and explode, which gave me some very painful moments in front of everyone else, especially when it was competition-time. The only way to calm him down was to hold him tightly.

Once, during a class, Daniel got into an argument with a little girl three years younger than him. Normally, we mothers would watch how the class was going, through a second floor window overlooking the pool. Daniel started shouting at the girl, which caused all the mothers to focus their attention on him. To my horror, he suddenly put his hand on the girl's head and pushed her down under the water. The mother instantly transformed into a fierce dragon, with flames shooting out of her mouth and daggers from her eyes piercing my very soul.

"Your son is drowning my daughter! Do something, for the love of God!"

"Daniel!" I shouted at the top of my lungs. "Get out of the pool right now!"

I flew down the stairs, taking them two or three at a time, to get there as fast as I could. The floor around the pool was slippery, and I slid along the floor as if on ice. It was all I could do not to end up in the water along with all the children. I stuck out my arm as far as I could to reach my son, grabbed him by the hair and yanked him, kicking and screaming, out of the water. The little girl, by this time, was hanging on to the edge of the pool, safe, though in shock. Daniel was completely beside himself and impervious to anything I could say, leaving me no choice but just to hug him tightly until he finally couldn't put up a fight any more and became limp in my arms. I ended up soaked to the skin and absolutely worn-out. My head was spinning and I could hardly breathe, but my heart, as always, behaved like a trooper and kept strong in the face of this new attack.

Fortunately, nothing more serious happened, but the mother was so angry that she got together with the other mothers to demand that Daniel be thrown out of the class. If he didn't go, they would!

I couldn't go back either, of course, so now I was without my course books and without the classes. Mind you, I don't blame the mother at all for how she reacted. I would have done the same thing, no question. Mothers can be fierce!

Arriving home, I felt defeated. I could see how my little boy suffered every time he was shouted at for something he had done. He would look at me with eyes that tore my soul in two. He would purse his mouth, his lips trembling, trying hard not to cry. His large, deep set eyes, wide open and wet with unshed tears, looked at me with such sadness, bracing himself for the inevitable scolding. At the same time, I knew that he hoped against hope that I would be behind him and not tell his daddy about what had happened, as he didn't want to be in even more trouble.

That day, my anger turned into a feeling of complete powerlessness, which turned into tears; all I could do was hold him and cuddle him for a good long while.

"Son, let's pray, shall we? We're going to ask God to help you to control yourself and be a good boy."

"Yes, Mommy, I promise I won't push any other little girl under the water. And I won't shout or lose my temper, ever again!"

He fell asleep in my arms and, once again, I begged God to give me strength and good health, so that I wouldn't fail Daniel at these times when he needed me most.

My young son went to eight different pre-schools, lasting only two or three months in each one, as they expelled him for lack of control. The list of his misdemeanors would get longer and longer, with detailed accounts of kicking, shouting and biting, among others, until finally, he would do something serious that was the final straw, like when he hit a pregnant teacher with a bat used for hitting the piñata. He had become obsessed with piñatas and, that particular day, he said the teacher's seven-month pregnant belly looked like a piñata, so he took a swipe at it. Another time, he was sent out for hitting boys in their testicles with his lunchbox. He had certain fixations and obsessions which were unfathomable to anyone else. He was just three years old.

Sometimes, he said he was scared and didn't want to sleep alone. He would appear in my bedroom, the fear showing in his eyes, and asking me to help him. I would calm him down, hug him and take him back to his room. The next day, I found several of his dolls under his mattress.

"What's going on, Daniel? Why did you put your dolls here?"

"Well, they talk in the night and won't let me sleep. They scare me."

"Dolls don't talk, son. It must be your imagination."

"No, they really do, Mommy. I can hear them."

I would never have guessed that, years later, we would finally understand that, for him, all this was real; his dolls talked and he was terribly scared.

Every day, there was a new battle to fight, and it was exhausting. There was never a "good" day, with no incidents, and there was always something new to deal with. When he was expelled from

Kindergarten, I arrived home with a pit in my stomach, and gave a forced smile to Ana Paula, as if everything were just fine. I knew God would help me, that no fight was in vain and that, eventually, we would find a way out. I was sure that, no matter how dark the night appeared, sooner or later, the sun would appear.

I wasn't going to give up, but I did ask myself what I was going to do next with the uniforms, shoes, school supplies to pay for, or how I would get the tuition fees returned to me. But, most of all, I worried about what I could do. I couldn't leave my son without any schooling; he had to be given the chance to be just a child and to learn, like everyone else. So, I kept looking for one more option to get him to mix with other children. I swore I would not be defeated.

My husband didn't involve himself much in my decision-making about schools, psychologists, special classes, and, actually, I was very guarded with what I told him, as he didn't respond well to hearing about more of Daniel's bad behavior. When he scolded his son, he was tough. But he did listen to me and support me, which helped me stay strong. I always felt he approved of my decisions and was a partner, albeit a silent one, in my struggles. Perhaps he couldn't do more, or he just felt it was my responsibility as the mother. The truth is, neither of us was equipped to deal with such a difficult case as Daniel's.

On many occasions during those years, I felt as if I was walking in an endless desert. Trudging through this arid and merciless wilderness, I was slowed down by the weakness in my physical heart, but the pain in my emotional heart, that part which my son inhabited, was even greater. I was parched from lack of drink and starved of food, and felt the burden of the child I was carrying on my back as I lifted each foot heavily to put one foot in front of the other. Besides that, there was another little girl following close behind, never letting me out of her sight. She needed me as well; she, too, was getting tired, was desperate for food and drink as we all plodded wearily onwards in the desert. But, most of all, what that little girl needed was to be hugged by her Mommy.

Not once did Ana Paula stop following me each step of the way. She was my guardian angel during my difficult journey with Daniel, unaware that she provided me with the love and strength I needed to keep going. Not only that, but the memory of my near-death experience lifted me up at all times. I knew I was not alone, that no day would go by without there being something to give thanks for. I had no choice but to get up and keep going, and give Daniel all the love I could. I never forgot for one second the message I had heard, and each time it became that much clearer: "live life to the fullest and enjoy the journey".

But still, there was something I needed to learn, and maybe others did, too.

In Daniel's eyes, Ana Paula was a very important figure, and she became his role model and his guiding light. He would draw, do handicrafts and watch movies with her. She took care of him, guided him and often gave him the balance he needed in his life. There was a problem, however: he couldn't stand her leaving him or having fun with her friends and not paying attention to him. Knowing what I do now, I can understand that it was not fair for her that she did so much or that so much was expected of her, as there came a point when, in Daniel's eyes, his sister only existed for his benefit, for him to play with and have fun with.

When Daniel was four, he was able to start in kindergarten at the same school where Ana Paula was in the first year of Primary School. But, here again, it wasn't long before the troubles began. One day, the director invited me to work in the school, teaching children from upper Primary, which meant that, if any problem arose with Daniel, I would be near at hand to calm him down. I was thrilled at the idea, and very grateful, especially as that would mean that both my children would receive a scholarship, and this would help us financially. The reality of it, though, was not ideal, as sometimes Daniel would barge into my classroom shouting and complaining about something he wasn't happy with in his class. The mothers of my pupils frequently complained, because they had been told by their children that a boy had come into the room shouting, and that I had to leave the classroom for a time, asking another teacher to stand in for me.

In spite of those demanding years with Daniel, I always tried to make time for Ana Paula, just to listen to her, as her conversations were incredible. She lit up my darker moments and made me forget my sadness, as once, when she was in kindergarten and was just learning the letters of the alphabet.

"Mommy, I've learned to write now and I want you to read what I did, and then tell us the story," she said, showing me a piece of paper, whilst the two of them snuggled up to me.

"Tell me what it says, Mommy," said my five-year-old, in her sweet and gentle little voice.

I invented a story and tried to relate it to what I supposed she was thinking or imagining when she filled the page of her notebook with letters and meaningless scribbles. I tried hard, but I think that, through me, she discovered some new story to write.

After a while, she went with her daddy for him to do the same, but was very upset when she realized that what he read was totally different from what I had said.

"Mommy! Daddy can't read!" she complained, in an absolutely firm and no-nonsense tone, sure that her daddy was incapable of understanding the marvels of her writings.

"It's true, Mommy. My Daddy can't read!" piped in Daniel, standing right behind her.

"OK. Now, I'll read it," she said.

And so began a long story full of all the adventures of the Sesame Street characters: Elmo, René the Frog and the Cookie Monster. I would never have imagined that so many characters could fit on to such a tiny scrap of paper. Daniel, for his part, listened spellbound, no doubt believing his sister to be a great literary writer.

I continued my search to find someone who could help me with Daniel: doctors, psychologists, schools and friends. I had him in language therapy, dietary control, medicine to counteract hyperactivity, but nothing seemed to work. We even took him to Houston to get a diagnosis, but the extent of damage that Daniel had suffered was still unclear.

Tests were done on him: a brain scan, psychological and cognitive examinations, amongst others. They told us the front right lobule was damaged, which accounted for his difficulty with self-control and inability to manage his emotions. They also pointed out that his brain didn't appear to have any physical damage, but his behavior did seem problematic, and they suspected that he was affected by his biological mother having consumed drugs during the pregnancy.

Shortly after that, we went to the institution where we had adopted him, and, sure enough, we found out that, somehow, some information had been withheld from us, for "administrative" reasons. Daniel's mother had never stopped taking drugs throughout her pregnancy. At first, we were livid, desperate and determined to sue them on the grounds that they had hidden vital data from us. Later on, however, at home, and having thought it through, we decided that, at least with us, Daniel was being given a chance that he would never have had if he had stayed in that place. Everything is for a reason.

It was all so difficult for us to accept. One the one hand, his behavior could now be explained, but on the other hand, I asked myself if I would be able to cope with him in the future. I still tired very easily and was worried about my own health, as Daniel was demanding more physical stamina from me to try and control him.

Whenever there was a children's party, I had to see where to leave Daniel as, if I took him, there was a risk that he would hit some child with the piñata bat when it was his turn. Sometimes, I couldn't stop him, and on several occasions we had the same kind of incident as with the pregnant teacher before. As a result, I was constantly under pressure, as I never knew how he would react, which explains why I eventually stopped taking him and had to separate him from his sister. I was tormented by feelings of guilt towards the one child for not taking him and towards the other for limiting her chances to have fun, which was so unfair, as she was always so well-behaved.

It broke my heart to leave him and, more often than not, I left him with my mother who looked after him, so that I could have a break and concentrate just on Ana Paula. That was until one day when I had to say, "Enough is enough!" Daniel put poor Max, my mother's dog, in the garbage, and then closed the lid on tight. Max was a miniature French poodle who the grandchildren loved to play with when they visited their grandparents. On that particular day, Daniel wanted to hide him, but then he totally forgot about him. Later that night, after frantically searching everywhere, my mother discovered Max, half-dead, dehydrated, without any oxygen to breathe and, generally, in a really poor state. Thank God the dog would make a full recovery, thanks to my parents' care, but my mother said she could no longer look after Daniel.

"Ana Cecilia, I love him very much, but I just can't watch over him on my own. I'm sorry to say this, but you'll have to find someone to help look after him whenever you leave him here."

"Yes, Mom, I understand perfectly."

I had a lump in my throat when I left, but I knew she was right.

Realizing that Daniel's schooling would continue to be a problem, with practically daily complaints about him, we made a decision. Together with the psychiatrist who would attend him for many years, and the director of the school, we decided that Daniel should take his classes on his own. We took him to a private teacher so he could complete the first year of Primary School, and, thanks to the small salary I was earning for my work there, I managed to pay part of the therapies, the psychiatrist and Daniel's teacher.

The only way to see past what we don't like in someone is to love them.

On one occasion, I took him for his usual doctor's appointment, and I can't imagine how I must have looked, but the doctor barely spent any time dealing with Daniel and dedicated the rest of the session to me.

"Mrs. Ana Cecilia, you look tired and worn-out. Tell me, how are you?"

"Well, yes, I am a bit tired, probably doing more than I should."

"I know you have a heart condition. Just tell me, out of interest, what do you do on a normal day?"

"Well, you know, doctor, the usual things we mothers do: get up, make breakfast, make sure the children get dressed, see that they eat and clean their teeth in good time. Then we all hurry out to the school where I work all morning. If Daniel has a good day, then everything goes smoothly, but if he's gotten into any kind of trouble then I have to go and sort it out. It's pretty draining. Then we go back home to have lunch. I take Daniel to his therapy and Ana Paula to her class, and then it's time for homework in the afternoon. Just the normal things, doctor."

"Yes, I agree, it' s normal when you do all this with normal children, but Daniel is very demanding, and takes a lot out of you, doesn't he? How is your heart? I reckon you're overdoing it. You really need to take care."

Hearing him say that was too much for me. I started to cry and could not stop. Yes, of course, I was tired and exhausted, both physically and emotionally. It was as if I was swimming against the tide and couldn't see how or when I would finally make it to the shore. Maybe I had been in that position before, in Intensive Care, but there, I didn't have enough strength to cry, not like I did that day. But this time, it was no longer a fight to survive for me alone; now, I had two children who needed me to be well.

I didn't speak much that day, but left there much lighter of spirit. Someone, besides my parents, had actually bothered to ask me how my health was. They and my husband had suggested more than once sending Daniel to a special home, but I had refused.

I had almost forgotten that the simple fact that I was alive was, in itself, a sheer miracle, and now it was my job to take care of myself. I had a purpose in life which couldn't be fulfilled if I became unbalanced or if my heart were to simply give up fighting. The doctor was absolutely right: something had to be done, but making a decision was difficult when there wasn't a clear diagnosis.

Many nights, I would go to Daniel's room while he was sleeping, and fall on my knees beside his bed. In the early days, when he was younger, I begged God to heal him, to help me look after him, to give me wisdom to guide him and not lose my way on this path, which was draining me of all my strength. I was exhausted, desperate and felt as if I had nothing more to give.

Ana Paula's friends had stopped calling round, for fear of her brother's aggressive ways. One day, she was in her bedroom with a few friends when Daniel started banging on the bedroom door with a skating boot, so powerfully that he made a great big hole in the door. The girls were terrified. He was annoyed because his sister hadn't let him into her room. Ana Paula complained angrily that he wouldn't leave her alone to enjoy hanging out with her friends, something all nine-or ten-year-old girls love to do. But he just didn't think that that was OK, and unleashed his anger on them.

By this time, Daniel was eight years old and the same height as Ana Paula, even though he was two years her junior. He was getting stronger, and was becoming a danger both to himself, his sister and to others who happened to be nearby. One day, he lit a fire in her dressing room. Another time, he was so excited to see the puppies of our pet dog Reinita that he took one of the newborn puppies and threw it across the room, killing it instantly. He destroyed toys and even threatened a neighbour with a knife. Needless to say, his ability to relate to others was depleting with each passing day.

Doctors, psychologists, the pediatrician, priest, family: everyone told us we should separate the children. Added to that, I was having a hard time, physically, trying to watch over him. At every turn, the general consensus was that we should have him institutionalized, which I absolutely, and in floods of tears, refused to do. But finally, after one incident which I actually witnessed, I made the painful decision to do just that.

That particular day, Daniel and Ana Paula were playing in the back yard, where there was a pile of rubble and some little stone steps. The steps had no railing on either side. Ana Paula started to go up the steps excitedly, at which point Daniel turned round and pushed her with all his might to make her get down again. Ana Paula lost her footing and flew backwards. If I didn't believe in angels, on that day I would have been converted. She did a somersault of 180°, just managed to put a foot on the next to the bottom step, gave another half-turn and ended up falling on her bottom on a mound of earth.

I watched the scene as if in slow motion. I saw her suspended in mid-air as if held aloft by strings which somehow prevented her from landing on her back and hitting her head on the sharp edge of the stone step. I charged out into the back yard and immediately lifted her up and hugged her. She was crying more from the shock than from the pain of the fall. Amazingly, she came to no harm, but, was understandably very scared and was crying inconsolably. Her voice was shaking as she tried to put the words together to tell me what had happened, little knowing that I had watched it all play out.

Daniel started to shout and cry, totally out of control. He expected to hear me yell at him to be more careful and to see the fury of my accusation in my eyes. Instead, I stayed silent and looked at him with the most loving expression I could. With absolute calm, I told him to get down and go to his room. Inside, I was trembling and I could feel my heart racing. He rushed down the steps and ran off, shouting and wailing out of fear and not knowing what to do. After waiting a short while, I went and calmed him down. Although I truly understood that Daniel had no control over what had happened, the reality was, it could have had fatal consequences. That was when I said: "Enough!"

I told my husband of my decision that night, which came as no surprise as it had been just a matter of time. On hearing my account of what had happened, he made as if to get up and go to Daniel's room, who by this time had nearly dropped off to sleep, but I asked him not to. I didn't want to hear any more shouting and scolding. It would do no good. My mind was made up: Daniel would leave the house, and now I would have the job of preparing him for that.

Letting him go without him having a clear understanding of why, seemed heartless and cruel. But I couldn't deny the high price I was paying in my effort to look after him. My heart, thank goodness, seemed to be functioning fine, but, nevertheless, I was very limited in what I could do, even after the surgery. I had been given a much better quality of life and yet I couldn't help noticing that I was beginning to suffer longer spells of tiredness again.

I started to think a lot again about *Ráfel*. I needed him near at hand now, so I could talk to him and ask him for a hug and words of advice. He had been there for me in so many trying times that I now felt in need of him. Perhaps he was near, and I just hadn't noticed. My life was most definitely not in danger at this time, but my heart was suffering more than ever. "Where are you, *Ráfel*?" I would ask him, tearfully.

My husband had everything arranged for Daniel's departure weeks before, and was just waiting for me to decide when. The following week, Daniel left.

This was one of the saddest days of my life. My heart and mind

211

both knew that it was the right decision, but all my senses were screaming that it was up to me to protect him. Letting him go was so heart -wrenching, I couldn't be the one to take him.

Ana Paula knew that he would be leaving at some point, as we had told her, but I didn't have the heart to tell her that it would be on that day. I felt I wouldn't have the strength to deal with the emotional trauma she would have to endure before saying goodbye to her Daniel. It was true that she was at her wits' end with him, but he was still her brother and she adored him.

It was a Saturday morning. I got up early and asked the mother of one of Ana Paula's friends if she would invite her over for lunch and let her stay for the afternoon, so that Ana Paula would be keeping busy and wouldn't be there when the final moment arrived. I also wanted to be alone with my son, so I dropped her off at her friend's and went home. My husband wasn't home, as he had gone to sort out the final details and was going to pick up his father, who would accompany him to take Daniel.

I went to Daniel's room, sat down on the bed, and he perched next to me.

"Darling, do you remember what happened outside the other day with Ana Paula?"

"Yes, I was naughty and pushed Ana Paula. Are you going to punish me for that?" he asked, his voice breaking.

"No, sweetheart, I'm not. I want you to know that I saw what happened and I could see you didn't do it on purpose. You couldn't control yourself and your first reaction was to push her."

We kept talking a little and I explained what the doctors had said and how important it was to seek help. He needed to learn to control himself and find the right medication to make him feel better, so he wouldn't get so desperate.

The psychiatrist had already explained to him that, one day, he might be going to a place where they would help him feel better and that, in time, he would be able to return home.

"So, I have to go to some place, like the doctor told me."

"Yes, darling. I think you'll have to go where the doctor suggests. They'll help you, and you'll see you won't get those fits of anger anymore and you'll be able to play safely."

"OK, Mommy. What clothes shall I take?" he asked, in a very sweet, soft voice, as if the news hadn't bothered him at all.

I pulled down a big suitcase and a bag, and we began to pack. One by one, he and I carefully and lovingly put in there his clothes, his toys, his treasures – his life.

I could hardly speak, and was shaking more with each new thing I put in the suitcase. I couldn't believe that I was going through with this, and, not only that, but my son was actually helping me to do it. He was so cooperative; I couldn't help feeling that he was enjoying it all. Maybe the thought of going to a different place was exciting for him, imagining new friends and adventures. Or, maybe he thought that this would be just a quick visit. I don't know, but my heart was trembling and I was finding it hard to breathe.

When they eventually came for Daniel, my whole body started to shake and I was in two minds as to whether we should abandon the whole idea. It was hard enough to see him ready and taking it all so calmly, whilst my whole body was bursting under the strain of the turmoil inside.

I went to Daniel, who was watching television, and hugged him tightly.

"Son, it's time to go. Your Daddy and Grandpa will take you there."

At that moment, Daniel stood up in front of me and said the words which I shall carry in my heart for the rest of my life.

"OK, Mommy. Let me give you a big hug, so big you'll feel it for days and days until I see you again."

I burst into tears and hugged him with all my body, heart and soul. Seeing me cry, tears flooded into his dark eyes and he blinked to try and stop them falling.

"I love you, my darling boy. We shall see each other very soon."

This was the son I was destined to have. He was not responsible for anything that was happening. He was a victim of circumstances and was paying the price –as we all were- for the decisions of his biological mother all those years before. I had to believe that.

So, there it was, and I cherished that hug until I next saw him, weeks later, on the advice of the doctor to give him time to settle in. I still carry that hug in my heart and his words will be forever engraved in my mind.

Daniel was never to come back to live in our home again.

The three of them went off without me. The institution was 2 hours drive away, so they would be home late, and, anyway, I was going to have to pick up Ana Paula and explain everything to her.

It must have been painful for my husband and his father to leave Daniel, but he himself actually helped relieve their distress, fortunately, by being so completely calm and trusting.

Now I had the job of telling Ana Paula, so, off I went, heartbroken, to pick her up and speak to her as calmly as I could. It was difficult for her, too. What at the beginning was a relief changed into a feeling of emptiness and sadness as the days without him went by. She missed her brother. We cried together on that first day and on many other days, too, when we touched on the subject. When all was said and done, he was her most constant playmate and suddenly he was gone. No matter how much they had fought and argued, they were two children, now 10 and 8 years' old, who would miss terribly their only sibling.

In time, Ana Paula accepted the situation and seemed to understand our decision.

That night, I suffered many attacks of tachycardia, which made me fear that my heart would finally give up now. I knew the surgery was not a permanent cure, but now I just had to keep going, as I had my daughter to care for. With my young son gone, and a huge void in my soul, I could feel *Ráfel* very near again. I closed my eyes, remembering the little trick I had always used: go deep inside myself, get in touch with what my heart said, and find the peace I so longed for. It worked.

Thank you, *Ráfel*... you are here with me. The tachycardia disappeared a while later.

We went to see Daniel as often as we could while he was in that institution. He seemed to understand very well why he had to be there, which helped us a great deal.

Thank God, all those years invested in him bore fruit. Once we started to deal with it, we found out that his acts of aggression were the result of his impulsiveness, which damaged him, as it was just so difficult for him to control his emotions. He needed medication and someone to watch him all the time. After some violent episodes, it was always him who suffered the most. It was years before we learned that Daniel had a complex form of paranoid schizophrenia.

I will never regret having brought him into our family. He taught me to fight until the end, to give of myself even when I didn't know if I would ever see the light at the end of the tunnel. He gave me the courage to let him go, and he gave me his precious hug just when I needed it the most.

I was left with an enormous emptiness in my life but, little by little, I found peace again and the certainty that I had done the right thing. I wrote a letter to Daniel, which I still have today:

April, 1999

My dear son,

Some days ago, you left the house. I trust you will return soon, but, for now, I want to write these words to you because you have left a tremendous feeling of emptiness in my heart, in the house and in our lives, and I want you to know this, somehow.

I don't know if you will ever read this letter, but I know that, in time, my life will be the proof to you that every word I write is true.

You arrived in our home because, one day, I conceived you in my heart. I didn't know where you were, but God knew that I was the one chosen to take care of you. Your first days at home were beautiful. The four of us were getting to know one another. Ana Paula wanted to play with you and wouldn't let anyone pull her away from you. Your father followed you everywhere because you were just taking your first baby steps and we didn't want to let you out of our sight. I loved your laughter, your games, and your happiness. It was as if you finally understood that you had come home.

With the passing of the years, we could see that you needed a special kind of help. For some reason, your development was not like that of a child of your age. We needed to help you, and that's what we did. We took you to special classes, with psychologists and doctors, all with a view to making you better. It wasn't always easy to look after you as put up some resistance, and your different way of being sometimes made our job that much more difficult.

Every day, you found it harder and harder to control your actions and respect our rules, so there came a time when we finally decided that you needed to be in a special place. I want you to know, son, that that was one of the hardest days of my life, the day I watched you go. You filled my life in many wonderful ways, and letting you go was the most difficult thing I have ever done. No mother should have to let her son go, but I had to, for your own good.

I know we shall be with each other again very soon, and I want you to know that I will carry you in my heart all the days of my life. You will be there when I wake up, as I go about my daily chores, and in my night-time prayers before I fall asleep. Never ever doubt how much your father and I love you, and the day you read this letter, you will understand without a doubt how much we have suffered, being so far away. You take a piece of my soul away with you, but I know you will be gentle and will cherish it.

I will forever treasure the moment when we are together again.

Always remember: live your life to the full.

I love you with all my heart,

Mommy.

SOME MONTHS BEFORE
DANIEL LEFT.

DANIEL´S DRAWING

●THE BALL UNRAVELS

Do not allow the silence to say what words dare not express.

I wanted to be happy, no matter what obstacles crossed my path, and despite the hardships we faced with Daniel. My married life took many turns right from the start; overcoming these was a great challenge.

When my husband and I embarked on our married life together, a friend of his planted the seed of doubt in his mind as to whether we were in the right church or not. Both of us were Catholic and we were both very interested in our spiritual growth. I had never had the opportunity to be in a Bible study group, and I was surprised to find some people encouraging us to participate in one. I agreed to join a small group from another church and met some wonderful people through that. I loved the topics we discussed and I could feel how I was getting stronger inside. And yet, it wasn't nice to feel this was not something I could share with my family and friends, as I was sure they wouldn't approve. All my life I had swum against the current, but this time I had my husband by my side, urging me on.

I wanted to please my husband and support him, so, if this was what made him happy, then that was fine by me. I learned a lot and realized how important my spiritual growth was to me in my life. In spite of always having been raised as a Christian, I had never thought to look beyond the Catholic Church and its rituals. But now, I was doing just that and loving the meetings, and I felt that this would bring us closer together as a couple.

The group to which we belonged met regularly during the first two years of our marriage, and it was shortly after I became pregnant that my mother found out we were part of an Evangelical group. I was so affected by my parents' disapproval that, for the first time, I went against my husband.

"We should reconsider what we are doing. God couldn't possibly have wanted us to be separated from the family."

My husband wasn't convinced about baptizing Ana Paula in the Catholic Church, but I wouldn't have it any other way. Fortunately, he respected my decision and the newly born Ana Paula was baptized according to both our families' customs.

A few months after she was born, we came across a very nice group for Catholic married couples called "Propagators of the Word". There, I met my friend Lilia who, afterwards, would guide me so that I could lead the courses myself. My husband wasn't too keen about this new direction we were taking, but he agreed, knowing how affected I had been by my family's reaction.

Unfortunately, this didn't last long. Some years after the surgery, we went back to the other Church. Although my husband had never quite fit in to the "Propagators of the Word" we remained friends with them, even though we didn't attend their meetings anymore. Something told me that my story, my life and my traditions didn't have to change as long as I was growing spiritually, but, anyway, I decided to follow my husband.

All our friends, no matter what denomination, were praying for me before my surgery and during my time in the hospital. They wanted to remain close and I'm very glad they did. I am convinced that all these prayers were what kept me alive. When two or more people come together in unison with a common purpose, an incredible outcome can be expected.

Once we returned from Houston in 1989 and I was feeling better, we were asked to bear witness in an Evangelical Church on the theme of my recovery. I was delighted, as I had plenty to say. I liked how open they were to listen to my testimony and saw it as a chance to give something back. I felt so full of love that all I wanted to do was share my after-death experience with them. I also had a clear message to share with them: in any adversity, we can give thanks and live a full life.

I shall never forget that day, how radiant I felt wearing my new navy blue dress. They asked my husband to introduce me. We only had ten minutes allotted to us and when we got up to the front, he took the microphone, introduced me, and then just carried on speaking.

He spoke about how hard our time in Houston had been, how difficult it was for him with me so seriously ill and so far away. He said how hard it had been to leave his ten-month-old baby daughter in the care of his parents and other relatives, but he knew that God had rewarded us with the improvement in my health.

Surely at any moment, he would stop talking and hand me the microphone. I had been so looking forward to this moment, but as he kept on talking, I started to feel an enormous weight pressing on my stomach, making me feel sick. It was me the people had come to hear, me who should give her testimony, so why wouldn't he stop talking? He told them about how he shared passages from the bible with other people in the waiting room, people who needed his words of solace. He said he never stopped praying for me and asking for God's help, and that what I had gone through in Houston was like an act of purification for me and, praise the Lord, I was back.

After nine and a half minutes had passed, he handed me the microphone. Through all that time, I never once stopped smiling, though my smile must have appeared frozen to my face as the minutes went on. I wanted to show my joy at being alive, how grateful I was to be there with them, but my smile had to transmit all that, as I was left with no time to express in words everything I longed to share with those people. How I would have loved to do that! All I was left with was a quick moment to thank them for inviting us to speak, and, to say that, well, my husband had said everything there was to say. My thirty seconds were up!

Outside the church, a woman came up to me and said how she had been looking forward to hearing me speak and what a shame it was that it hadn't happened. "Me, too," I would have liked to say. It's not that I wasn't grateful, but I was left with this awful empty feeling in my stomach which I couldn't quite explain. I duly adjusted my imaginary "veil" that covered my eyes so as not to see what my heart was starting to perceive: my husband and I would agree on one thing, and he somehow managed to do something totally different.

My husband cheated me out of the opportunity to share my experience and I just went ahead and let him do it. Why would I do that? In spite of everything, I wanted to be happy and part of that meant keeping him happy. If he wanted to be the center of attention, then so be it. I let him get his way.

Very soon after our return to Monterrey, we started to have problems with how we administered our household budget, because my husband never quite sorted out when he should give me the money to make our payments on time. As this led to frequent arguments, he decided to pay the bills from the office, so I wouldn't be involved, so I only received enough money for the food and the daily help.

I got used to living like this and felt I was happy. My life was more than fulfilled by giving Bible classes. Lilia guided me through this and I felt better prepared each day. I was starting to make sense of the wonderful experience I had had in Houston, and, as the days went by, I understood that everything was important, everyone had something to contribute and each of us living beings is connected in an intricate network. This meant that whatever I did would affect others in some way. My actions, albeit not directed specifically towards someone in particular, would, sooner or later, either harm them or be to their advantage. Each day, I discovered new things, fascinating things, some through intuition and others from the amount of reading I was doing. The spiritual strength I gained by sharing all of this was immense, and it helped me feel more confident in myself and gave me the basis for raising my children.

In contrast to this, my marriage left me confused. Some of my reactions were even hard for me to understand, and I know my friends couldn't understand the transformation in me just a few years into the marriage. That reckless young woman, ready to devour the world, always with lots to say and a smile on her face, never accepting "no" for an answer in order to get what she had set her mind on, was practically gone. Was it my immaturity, my preconceived idea about what marriage meant, or was it my fragility because of my health issues? I honestly don't know how it all came about, whether it was a gradual thing or just happened from one day to the next, but sadly I distanced myself from all those wonderful unconditional friends. It's hard for me now to pinpoint the moment when I started to view my husband in a different way. All I know is that when my physical and emotional stability were so precarious, I began to put my husband on a kind of pedestal for how much he cared for me and protected me. I even went to the extreme of not trusting my own judgment and felt the need to consult with him before any kind of decision-taking.

I can see now, of course, that I should have demanded what I truly believe in and thought was right, but somehow I didn't. I felt grateful that my husband was still by my side in spite of my illness, my surgery and my many limitations. The vulnerability which I felt after the surgery turned into a blind dependency, to such an extent that I believed everything, absolutely everything had to be given his seal of approval.

I learned to live on promises that were never kept and plans that ended up bearing no resemblance to anything we had agreed on, simply because he chose to do things differently. His lack of punctuality, which had bothered me for years, was just one more sign that he would forever be failing to keep to any arrangements we had made. I learned to survive on illusions and daydreams that he planted in my head and in his children's, but which rarely came to fruition. I learned to live like that and to enjoy the meagre crop of pleasures I had to live on.

When Daniel was three, I stopped giving the classes I had enjoyed so much. In public, I showed the world that I was self-assured and confident, but, in private, it was a different story. Whenever we couldn't agree on something, my husband wouldn't shout or get angry, he just would keep up a stony, punishing silence which seemed to last forever. His replies to me were distant and condescending, and the look he gave me was so icy and harsh that I felt intimidated and unsure of myself. It took me years to realize that his silence was an act of violence and his look, an act of aggression.

My days were exhausting when the children were little, and my heart would still cause problems occasionally, especially when I was over-tired. What brightened my days was the memory and the certainty of that unique experience I had had and which helped give meaning to my hardships. I knew I was living life to the full, which lifted me up when things got tough.

I established a simple routine for the children. Every day, I got up and put music of praise or classical music on, to wake them up. Then, I would go and fill them with kisses and hugs until they got up, the complete ritual taking up about ten minutes in all. Then, I made breakfast and prepared their lunchboxes for their morning snack. Their father took them to school and it was my job to take them to and from their afternoon activities. Before they went to sleep, I would play with them and sing funny songs.

I always longed for that time when I was in bed and their father took charge of them for a while, especially when I had had a difficult day with Daniel. Any woman would have felt tired after the kinds of days I had.

Shortly after we adopted Daniel, we became involved in a business which, supposedly, was to bring in an extra income. We hoped that together we would make a success of it and have more money coming in. Much of our time was spent encouraging other couples to join the business and he loved giving talks and being the center of attention, whereas I would give simultaneous translation into Spanish of the guest-speakers and demonstrate the products.

Now that I think about it, I wonder where I got the energy from to do everything I did.

The Bible study group for married couples and the business kept us together and I felt it made us better people and trained us to contribute to the world. As often occurs, the business started to demand more and more of my time and I decided to stop after various years. I felt exhausted and Daniel needed me more than ever, demanding that I devote all my energy to him.

I missed my friends as, even though they kept inviting me to get-togethers, piñatas and birthday parties, we saw one another very little. My husband never got close to the group nor to my friends' husbands. He believed we were going in opposite directions, which meant that, when I challenged him about it, he would convince me it wasn't in my interests to let them get too close, as they were, in his words, "liberal". The way he saw it, it was unthinkable that at eight o'clock they could still be out somewhere and not, where they should be, at home. Wives should be there waiting for their husbands to arrive home from work. I, in my desire to be a good wife, convinced myself that whatever he considered wrong must, in fact, be wrong.

One day, my friends confronted me, and I just couldn't bring myself to tell them the real reason why I had distanced myself from them.

"As far as your husband's concerned, we're not "appropriate" friends, are we?" one of them said.

"It's not that. It's just that he doesn't think the same way as your husbands do. He believes a wife should be much more submissive and that her happiness can only be found at her husband's side. He thinks all of you spend too much time having fun together, when you should really be at home, with your husbands," I replied, rather tamely, not believing a word of what I was saying.

They kept quiet and didn't argue. They didn't go along with those ideas, but they did make me feel they would always be there for me, anyway. I honestly thought I was doing the right thing, putting my husband first, not realizing that I was giving him such power over what I did and what I thought that, in the process, I was damaging myself. Now, I know that a basic trust and a desire to communicate honestly are the foundation of any relationship, certainly not one of the couple just trying to keep the other one happy, at all costs.

When things got tough financially, we often had the electricity, gas or telephone cut off, fortunately for us, not usually at the same time! When we were without gas, we could use the electric oven for cooking. When there was no electricity, we used gas and could light up the house with candles and pretend we were on a camping holiday, trying to make the best of a bad situation, for the children's sakes.

I was convinced that this was all part of the struggles that married couples go through, and I was always aware of the promise I made before God when we married, to support my husband for better, for worse, for richer, for poorer, in sickness and in health. We had more or less survived my sickness issues and now it was my turn to help him in the other areas.

Ana Paula was seven when I started to teach at the school, which paid for extra afternoon classes and psychological help for Daniel. On those occasions when I didn't have to take the children anywhere, I would give special classes to pupils who were under-achieving at school. Whatever I did, the money was never enough.

I convinced myself that I didn't need anything for myself, and it was rare that I asked for clothes or shoes and, much less, jewelry, trips or special treats. I normally pushed this to the back of my mind, as I focused on the children's needs. I took our shoes to be repaired, soled and heeled whenever necessary. I mended socks, lowered hems on skirts and pants and patched worn-out clothing. Rarely did we go to concerts or on little family outings, which I would have liked. Maybe I was fooling myself, as I really did need new shoes, pants, dresses, but I felt too guilty to ask for them, considering the constant shortage of money. Besides that, we still had the hefty hospital debt to pay off, so I only asked for the bare necessities. Deep down, I felt I owed my life to my husband and couldn't possibly dare to ask for more.

My mother gave me clothes when she saw me wearing things that had worn out. She never asked why I wasn't buying clothes for myself, and I suppose she just presumed we didn't have the money, which was basically true, as if I needed something and couldn't pay for it myself, then I went without. On one occasion I had the nerve to ask for something which wasn't even for me, and the response it was met with made me determined never to ask my husband again for anything.

"Do you realize we still owe the hospital in Houston? We can't afford to spend any more."

"How is it possible that we can find money to buy your bicycle and all the fancy gear that goes with it, when we often can't even provide for our children's basic needs?"

"I can't believe you want to kill the hen that lays the golden eggs! That is all I spend my money on," he said, with looks that could kill.

How do you argue against that? I would love to have said: "OK. You spend on bikes and I spend on doctors, so we're quits." But I said nothing.

Having to justify myself was a pain. I always preferred to believe that this was our lot and sharing the hard times was making us grow as people. I tried not to lose my natural optimism and many times suggested that he look for other ways of making some money, but he never did.

It is not necessary to offend; by simply stating the truth, it is enough.

I was always grateful that he never suggested we should get rid of the daily help, whose wage I partly paid for, if truth be told, with my very modest salary, but I didn't mind, as she was such a help. When I had to do all the work myself, I sometimes ended up in the hospital due to exhaustion. My husband knew that the choice was between me teaching or cleaning the house: to do both was physically impossible.

With hindsight, I now see things more clearly. The truth is that my husband didn't buy much for himself, just things related to what really gave him pleasure: cycling, swimming and climbing. Everything else was not urgent. I mistakenly believed that he had the right to do this, as I had already spent my share, on medical things, and it was up to him to decide where the money went.

When we were out clothes shopping for the children, hard to avoid as they were forever outgrowing their clothes, my husband chose, not only their clothes, but also mine. That was what he liked to do, and I thought I didn't mind. I was very grateful for his help and didn't quite catch on to the fact that, funnily enough, he always ended up buying whatever he liked. It was rare that we bought anything I actually liked. I don't blame him. I let him do it. I may have believed that, this way, I was making him happy. I don't know, but, eventually, all of this affected my self-confidence

The truth is that, as time went by, we were started to speak two different languages. What I first saw as protection and loving care on his part ended with me feeling trapped and controlled. I also saw clearly that what he said and what he did were two very different things. He said he loved me, and I believed him. Why wouldn't I? Surely, the fact that he was paying off my hospital debt was proof enough of that, wasn't it?

I do not doubt that, indeed, my husband did love me, in the same way he loved his children, but perhaps he just couldn't help always putting himself as number 1. I can't say. I did know that we were connected somehow and the fact that he and I had got married meant that we were destined to be together and grow together, and there were lessons we had to learn. I wasn't prepared to give up easily.

Sometimes, I thought it was me who had changed so radically after my experience in Houston and was now seeing things very differently. I was determined to focus on what was worthwhile about being with him. We were so happy, before the economic crisis in the country hit hard, when we sold our house and used part of the money to pay off the debt in Houston, after 8 years and part to start building our new home.

I was in charge of much of the designing of the house, together with the architect, and I enjoyed the project enormously, as it allowed me time for myself, which made me feel so good. The house was designed to be the perfect home for a growing family, and the living area was all on one floor, just in case my health issues cropped up again.

Before the house was finally completed, we moved in, and, even though there was much that still needed to be done, we enjoyed our new house. My husband would go off on his bike whilst I would go to my special part of the house where I could spend hours listening to music and writing. The children would go outside and had great fun playing on the piles of earth and stones at the back of the house. It was many years later when I finally got this area to my liking.

Three years after we moved in there, Daniel left us to go to his special home. The void which remained was not only emotional but also one of time, as I had spent so many years attending to his needs, plus looking after my daughter and holding down a job. Now, I wasn't sure how to fill all my empty hours, as my greatest joy was feeling useful for my children. Looking after Daniel, in particular, was part of what had kept me alive all those years. As for my husband and me, it was as if we were on two different planets. My daughter, meanwhile, was just entering adolescence, which meant she would be withdrawing more into her own world and spending less time with me.

Many times, amidst this gloom which I couldn't shake off, I would talk to myself, as before. I never entirely abandoned my "escape routes", where I would cut myself off from what was upsetting me, and, thanks to these, I had the strength to keep going. I relived all the details of my experience in Houston, when I was sick there. The more I thought about it, the more convinced I became that the immense love I had felt was more than enough to help me rise above any obstacles. I wasn't alone. God was with me and held me, just like when I was a girl. Besides that, I never went anywhere without *Ráfel* holding my hand, and, curiously, rather than being concerned by that, it was a comfort. He never failed to appear when danger loomed. And yet, wasn't as if I went out of my way to "conjure him up" out of nowhere. He, very simply, was there.

It didn't help that, on many occasions throughout the marriage, I was in and out of hospital. My arrhythmias never seemed to go away completely. How could they, when I was always dangerously on the brink of losing myself for ever?

Even though I was very strict about taking my medicines, there was always something that would upset me and trigger them off and I would be hospitalized again for a few days.

What made this even more of a delicate issue in our home was the fact that I wasn't covered by medical insurance. Each time I stepped foot inside a hospital meant more expense, which put more of a strain on our relationship. No matter how much I worked, it was never enough to cover the bills, and I continually felt that I was a financial burden to my husband. My parents often helped us out by paying the bills, and he would begrudgingly accept their financial help, whilst giving me the obligatory icy stare, followed by the perpetual punishing silence.

One day, for example, I showed up early for work, as usual, but I had woken up that morning with tachycardia. We'd now been married about thirteen years and, whenever I could, I put up with these "nuisances" so as not to bother him or put more stress on our relationship. There was no problem, but, even so, if there was something the matter with my heart, money had to be found from somewhere. That day, I got to the point where I just couldn't stand it anymore. I was going up the school stairs but there came a point where I had to stop and take some air into my lungs. I had no more strength left in me and just plopped down there and then, halfway up the stairs.

"Miss, Ana Cecy, is something wrong?" asked the School Director, who just happened to be passing by at that moment.

It was all I could manage to give some kind of a reply.

"Yes there is. I'm sorry. I can't breathe properly.. no more energy. I have tachycardia..very strong."

"OK. Stay right where you are. Don't move. I'll get some medical help."

I reached my husband on the phone, saying that either the ambulance would come to take me to the hospital or else, he could. He was quite close, so he came for me.

He took me to the usual hospital, but not without mentioning that, if I had to be hospitalized, we would go elsewhere. I tried to process what he meant, but I was deteriorating quickly. During the short journey, I remembered that time I was in the car with my parents and they told me about my illness. Now, just as I had done back then, I felt the presence of someone else in the car: *Ráfel*. Very silent, as always, but so clearly there in the back seat with me, in the same place as before. I wanted him to speak up for me, let my husband know that I really did feel bad and not to worry as it wouldn't cost too much for me to be attended to.

Finally, we arrived and I was whisked off to the Emergency Room where Dr. Assad immediately appeared. It was serious. My heart rate was greater than 200 heartbeats per minute at rest. The doctor asked for me to be connected to an IV and taken to the intensive care unit. I couldn't believe my ears! I didn't feel bad enough to be taken to intensive care, but, then again, he was the expert, after all.

Ráfel was by my side, not disturbing me in any way, but he didn't leave me for one moment. I could feel him. It was so good not to have lost the ability to feel his presence and know he would always be near.

Dr. Assad went out to speak to my husband and parents, who had just arrived. But before leaving the room where I was, my husband looked me straight in the eyes.

"We have to go right now. I cannot pay for this. Let's go!"

I saw how desperate and helpless he felt, but what could I do? There was no way back: I was connected to the IV and my heart was still racing out of control. No way were they going to let me leave. I shed a few tears, and he left. I begged his forgiveness in my heart, but in my mind, I was shouting out to him to help me.

Just then, my sister, Sandra, came in and told my husband she would stay with me. All I could do was ask her, tearfully, to help me.

"Sandra, please don't go. Don't let him take me out of here. Please pay the bill for me or ask Mom and Dad to pay just this once, but I have to stay. I feel so bad. My heart is really pounding away."

Sandra opened her eyes wide, so shocked was she at what she'd just heard. She took my hand in hers.

"I'm not going anywhere. I will pay."

I was only in Intensive Care for two days and another day in a regular room. My arrhythmias disappeared and I was back to normal. My parents took care of the bill. This series of events marked the beginning of the end of my relationship with my husband.

Days later, I managed to speak to Sandra again and she commented that, for some years now, the family had noticed that my personality had changed, that something was not right. Although it was not my intention, the door had been opened for me to speak openly with her. We talked about a lot of things, but one of her comments in particular stayed with me.

"You have paid a very high price for being ill, and you have paid off the debt many times over."

Maybe she was right but, deep down, I needed to believe that my husband loved me. Otherwise, my world, as I knew it, would no longer exist.

A few months after Daniel's departure, and with so much time on my hands, I reflected deeply on my life. My husband and I spoke very little and almost never went out together. I then remembered what Daniel's godmother once said to me. She could never have imagined that, years later, her words would come back to me and set me off on a path of no return.

"Ana Cecy," she said. "Does your husband like to see you going round in dowdy clothes, looking like an old spinster?"

I knew I didn't want to cover up for him anymore, so I said, half-jokingly, "You know what? You're right. Maybe he's scared of losing his little princess and so he goes to great lengths to make sure nothing happens to her!" And I burst out laughing, when, in reality, I now saw clearly what I had been blind to. The veil before my eyes had slipped away forever.

I, unwittingly, had believed that I was in control, when the sad truth was that I was a mere puppet, letting him pull all my strings, while thinking that that would keep him happy.

I went home that day, and headed straight for my wardrobe. For a long time, I just stood gazing at the clothes hanging there, slowly observing each garment, and it was then I realized that the only brightly colored piece of clothing that I owned was what my mother had given me. Everything else was dull and sad. My mother had brought color to my life. At that moment, I saw just how many, many things I had stopped doing and how I had stopped making my own choices. But what I couldn't quite get my head around was why on earth would I have allowed that.

Some weeks later, I received an invitation from my lifelong friends. It was as if they were trying to drag me by force out of my imprisonment. I said yes, and simply told my husband what I was going to do. I didn't have any money to go out on a shopping spree, but my mother, when she found out what the plan was, gave me some cash to treat myself. The plan was to go to McAllen, Texas, and return the same day. In the end, however, we had to stay overnight, due to a problem with the car. We all called our husbands to tell them what had happened. We split the expenses and the four of us stayed in one room. It was the most wonderful evening. It took me back to when we were teenagers and the endless nights when we would have pajama parties and never stop talking. My friends saw their chance and helped me to choose clothes, shoes and makeup. I loved talking to them, feeling free and just revelling in being together with my Soul Mates.

That was the beginning of my finding my inner freedom.

When I arrived home, I was met with the same atmosphere of reproach: the stony silence, and the accusing look which spoke volumes of downright disapproval at what I had done. But this time, I didn´t care in the least about what my husband did or insinuated. I knew I looked good and felt, for the first time in years, that I had chosen exactly the clothes that I wanted, and, more to the point, I had done so with excellent taste!

Things are not always what they seem, as I was about to find out.

"PROPAGATORS OF THE WORD" TODAY

FINDING MY HEART ONCE MORE

If you don't love and respect yourself,
how do you expect anyone else to?

As the years came and went, I understood that I was wrong, that at no time did I or my husband owe anything to each other. We were there out of love but, unknowingly, we both conditioned that love. We paid a high price for having set off with the confused idea that I was somehow for sale and that my husband was buying me. These are unfortunately unspoken codes which are assumed in many relationships.

I also know now that he took advantage of the territory which I so willingly conceded to him. So many times in the early days, I tried to mark my boundaries, until the day came when I stopped trying, stopped wanting to fight. That was when I started to die inside. There are different kinds of deaths: physical, emotional and spiritual. My near-death experience in Houston had given me more life than ever so that my spirit could stay strong and healthy enough to move forward. In time, however, I misinterpreted things, got confused. Faced with the life I was leading, I seemed to be fading away, until the point came where I almost lost myself. What we were really doing was misinterpreting God's will. I was never as close to dying in my body as I was to dying in my soul, deep inside, at my very core. That magnificent and great energy, which for one moment had completely illuminated my being, was now withering, slowly but surely.

My spirit was dying, and I didn't know it. What had kept me alive was the certainty of what I had experienced after dying. But I am sure that, if I had died at that moment, the way I was now, God Himself would not have recognized me. I don't put all the blame on my husband. We were both accomplices. In any relationship, there is never just one partner who is completely guilty and one who is completely innocent.

We both distorted many of the teachings from the Bible and we lost ourselves in following the rules without considering the spirit intended, which was what happened when we interpreted the reading of St. Paul in his letter to the Ephesians: "The woman should be submissive to her husband." I believed that, by pleasing my husband, I would be pleasing God. What I didn't know was that "submission" does not mean "obedience". The Greek word for "submit oneself" (hupotasso) means "position oneself beneath", which has the idea of placing oneself below another, but not implying any true inferiority as such. Neither does it degrade the woman to a second-class state either in the home or in the marriage. It speaks of a functional classification rather than an essential inferiority.

As my grandfather, Enrique, used to say, "My dear, the spirit of the law is what prevails; the words themselves are open to interpretation." That divine law was what I had read before in Saint Augustin, that which guides us naturally. I had no need to feel as if I owed my husband anything. I had to find the way to put an end for once and for all with this way of thinking and to see once again that light which had illuminated me years before. Something was very wrong, and I was not happy.

For months I begged my husband to seek professional help if our marriage was to be saved. At every turn, we were growing farther apart, and I was growing more and more out of touch with him and with myself. I had an enormous void within, and instead of feeling grateful to God for what I had, which I had always done before, now I became apathetic and sad. But my husband refused to go to therapy, stating that he didn't believe in psychologists and, therefore, would never go to one.

Once he acknowledged that I had become withdrawn, and showed no interest in anything we did together, and no desire to go with him anywhere, he knew that the situation was serious, at which point, he started to get worried and tried to find ways to cheer me up. He even agreed to have Internet installed in the house, which I had been asking for months, so as to investigate and learn more about Daniel's illness. He brought me flowers, bought me my favorite music, he even bought me a new television with cable so that we could see the programs he had previously said Ana Paula shouldn't watch. I just kept going about my business, not reacting one bit to any of these gestures. I was beyond caring about anything except my daughter and my classes. Nothing and no one could shake me out of the depression I had sunk into over the years: not my friends, my Bible studies, my parents or my brother and sisters.

Emotionally, I switched off completely and spent hours on the computer, giving the excuse that I needed to organize my classes and learn about ways to help Daniel.

The truth was that the computer offered me a way to escape to another world: the world of technology, research, knowledge. It was all new. Now that I couldn't escape the reality of the life I was living at home, at least I could escape by means of the virtual world of the Internet.

My husband, meanwhile, tried taking me to get-togethers organized by his friends, who he swam and cycled with, and their wives, but I wasn't in the least bit interested. He took me out to dine in places that he would never have dreamed of taking me before, but it was all the same to me. Nothing could shake me out of my numb state of mind.

It was at that point that he started to look for someone who could help me come out of my depression, which he attributed to Daniel's departure; for him that accounted for it, and that in a nutshell, was my problem. One day, a friend persuaded him that, yes, he did actually need to help me, and the friend recommended Dr. Lorena Gutierrez who had helped his family. It entailed a family therapy , including individual and couple sessions. As far as my husband was concerned, the idea was that the therapies would help me stay happily by his side, which is how he put it to the doctor. The greatest blessing of all this for me was that it was he who said who we should go with, which amounted to another example of him somehow always getting his way, but which suited me, for once. Now, there was no way he could say it was a bad idea.

As sometimes happens, you arrive somewhere believing you will solve one thing and you end up solving another, which is what happened in our case.

We were in therapy for about one year. At first, I blamed myself terribly for not being able to react to anything my husband did. I was carrying an enormous burden on my shoulders, believing that I was responsible for not loving my husband in the way he needed and deserved, given that he had always been so good to me. I constantly misread our relationship and didn't see what I had in fact brought to it.

In the process, I realized that what I needed to do was save myself before attempting to save the marriage. I had lost myself amidst the drudgery of day-to-day living. I had stopped smiling, singing and playing the guitar. I distanced myself from my friends and hardly saw my family. And I was the one who had allowed this to happen. I was alive, and had recovered from a physical condition that few people recover from. I had so much to give, so much locked up inside me, which I needed to share. I understood that there was nothing I could do to change what had happened to Daniel, and I would continue to give him everything I could. But I, Ana Cecilia, wanted and needed and longed to be the happy woman I had always been as a young girl.

I don't know what my husband found out in the therapy sessions, but I discovered personal things, and things about him, too. I learned that both my husband and I had the divine right to proceed in and guide our own lives as best we thought, whilst not hurting a third party. Nobody belongs to us, and neither do we belong to anyone else. I knew that one of the greatest offences we could have brought on each other was to try to impose our point of view on the other. In our different ways, we were both guilty of that. I also realized that he could not keep me at his side if I felt repressed and needed to be free of him. But, first, I needed to free myself within me, so I could understand that the answer lay in me. I had allowed myself to get caught, albeit unwittingly. And so, I stopped blaming others for my difficult situation and started to be responsible for myself.

Maybe my husband didn't have anything to hold on to, either, and had also lost himself somewhere between what he thought should be, and what actually was, happening between the two of us. Without consciously meaning to, we had moved away from the solid bases and principles that our families had inculcated in us while they were raising us, to the point where we were completely alienated from our beliefs.

We were living in a kind of fanaticism. I took away many good things and will never regret all that we learned with our friends from other churches, but that wasn't what I wanted to do. I had years of being emotionally distant from my husband and I submerged myself in the study of the Bible. Because I couldn't rely on him for support, I turned to the Bible for my strength and relief. There was so much more I had to give in the place where I had always grown up, and had no need to distance myself from family and friends, but the Bible was what I turned to that saved my life, and even today I find my sustenance in it. It was the life-jacket that kept me afloat during those many years when I was lost at sea, adrift, and only God and dear friends could hold me up out of harm's way.

I stopped going along certain paths as they led me away from where I wanted to go.

Recognizing the problem was the first step. I understood that I was not happy, that I loved my children deeply and also their father, but only as that: as the father of my children. In truth, it was my spiritual sustenance that held me up, not my relationship with my partner.

During my therapy, I came to see that I didn't really know the man I was living with, and he didn't know me, either. We were two perfect strangers who had been living together for 16 years. We played at being happy, but we weren't. We were bonded by our children and our shared activities, but we had nothing in common. I was fixed on this idea of me being grateful to him, but this was holding me back even more.

Today, I can understand that any relationship is not a question of stereotypes, conforming to paradigms of power or of role playing of those involved. Any couple's managing of their relationship must be based on communication rather than on confusing Biblical passages which they apply in favour of one partner or to the disadvantage of the other. Otherwise, they run the risk of living their lives based on obligation and not on conviction. I am sure that God brought me to this world to be happy and fulfilled and to play my part in helping others, while at the same time respecting them. I believe we should do what we want to do, as long as we avoid hurting other people along the way.

I also realized that my husband wasn't happy, either. He tried to be, and made a great effort to be the perfect husband. From being a young child, I learned to listen to what is not said and read what is not written, but that sharpness of perception which I had honed back then became blunted with the years. My newly aroused sensitivity told me that, in all truth, I had not the faintest idea of what was going through the mind of the man I shared my life with.

I think he was sure, as was I, that a few years into the marriage, I would die. We never imagined that I would live so long as, even after the surgery, the prognosis, according to the doctors, was unclear. But the vows we had made in the church of "till death do us part" never came to be.

After one of the last therapy sessions, I announced to him that I definitely did not want the marriage to continue, and I asked for a divorce. Upon hearing these words, he went absolutely berserk and lost all of his sophisticated façade. In the midst of his frustration, he had a total meltdown.

"This shouldn't be happening! You weren't supposed to live for so many years, and now you want to leave me! What's the matter with you?"

At that moment, I understood that when my parents had spoken to him, before we got married, about my heart condition and the risks involved, he took it as a promise, as a sure thing, not as a warning of what may happen. I would die soon, and that was that. Both of us believed it.

"What are you going to tell everyone? Why do you want to leave me?" he shouted out in desperation. And then he went on, "Just to be clear about this, it's you that's breaking the promise you made to me in the Church. It's you that's breaking up this family. Do you get that?" he shouted, beside himself.

And then, I blurted out the question which I had kept under lock and key in the depths of my heart.

"You thought that I would be dead by now, didn't you?"

"Of course I did! And that's the truth!"

At that moment, my heart broke into a thousand pieces, the one thing that had held me together, and I cried. What my heart problem, my childhood sicknesses, the surgery, the pregnancy, what none of these things had succeeded in doing, he, with those words, had finally managed. The pain I felt, the anger and the frustration from what he had just said to me knew no bounds. For years, even before the therapy, I had thought that I was being unfair to him for becoming a wife who probably wouldn't survive, who had made him spend so much money, and that only he was the one being hard done to. I blamed myself for not bearing him more children, and I wanted to make up for that by adopting Daniel. And I thought I was making him happy.

He tried to get close to me, suddenly realizing the awfulness of what he had blurted out in his rage. I pushed him away.

"My mind is made up. We cannot live together any more. It takes two to tango and you and I have danced enough. I have no intention of dying soon and I want to be happy!" I cried out, and disappeared into my bedroom in a flood of tears.

During the following weeks, he made many attempts to get close and convince me that we should talk things through, which we did, but each time we came back to the same dead end.

He stood his ground, claiming that I would be the one to lose out and that nobody would ever love me as he had done. The more he tried to win me over and make me stay, the more convinced I was to go in the exact opposite direction. I simply could not stay with him. Something inside me said it was time to leave. I had to take heed of my inner voice, no matter how hard it was.

I knew he wasn't happy and couldn't quite understand why he was so adamant about me staying with him, when clearly I hadn't figured in his life plan for some time.

I don't know what he told his parents, family or friends, and I didn't honestly care at that moment. All I wanted to do was finish the relationship as soon as possible. As for me, I only went into the details with my parents and my siblings, but didn't share any of this with anyone else.

Sometimes, all you need is to forgive. If you don't, it will be difficult for you to start again.

The separation was a difficult process for Ana Paula, even though she had been noticing that something was wrong. She was thirteen years old, and yet showed an incredible maturity. One day, I decided that she and I should go for the weekend to the beach. We talked a lot, but I didn't come out and say that the decision to separate was definite. I mentioned that her daddy and I were having some problems.

"Are you going to get divorced, Mommy?"

"Maybe, darling. We are trying to work things out, but in the end, it might come to that."

"I don't think it would be so bad. After all, you're not happy and I hardly ever see daddy. He always gets home so late."

Her words left me ice-cold. She had already noticed many of the things we talked about that day, but she had never said anything until I prepared the groundwork for her to do so. She had noticed how distant we were and felt that her father was even more distant from her than ever. For our parents, too, it was hard to hear our news and to accept the decision. We decided not to let Daniel know for the time being. He was a long way away and it was best to wait a bit.

Even though I have never been in favor of divorce, I know that there are times when convictions and beliefs are put into question, when you realize that it does more harm than good to keep going down a path that is leading you nowhere.

When something is broken, you must fix it. When something is damaged, it's important to try to save it, not just throw it away. But you must also admit that when a crystal wine glass is broken from the moment you bought it, no matter how often you try to repair it, there will always be cracks, and even the finest wine will seep through those cracks, drop by drop, until the glass empties. There are some situations in which it's better to accept the inevitable, move on and start again.

Sometimes, it's better to close the book, when simply turning the page was not enough.

With time, I also came to see that, just like my husband, I had married thinking that I would die soon. The emotional pressure I was under in those days , while dating, perhaps prevented me from delving too deeply into the things I didn't like or didn't understand. It wasn't a topic that we discussed much. He made me believe that everything would be fine and I was carried away by his dreams, so I believed him. I felt that I was in love and, for me, he was my savior, my knight in shining armor, who would let me know the true meaning of happiness before I died. And, in his eyes, I was the damsel in distress, ready to be saved by him, the valiant hero. We both got it wrong. We were blinded by the fairy tale, and neither of us imagined that the romantic tales of princes and princesses don't always have a happy ending.

Today, I can say that the separation was the best decision I could have taken. I know that the therapy helped me understand the irreversible and complicated situation we had unwittingly let ourselves become submerged in. I will always be grateful to the father of my children and will love him for just that, for having stayed by my side through such harrowing times, and for being part of the adventure of having a daughter and adopting a son. Both he and I gave whatever we could, which was no small thing. From the bottom of my heart, I asked for his forgiveness some time later for any damage I might have caused him, and he did the same. Neither of us had any wish to harm the other, even though we did. We forgave each other sincerely, and from that point on, I began the beautiful process of healing my inner self. I knew I had to rediscover my tranquility and peace of mind, which I had experienced in Houston and never should have lost.

Now I know that he, my former husband, is well and at peace, and so are my children.

●PUEBLA; ONE MORE CHALLENGE

*I stopped blaming others for my problems
and started finding all the solutions.*

With the separation and subsequent divorce, I had to remake my life, and one of the things that seemed most important was to stand on my own two feet and have faith that everything would turn out well. The divorce settlement hadn't been very favorable to me, especially regarding financial help towards Ana Paula's upkeep, and so I resolved to do whatever necessary to see that she received the best education.

I had work, but earned very little, so I had to explore other options for making more money. Fortunately, the house was in my name, otherwise I would have lost it, as my then ex-husband wanted to sell it and split the money between the two of us, which I was not going to allow. I knew that, if we were to rent it out, it would bring in enough money to provide for our living expenses. Besides, it was our children's inheritance. So, I decided we would look for a smaller house and I would look for a job.

When I received a job offer in the city of Puebla, I jumped at the chance immediately. I was a tempting offer and it would mean that I would get away completely for a time, which my therapist, Lorena, recommended wholeheartedly, encouraging me to make the most of this opportunity. I knew thatputting some distance between us would help us both. My parents were nervous about this new project, but in the end, they supported me, knowing I needed to make my own way and act in my daughter's best interests. In any case, before taking a final decision, I talked to Ana Paula, whose opinion was of the utmost importance to me. Even though she was an adolescent and at the age when they don't want to leave their friends or make drastic changes to their lives, she was in favor of the move.

So, my fourteen-year-old Ana Paula and I, a 36-year-old woman, agreed to give it a go for one year, just to get away from all the messiness in Monterrey with the upcoming divorce. She was the one who suggested we needed a change and that to go far away would do us both good. It may have been she who gave me the courage to go through with this adventure, not knowing it turned out to be the best thing that could have happened to her. Although in age she was still a child, she had the maturity of a much older person. Daniel was still living in the institution and his father took responsibility for him. I called him whenever I could but, as might be expected, we lost touch a little. Even so, I was calm about the arrangements, knowing that his father would be looking out for him.

It never crossed my mind that I might be affected by the altitude of Puebla, much higher than my hometown of Monterrey. I was feeling in good health, everything was under control and my cardiologist gave me the name of a doctor who could see me in Puebla. He and I never even mentioned the possibility of the altitude, but, some years later, we knew that it was.

We travelled there by car in a new Jetta, which my father helped me to pay for and which, as it turned out, he wouldn't let me pay for. So, I felt safe driving all the way from Monterrey in the north to Puebla in the center of Mexico. I had never driven alone on the highway and much less with a young girl on board. The car was full to busting, even though we were only taking what was indispensable. It was decided that once we had rented a new home, we would move down the remaining furniture.

We lived in Puebla for nearly five years and it was during this time that I grew most, both professionally and personally. However, the altitude of Puebla seriously affected my heart and my health.

A friend took us into her home. She was a widow with no children, so we stayed with her until we found our feet. I shall always be grateful to her for her encouragement, as we started on this new chapter in my life.

My job was to give English classes to teachers at the Universidad de las Americas de Puebla. As I was only used to working with children and adolescents, this was quite an experience. I sometimes battled with them more than I had with the children: they didn't bring their homework, they always seemed to find some kind of excuse to be absent, and they were forever leaving a mess in the classroom. Anyway, I managed to get the group under control, and these were classes that I really enjoyed. In the afternoons, I would give private classes to university students.

With the money coming in from my rented house in Monterrey, together with the salary from my job, I could now pay my own way and provide a good education to Ana Paula. I still didn't have enough to rent a house, but my friend assured me she was in no hurry for us to leave, which was a huge relief.

Ana Paula still had two years to go before she finished Junior High, so I decided to stay on in Puebla until she finished. I enrolled her in one of the best schools in Puebla, which actually cost half of what it would have cost me in Monterrey: the American School of Puebla.* This represented quite a change for her, but she adapted immediately and made many good friendships which have lasted up to today.

During these years, I enjoyed my daughter like never before. For the first time, we weren't in the same school as teacher and pupil, but now we were closer than ever.

Six months after arriving in Puebla, I decided it was time to look for a job in another university, so I applied to the Tecnológico de Monterrey, where I had studied in High School in my hometown. The director of foreign languages, Helen Rowland, who would later become one of my best friends, interviewed me and hired me the very same day. The salary was much better, so I wouldn't have to be giving extra classes in the afternoons to make ends meet.

I started working immediately and took to it like a fish to water, and had the chance to take all kinds of training courses. I started doing an online Master's in Education degree, and at every step, I felt freer, more self-confident and with more control over my life, all of which was long overdue. I had hardly been there for six months, when I was offered a full-time contract. I initially hesitated, as I didn't want to take on too much, but I knew that if Ana Paula went to the High School section of the same institute where I was employed, she would be entitled to a scholarship which would represent a considerable saving on school fees.

After a year, I was offered the post of Director of the Foreign language Department, which was a great opportunity for me. Ana Paula finished Junior High and was about to start High School. Our original plans changed as these new opportunities arose, as now I had a good, permanent job, a scholarship for my daughter, and, apart from that, the money I was receiving as part of the divorce settlement was kept on one side, untouched. It wasn't much, but it was something to fall back on if necessary.

Six months into my new position, I was feeling very confident and so we moved to a bigger house which we really liked, so now I could pay rent, cover all our needs and start to enjoy this phase of our lives. Ana Paul was a young woman who was full of life and had much to offer the world. We treated ourselves to long hours of just sitting and chatting in the center of Cholula or in our back yard. hilst we relaxed together, preparing delicious barbecues.

Dare to be the captain of your life and not just a spectator

I had my own bank account, and I even had enough money left over to afford a few luxuries and do what I loved most: going to concerts. The first concert was with Pablo Milanés. I loved music so much that, for me, this was the best way to enjoy the fruits of my labor; and, of course, Ana Paula went with me at all times. After the concert, we would go to have dinner and just chat about anything, which meant that I got to know my daughter much better as we shared these moments together, but now, the time I devoted to her was different: I listened to her.

The second concert was to see one of my favorite groups, Mocedades. By now, some of their original members had formed a new group called El Consorcio.I had listened to them as a teenager, never dreaming I would one day hear them live. I went to as many concerts as I could afford and whenever someone agreed to go with me. How I enjoyed those outings!

I studied hard and prepared my classes down to the last detail, always aiming to give my absolute best. As the months went by, I had very little time to rest and, little by little, that affected my health. What with being in charge of the department, studying for the Master's online and giving my classes, I ended up totally exhausted.

I tried not to complain, either at home or at work, but each day I was finding it harder to keeping everything going.

The offices of both teachers and directors were up on the fifth floor. As there was no elevator, and no plans to install one, I had to go up and down those five gruelling flights of stairs many times a day, having to rest and catch my breath after each flight on the way up. Whenever there was a meeting with the other directors, I went down to the first floor, and then, I had to return to the fifth floor to carry on my working day. It was like running a double marathon. I did try to rearrange some classes to be on the fourth floor just to make life a bit easier for me.

Having lunch was another challenge, as the microwave oven for heating food brought from home was on the first floor, so I solved that by buying my own small microwave and placing it in my office, so I wouldn't have to move. I looked for other ways, too, to ease my physical load, holding meetings with teachers, my classes , interviews, lunch and tutoring sessions as near to my office as possible, until the day finished and I could go home.

When my Director of High School moved to another city, she was replaced by a new director, who turned out to be quite a learning experience for me. My previous boss and I were in the habit of discussing things and coming to an agreement on how best to run the department but, with this new boss, everything changed. With him, I certainly learned a lot because, in my view, and that of a good-size number of colleagues, he was someone who was intolerant, imposing, controlling and who questioned everything, mistrusting whatever was said to him.

He questioned why I organized my schedule so that I was always on the top two floors, without the need to move, like everyone else. Notwithstanding the numerous occasions when I explained to him that I did this so as not to tire myself out physically, he was harsh and belligerent, determined to impose his own will and often forced me to make changes, just because he disagreed. At no point did he exhibit any empathy or understanding, except towards the people whom he himself had hand-picked.

All of this made me question whether I was really in the right place. Admittedly, I did learn to see beyond his words and apparent cruelty. He was suffering, and suffering a lot. He was a man who hid his loneliness and pain by being the way he was. He didn't listen to reason and he put me through some very difficult times. Before too long, I saw that he, in fact, did the same to many of my colleagues.

Once, I was in his office in a departmental meeting which was just getting underway when I started to feel a tachycardia that grew stronger by the minute. I had been getting rather upset about the topic in question as he was not listening to what I was saying. I pointed out to him that I couldn't give a summer course, which was what he wanted, as I had to revise many course programs for the following semester: 9 levels of 4 different languages. No other director was being given summer courses precisely because of the workload involved. On seeing his attitude and realizing I was fighting a losing battle, I sat back in my chair and started to feel dizzy.

"I'm sorry, I don't feel well. I feel dizzy and my head's hurting. Could we call the campus doctor and ask him to look at me? I can feel a very strong tachycardia, and I am worried."

"Call him if you want. He can see you here. Tomorrow we'll pick up where we left off, because you are going to work just like everyone else. It doesn't matter how many courses you have to revise, you will give the summer course!" he said in a totally dismissive and matter-of-fact tone, as he left the office.

Perhaps he was feeling nervous and preferred to leave, but I was left not knowing whether to cry or to yell at him that he must help me. I called the University doctor on the office telephone, and he arrived almost immediately. He told me in no uncertain terms that I should go home and rest, as my condition was dangerous. Just when the doctor was about to leave, my boss came in and heard his pronouncement.

"I recommend that Ana Cecilia leave. Her heart is suffering from an irregular beat and needs to be checked by a cardiologist."

At this, my boss's eyes opened wide. He breathed in deeply and looked straight at me for several seconds before, finally, looking down at his desk.

"If you want to leave, please let your teachers know, and then we shall make sure these lost hours are replaced, very possibly one

Saturday, if I consider it necessary."

My heart wept inside. Not one inquiry as to how I was feeling. Not one word to ask if I needed anything. I was standing before a man who knew only too well that I was doing my very best, both physically and professionally, in order to do things right. He knew that I had received only excellent evaluations from my students each semester, with no exception. He had received not one complaint of any sort about me. And here he was, treating me as if I had absolutely no value at all, in his eyes.

Today, I know that in that office, that day, there was only one being who felt any affection towards me and who showed me any understanding: *Ráfel*, who was without any doubt hovering attentively nearby. When I arrived home, I called my cardiologist in Puebla, went to see him and he made some adjustments to my medicines. Fortunately, I managed to calm down and slept much better that night.

Don't expect everyone to understand what you do, and why. Especially if they haven't had to follow the same path as you.

That episode with my boss gave me insight into how much he was suffering. He couldn't admit that he was vulnerable and didn't know what to do, which is why he left the office. I sensed that, had he stayed and realized how bad I was, he would have gone to pieces right there in front of me. Maybe he thought that putting on this air of toughness would make him popular and respected by all of us. Unfortunately for him, he couldn't have been more mistaken. By acting as he did, he lost the trust and respect of many very worthy people working there.

Even though, when this was happening, I naturally felt hurt, with time I came not only to forgive him but I even took it upon myself to write him a letter, which helped me to free myself and stop being weighed-down by his behavior which, actually, had nothing to do with me at all. The therapy sessions I took helped me a great deal to recognize and identify what exactly was going on. I learned that there are some people who, consciously or unconsciously, abuse others. The truth is that this man would indeed have ended up abusing me if I had let him.

Once this incident had passed, I decided to go to Monterrey to get a medical check-up and see my family. I asked for two days of vacation leave, and Ana Paula stayed with a friend. After examining me very thoroughly and making some tests, Dr. Assad, my dear cardiologist, spoke to me very seriously. He was extremely concerned.

"What on earth are you doing up on the fifth floor, for goodness' sake, Ana Cecilia? Not even an athlete, no matter how healthy, can go up and down five flights of stairs without experiencing some element of tiredness. Imagine how it is for you! Your heart is very tired, and all this isn't doing it the slightest bit of good."

He wrote a letter addressed to the University, asking me to be relocated to an office on the first floor, for health reasons. As always, I appreciated his support and I gave him a big hug. He was like a father to me, he really was. And he was right: I was over-exerting my heart.

It had been seventeen years since my first surgery, but they had made it very clear back then that this was just a temporary measure, and it would probably be effective for ten years. The doctors were certain that I would need another surgery to at some time in the future. Perhaps, that time was now approaching; no one knew, but my heart was certainly tired.

That weekend, I went to the beach with my parents, Sandra, Enrique Luis and two of his children: Juan Diego and Sandrita. This was a great time for making plans and discussing projects for the future. We talked a lot and they were all very supportive. My brother got me thinking when he asked me what I wanted to do.

"Well," I said, "I want to come back to Monterrey and work in something which isn't so physically demanding. Plus, I want to finish my Master's and then....have a little rest!"

I had been gone for over four years. I missed my parents, my family, my friends who were always there for me and never forgot to invite me to their get-togethers. But, above all, I missed Daniel. I wanted to see him and feel him close to me again.

Ana Paula missed her cousins and grandparents, too. She didn't have much communication with her father at that time. He went to see her occasionally, but she rarely went out of her way to contact him. Clearly, she needed to keep a distance between them.

Things were very much calmer after the divorce was finalized, even though my ex-husband, after so many years together, called me almost daily to ask me to sell the house, as he wanted his share of its value, besides which he never failed to remind me that I was the one who had broken up the family. After three years, thankfully, the calls stopped. He also stopped trying to speak to Ana Paula, just to tell her that he wanted us all to get back together again and that, clearly, I hadn't been thinking properly, as nobody in their right mind would have left him. She would tell me about these calls, but didn't give them much importance. Her reaction made it obvious to him that we had both changed for the good and had come a long way. Distance had worked its magic.

Back in Puebla, I handed the letter from Dr. Assad to the Director of the Campus, who promptly issued the order that I should have my office moved to the first floor. So, I was pleasantly surprised to be offered an office much more spacious and more accessible than my previous one. All the teachers in my department helped me with the move. What a wonderful team we made! I can say that I had earned the respect and affection of each one of them. Now, more than ever, my boss felt threatened, which didn't help our relationship at all. But, even then, I did make a considerable effort to support him and work alongside him.

That talk with Enrique Luis on the beach had made one thing very clear as to what I wanted to do. That was it. I would look for work in Monterrey and see a way to gain a scholarship for Ana Paul wherever I decided to work. I sent out various applications to different educational institutions including the University of Monterrey, which, as it happens, was where Ana Paula wanted to study. They called me a few days later, offering me an interview, which was really exciting, and I went along the next week, feeling very hopeful. That Friday afternoon, I was interviewed by the Director of the Department for International Programs: Thomas Buntru.

The interview went incredibly smoothly, and he and I made an instant connection. He was a very nice man, polite and extremely professional. I made it absolutely clear from the onset what I was looking for, and he seemed to be open to all my requirements. Apparently, I was a perfect fit for the job, and all that was needed now was for them to hire me.

Initially, I thought that I would have to have their job offer before handing in my notice in Puebla, but I was so desperate to be back in Monterrey that I immediately quit my job. Four days later, I was made a formal offer by the University of Monterrey, just one day shy of my birthday. Many people would call this reckless, making such an important decision before weighing everything. And they would be right. Except that, I had the absolute certainty that I had to return to Monterrey and I had to trust that everything would turn out fine. A leap of faith, indeed!

Each and every one of my wishes was coming true, slowly but surely. I visualized what I wanted and needed and asked God to help me achieve it so that I, and others, could benefit from it. Everything fell into place. I asked the Director of the Puebla Campus, who I got on very well with, for his help, putting him in the picture as to how things were with my boss. He saw me straightaway and came to the same conclusion as I did, that talking to my boss would be an utter waste of time.

In fact, the Director couldn't have been more helpful. In the beginning, he was reluctant to let me go, but he and I both knew that it was in everybody's best interests. My boss wasn't going to change and I was not happy in my job. He generously said he would respect Ana Paula's scholarship for her final semester at school in recognition of my excellent work as a teacher there. He helped me sort out my severance pay and even offered to be Ana Paula's tutor. To top it all, we were even given a discount for the students' residence where she would have to live for her last semester of High School.

Four days later, I received the formal offer from the University of Monterrey. I was to be the Coordinator of International Programs, which would mean a 40% increase in my salary, plus a 100% scholarship for Ana Paula to study there. My duties would be to travel, organize events and talks to parents and present options for new student exchanges. This was going to be demanding, no doubt, but it paled in comparison to the exhausting responsibility of coordinating fifteen teachers, together with teaching classes and being the Director of the whole Department of Languages. I was ready for it!

●MY RETURN TO MONTERREY

Home is where my people are and where my soul is at peace.
SANDRA, ME, DR. TORRE, MY MOTHER AND AUNT MARTHA

I returned happily to Monterrey in December of 2006. Even though I had, of course, been happy in many ways in Puebla, my constant tiredness just didn't allow me to enjoy the city any more. I needed to rest.

Work at the University of Monterrey began on January 8th, 2007. The atmosphere was marvelous. My colleagues made me most welcome and I immediately felt at home. I found the best boss I have ever known. Thomas is a great person, with a human quality I have rarely seen, ever. It was easy to develop an excellent working relationship with him. God gave me a respite in every sense of the word: a great boss, a wonderful and less demanding job, my daughter's scholarship, and what I longed for most-to be close to my family.

Part of my job entailed traveling to different places in the world with a view to sending our students there. Some of these trips were a real joy, as I could get to know other countries and cities I had never been to. It wasn't long before I had signed many agreements for the International Exchange Programs and I met many wonderful people in the process. However, every day I would notice that I was getting tired very easily and I was finding it hard to even speak. My heart was working overtime. My boss called my attention to it on several occasions and was concerned that I couldn't elaborate long sentences without having to take a deep breath first.

Today, reflecting on all this, I still don't understand how my body withstood so much.

Eight months into my new job, my heart started to fail. Now, it wasn't just a case of feeling tired; I was having tachycardias every day and sometimes they lasted for hours before finally stabilizing. On one occasion, they lasted so long I had to be taken to hospital, where I spent three or four days.

Now, it was only too evident how extremely tired and weak my body was. My heart simply wasn't responding like before. On one particular occasion, Dr. Assad spoke to my parents and my daughter, and told them that the time had come; I needed another operation, but he added that this time there might be no way to repair my heart. He said there were very few cases of successfully undoing a previous surgery in order to do it again performing the necessary corrective procedures. But there was always the possibility of a heart transplant.

The doctor spoke to me and explained that we couldn't ignore so many episodes of arrhythmia and shortness of breath, and major steps needed to be taken. In Mexico, no adult with a similar heart condition to mine had ever been operated on, and they were just starting to perform such operations on children. It would be extremely risky to undergo such an operation in my country, as I was still the only person with this heart disease to reach my age. So much time had passed that I had forgotten that small detail: it was a pure miracle that I was alive. There was no getting round it; I had to do whatever it took.

And so, once again, I felt the need to go on that same journey deep inside myself in order to assimilate this new turn of events. Another surgery, and even more so, if a transplant was involved, would mean a huge risk, not to mention the tremendous expense. The chances of success were quite remote. I was fully aware of that, but I kept repeating to myself that I just had to get well and that my heart would not give up without a fight. The risks of another operation were only too obvious, but I decided not to think about that. I focused on the future once again, and started to get mentally prepared for my second operation.

Dr. Assad wasted no time in putting me in contact with Dr. Guillermo Torre: a Mexican cardiologist born in Monterrey who now worked in the Methodist Hospital in Houston and who just happened to be in Monterrey at that very moment. Dr. Assad sent my medical records to Dr. Torre. Naturally, we all expressed to him our misgivings about me undertaking such a complex operation. He was kindness itself to us, and I felt I could trust him implicitly. He would see us in Houston and would arrange a series of appointments with different doctors. He paved the way for me to have visits all over the city with three cardiologists, specialists in heart transplants, and a cardiologist at Texas Children's Hospital.

I asked my boss if I might take a few days leave in order to go to these appointments and he was very understanding, wanting to help in any way he could. He wasn't going to discount my pay for those days and only asked that I keep working at a distance as much as was possible, which I did.

So, off we went to Houston: my parents, brother and I, and all three of us attended each appointment together. The doctors all reacted the same way to what they saw before them: they simply could not believe that I was still alive! For them, it was amazing beyond words and the inevitable question would always arise eventually: "How have you managed to keep so well? Tell us about yourself."

We couldn't give any explanation, but it was undeniable: just my being alive was nothing short of a miracle, and there was no way I was going to give up the fight now! It took me back to those moments in 1989 before my first surgery in that very same city, with me sitting in front of Dr. Nihill as he bombarded me with endless questions. Then, as now, I was deeply conscious of the privilege of being alive. So many years had passed that I had forgotten that my precious heart was an indefatigable warrior, a source of wonder and awe that left so many doctors totally baffled.

This trip to Houston was not easy. It was tiring for us all, both physically and emotionally, as we tried to assimilate the tremendous amount of information we were given. One of the doctors said I was in urgent need of a heart transplant, whereas another said I would need a transplant of both heart and lungs. Yet another stated it was only a matter of time before we would see if a lung transplant was necessary, too, and that maybe just a new heart would be enough. The social worker warned us that if I were to be approved as a candidate for a heart transplant, I would have to stay in Houston and wait for a suitable donor, whenever that might be.

We ended up worn out and scared, realizing that the whole procedure was complicated and that any decisions taken would be far from simple.

Finally, we made our way to the Texas Children's Hospital, hoping against hope that they would somehow offer us an alternative for treating my particular case of single ventricular heart disease. The doctors there had come across many cases like mine, but with the only difference that they had never performed this kind of surgery on someone of my age.

After I had undergone a series of tests including an echocardiogram and an electrocardiogram, I was presented to Dr. Wayne Franklin, who entered the consulting room with a broad smile on his face.

"Let's meet the beautiful lady who wants a surgery!" he said, rolling his eyes and pretending to look round the room for me.

He introduced himself and his team to us. The doctor was sure that he could help me. They would have to do a catheterization to see the status of the previous surgery, after which they would decide how to proceed with a new surgery. My heart, indeed, was very tired, but if it was well repaired, it would allow me to live some years more. The more he spoke, the more his attitude succeeded in calming us down. He explained in minute detail the nature of the procedure and how they intended to go about dealing with my case. We were amazed by how much medicine had advanced in those twenty years since the first surgery. Yes, they were only too aware that this was far from being a simple procedure, but, on the other hand, they knew perfectly well what needed to be done: undo the previous surgery and do it again with a modified Fontan surgery. The doctors were optimistic and confident.

They pointed out that I would be the oldest patient that they had operated on with this malformation. Normally, their patients were much younger. But that didn't put them off. What they did say, quite categorically, was that I should not have a heart transplant and that they would do all within their power to fix my heart.

"We are not giving up on this beautiful lady's heart," Dr. Franklin said, smiling, as he put his arm round my shoulders.

My mother couldn't stop beaming, she was so overcome with excitement. "That's fantastic!" she said. "It's a miracle!"

My father didn't stop smiling, either, but he was clearly nervous.

My brother hugged me and we all shed some tears. My heart had proved to be strong in spite of the circumstances, and the doctors wanted to save it. They told me I had the physical tiredness of a 70-year-old woman, but I was strong and in urgent need of surgical attention. I was just 42 at the time. My heart had had to suffer the wear and tear of nearly an extra 30 years in order to survive.

It was decided; they would operate at the start of the New Year. I would have to undergo a series of tests and take certain precautions before the operation.

I went back to work and could, fortunately, postpone the trip abroad which we had planned. I dedicated myself to working as much as I could from home. I was exhausted but happy that, very soon, I would be having my operation that would surely change my life.

The year came to an end and I made the most of two weeks of Christmas vacation, in order to rest. We all had a wonderful time as a family and I was constantly reminded of their unconditional support. I had to start getting things ready as, if the operation was to be in February, there wasn't going to be much time to put everything in order: namely, my will and decisions to be taken about Ana Paula's future. There was much to discuss. I knew this had to be done as anything could happen during the surgery. And yet, my mind stayed absolutely focused on the future: my daughter's graduation, watching her grow professionally, her wedding, my grandchildren. I had to cling to this for all I was worth, whilst at the same time doing what any responsible parent would do: prepare to die.

Once back to normal life after the vacation, I could feel my condition worsening. I was so devastatingly tired. My boss suggested I go along to the Public Health Service so they could advise me on how to obtain sick leave benefits. I had no idea about how all this worked and I needed to know before the operation. doctor there checked me, looked over my studies, my medical history and my present situation, then he just looked at me, dumbfounded, and asked how I could possibly be still working. Looking at all the evidence in front of him, he said there was no way he could allow me to return to work. I froze at these words. He handed me a sick-leave permit for 28 days and said quite simply I was not to return to work. I didn't know then, but I wouldn't return to the University of Monterrey.

Surprised as I was by this turn of events, if truth be told, I was glad, as I needed to rest. By now, the slightest effort on my part was draining me of all my strength, and each day it was becoming more and more obvious. Of course, the news caught my boss and colleagues off-guard, but they were behind me all the way and we promised to stay in touch.

DR. WAYNE FRANKLIN

●DIFFICULT CONVERSATIONS

You can only reap that which,
in one way or another, you have sown.

My daughter, just like the rest of the family, was worried about the upcoming days. The great advantage I have always had, up till today, is that the communication between us has always been marvelous. Now, we had the time to have long conversations and, one day, we had the most difficult.

That night, Ana Paul stayed home and together we prepared a delicious meal and opened a bottle of wine. I put some nice music on and we sat down to chat in the lounge.

"I want to touch on a subject that's hard to talk about, but we have to. I'm hoping that my surgery will go really well and we can share many years together. But I cannot deny that things might not go the way we want. Sweetheart, have you thought about what you want to do if I go? Who do you want to live with?"

I felt as if I was asking the question to a small child as, for me, she still was a child, my 19-year-old daughter. Just then, Ana Paula's eyes filled with tears and she came up to me and hugged me. I held her in my arms and could feel her warmth and her sweet softness. The tears rolled down her face and her voice trembled.

"Mommy, I don't want you to go. I need to have you near me. You're the one person who lifts me up and gives me the strength I need. I can understand that you want to talk about this, but it's really, really hard, Mommy."

We stayed silent a while. Just listening to the music and enjoying the wine, whilst we held on to each other. My fingers caressed her hair and I gently kissed her forehead until she calmed down.

She told me, in a voice full of emotion, that she would like to rent a small apartment and continue studying. She wanted to be near the family, but not get in anybody's way. She felt that she could be at an age when she could be independent and she would like to live on her own. With the rent of the house where we lived, together with the life insurance she was due if I died, she could easily do that.

As I could now feel she was feeling more comfortable talking about all this, we discussed how I would like my funeral to be and what should be done with the ashes.

"What I would like, darling, is that your grandparents, Sandra, Enrique Luis, Marcela and you all make a special trip to the beaches of the Riviera Maya. I want you to scatter my ashes in the sea and, while you do that, please think about one thing: that I am finally free, that I'm happy and at peace."

"But, Mommy, why do you want it to be in the sea? We'll lose you completely then. We'll have nothing left of you."

"On the contrary. For me, the sea means life. It's a deep and mysterious place which I would have loved to have known better. Traveling through water is the best way to go around the world. But, spiritually speaking, I know I won't be there. I'll have gone to a much better place and I shall always be there with you and your brother."

She looked at me with the eyes of a child, amazed at what I was saying.

"What we see is not what we are, not really; it's just a taste of what lives inside each of us. You will keep my heart, my teachings, my words and everything we've lived through, side by side. You will keep all that my soul told you through my actions and not only my words."

We laughed, cried and hugged while taking small sips of our wine. At times, she would stay quiet, pensive, and I had no idea what could be going through her mind.

"Yes, Mommy, I understand you and I admire you so much, but you know what? I 'm sure you'll be fine with the surgery. Don't forget you have to see me as a bride on my wedding day and then hold your grandchildren."

She brought us back to the reality and the struggle we were both going to have to face in a few days.

"Yes, darling. I'll be fine, especially now that we've been able to cut through this taboo of talking about death. So, now, let's get on with living life to the fullest!"

It was incredible to be talking about this so calmly, so serenely, but I can honestly say it was one of the most liberating moments of my existence. I realized that, not only was I able to talk to my daughter about my death, but also I could see how she grew in confidence and acquired a new strength right before my eyes.

She knew what her mother wanted and was prepared to speak to me on any topic. I felt grateful to have this chance and prepare her for what might come.

I knew only too well that the surgery I was going to go through was much more complicated and laborious than the first. The only saving grace was the advances in technology.

●BREAKFAST AND MASS

Our true friends are a reflection of ourselves.
MY SOULMATES

My mother organized a breakfast in her home to celebrate my birthday on November 24th. I knew that, deep down, she knew only too well that this might be my last celebration. The poor woman had been living with this torment for years. We invited all my aunts and friends and it was a beautiful get-together, which I enjoyed immensely in spite of my tiredness.

My Soulmates had written something especially for the occasion:

Dear friend: we're so happy to be here with you to celebrate your forty three years of life. For those of us who have had the chance to know you for the last thirty years, we know everything you've had to go through to come this far. And, in spite of everything, we've never told you this to your face, but you have been a great example for us all. You have taught us to see and value life in a different way. Through you, we've learned that we must live each day to the maximum, giving thanks to God for the abundance of blessings He has given us.

We know you are about to face yet another challenge and we're sure that, with your strength and God's help, you will come through this victorious, you know you can count on our unconditional friendship and all our prayers. Don't forget, we're counting on you to be with us on our trips when we turn forty-five, fifty, sixty, seventy-five......

We love you very much.

Your friends"

In January, this same group of friends organized a mass to pray for my health. They spoke to the priest and he asked to speak to me beforehand. I talked to him and told him I had all the will in the world to keep on living, that I wanted to see my daughter get married and have the joy of knowing my grandchildren if that was God's plan, and that I wanted to accompany my children along their paths as far as I could, but I also confessed to feeling very, very tired.

"You know, Father? Sometimes, I am overwhelmed by tiredness, but it's purely physical. My strength fails me and I have to finish off whatever I was doing in my mind, as my body just gives up. I need to stop."

"What plan do you think God has for you?"

"I know I came to this world to be happy and to give whatever is in my power in order to help others. That's what I've dedicated myself to, to live my life intensely."

"So then, you've no need to worry about anything; you'll be fine."

His words were few, but I heard what I needed to: you'll be fine.

The mass was about to come to an end when the priest looked straight at me.

"We're celebrating today a mass as if it were for a person who has died. The difference is that the person for whom we are gathered is right here amongst us, alive, and listening attentively to these words. God is giving us the chance to be with her and to bid our farewells while she is alive. Ana Cecilia is about to face a difficult situation, but this is nothing compared to what she has already been through throughout her whole life. She is ready and strong of spirit. We must accompany her with our prayers so that her body is also strengthened very soon. That is what friends do."

He added that we must have faith and trust that God would help me to heal.

"Ana Cecilia, God is allowing you to come together, in life, with everyone who loves you: your parents, brother and sisters, children and many friends. What a privilege for you to be here!"

It was a very special service. When it was over, I looked around and saw that the church was absolutely full, and I saw many people whom I hadn't seen for years. They hugged me and gave me all the support I needed before I set off for Houston.

The priest's words touched me deeply. It was true; I was witnessing what could have been my funeral service. *Ráfel* held on tightly to my hand.

A VISIT FROM MARCELA

Problems never seem so great when seen through the veil of humor and love.

Marcela was living in Spain and I missed her very much. I saw a lot of my family in Monterrey, but I felt incomplete not having Marcela, her husband and her children nearby. When I spoke to her, she asked if I'd like her to visit me. I knew she couldn't go to Houston with me for my operation as she couldn't sort out her visa and passport in such a short time.

Of course, I said yes. We both knew of the great risk attached to the upcoming surgery. I believed I would survive it, but we couldn't be sure of seeing each other again if things didn't work out as expected.

Her two-week visit was like a breath of fresh air. We went around everywhere together, shopping and just having lots of fun. She slowed down to keep at my pace, but during those two weeks, I enjoyed her more than I had for many years. It was the best gift she could have given me. When the time came for her to leave, we cried, hugged and smiled.

"We'll see each other again in summer. I want to see you and the kids. Tell Jaime that he has to come, I won't take no for an answer. I want to see him in person and give him a big hug!"

Family is the greatest treasure I have. Absolutely nothing can take its place.

WITH MY SISTER MARCELA.

MY BROTHER AND SISTERS

●ANA PAULA'S LETTER TO ME…
STAY CALM AND AT PEACE

The same path can be seen to be full of light or darkness; you decide.

Before I went to Houston, Ana Paula handed me a letter:

We don't exactly know the reason for what is happening now, (I mean, broadly speaking, as obviously your heart problems are at the root of it all.) Neither of us knows what will happen. God does this as part of a plan which we cannot possibly understand now, but which will come clear sooner or later. You and I are both learning from this. Everything we have lived through (good, bad, weird, beautiful) has been to help us grow and become so close that now we are the best of friends.

I just want you to know this and it's very important that you don't forget: I love you with all my heart, Mommy. I love you as much as the very life that you gave to me.

You have been to me so many things: a mother, a best friend, a companion, a support, love, wisdom, values, affection, security, protection, bravery, courage, confidence…what God has given us is an extraordinary life.

I want you to feel calm and at peace when you are in Houston. I shall be fine, what with all my friends you've entrusted me to. (I'll also do my bit to make things work, I promise!) I want you to feel calm when you go, with no fears, no remorse. Go to Houston, enjoy what you can of the trip (it is a trip after all, and trips are to be enjoyed!) I hope the doctors give us good news, but whatever they say, it will be what God wants for you. You might even take a moment to talk to my grandparents about it, as there's no time like the present to get everything out into the open.

I LOVE YOU!!!

Yours,

Ana Paula

P.S. Remember you will need to meet your grandchildren and I'm not in a hurry…. so you're going to have a long wait before that happens!

There it was again; my daughter was saying, "Stay calm." Those words were constantly going round my head, and now it was she who was saying the exact same thing as in my after-death experience. "Stay calm and be at peace, and do everything I have asked you to do." I was sure that, up to that point, I had followed those instructions to the letter: live life to the fullest and always give thanks.

Of course, I had to be calm and at peace; I was heading for yet another test which I would do everything in my power to come through with flying colors. Besides, I was ready to enjoy the trip!

●HOUSTON 2008

You decide whether to see only the obstacles in your path or the way to get round them so you can go on your way.

I moved to Houston a few days before the surgery as they had to perform a catheterization and evaluate the complexity of the situation. Four of us travelled: my parents, my brother and I.

Enrique Luis took the initiative to ask me for all my friends' emails to keep them up-to-date with the proceedings.

They performed the catheterization and concluded that the surgery would be of a much more complex nature than previously thought. They couldn't operate on me in the hospital they had originally recommended, St. Luke's Hospital, and it was decided that I should be operated on for the second time at Texas Children's Hospital, because of their vast experience of working with cases like mine. They had never operated on a 43-year-old woman with my particular kind of malformation. Even though I was an adult, it was more likely that they would know what to do in the Pediatric Unit, were any complication to arise. The operation was postponed for two weeks.

This gave me time to write letters to my siblings and my children and I was able to spend hours chatting with my parents about anything that came into our minds. We visited places, went shopping and just enjoyed one another's company.

My friend Pamela stayed close and often visited me, together with her mother, Silvia, who is a church minister and tried to go and give me communion every day. I was so grateful to her for her visits and her company.

I felt strong and ready for the surgery. The fact that I had had to wait those extra days made me stronger rather than more anxious, as could have been expected. I am sure that the prayer chains, the encouraging messages and the fact that hundreds of people joined in wishing me well, gave me the necessary strength.

My mother's sister, Aunt Martha, who had taken charge of Ana Paula during my first surgery, arrived one or two days before, in order to keep my mother company and help keep our spirits up. These were special days in which we spent a lot of time together, creating an even closer bond between us, and it was a true joy to see again what a great human being she was.

I am convinced that when people come together in prayer, with a common goal, the entire universe conspires to achieve the desired result. I call this "a miracle". I know this happened to me, because I could feel it. My heart and spirit strengthened enormously during those days. My body began to relax completely and all of my being was at peace.

●LETTERS TO MY BROTHER AND SISTERS

The greatness of a person is not measured by what he or she finally managed to achieve but rather by the love, respect and commitment they left along the way.

My brother and sisters have always been my fortress, one of the greatest treasures life has afforded me. Each of them was a support to me in ways that perhaps they themselves could never have imagined. So now, during these moments before my surgery, I felt compelled to thank them and express my love for them, putting my thoughts on paper.

I always admired Sandra very much, for her astute words of advice and support just when I needed them. She was the epitome of an obedient daughter, studious and steady. Not only did I admire her, I was also jealous of her because I was in many ways just the opposite: naughty, disobedient and forever restless. Even so, it didn't mean I couldn't recognize noble qualities in a person when I saw them.

January, 2008
Sandra,
I've been trying to write this letter for weeks. I think the reason I haven't done so is because I know I'll end up in a flood of tears. So, I have changed my tactics: I decided to cry my eyes out first, and get it out of my system, and then do the writing. That way, I wouldn't have to stop the flow.

I know only too well there were many occasions when I was far from easy to deal with, but I also know that, when all was said and done, you realized the deep love I felt for you.

You have made me feel your warmth, your love and your deep convictions, which make you stand firm as a rock at all times. Just to see how much you love your husband, how you bring up your children and the wholehearted devotion you show towards everyone; it's awe-inspiring. You have no idea how much I admire your ability to find time for everyone and everything. You have amazing sensitivity and somehow always manage to be at hand when someone needs your help. And I don't just mean family; I'm talking about anyone who comes across your path.

I think that there was many a time when you felt the need to put the brake on my crazy way of wanting to live my life. Today, I can see that that was how I had to live in order to survive, as I was always conscious of my ghost being close at hand. I desperately needed to suck every last drop out of life. But whenever I stopped my madness and looked around for a role model to follow in my childhood, I turned to you.

Nothing and nobody will ever appreciate what you mean to me. Thank you for being Ana Paula's godmother. Thank you for the love you have always shown her and for the calmness I can feel now, knowing that she will always be able to count on you and will not be alone. Thank you for the way your children love us both, their aunt and their cousin; I know that you and Tacho are, in the main part, responsible for that, by your example. I thank God for the chance to be so close to them.

Thank you for your love, dear sister.
I love you with all my heart and soul.
Ana Cecilia

Enrique Luis is the most loyal companion and friend that any sister could wish for, and it's impossible not to feel his love. He was always my favorite, no doubt because he was the only boy. He has been, and always will be, an unconditional support for me as well as for Ana Paula. For her, especially, he has been one of her greatest pillars to lean on. His way of being, sometimes a bit scatter-brained and carefree, has sprinkled that element of fun over my life. He's an amazing father and a great example to follow as a human being.

The letter I wrote to Enrique Luis shortly before my second surgery:

"January, 2008
Enrique Luis,

I remember how you were always my kind of hero, even from when we were little. I admired you so much; I often wanted to be just like you. It was only when we started to grow up and when I saw how you were getting taller, more handsome and more interesting by the minute that I started to see that now it was you who could protect me. I don't think you ever realized, but you made me feel safe.

The divorces we both went through, yours a year before mine, brought us closer together. Not only were you someone I could always talk to about anything, but with you, I never felt judged or criticized. Actually, it was as if I was talking to myself. I saw how much you suffered, wept and so deeply regretted your divorce, and I was glad to have gone through it all with you in some way. Who would guess that it was only a year later that I would be in the same situation, and it was your turn to stand by me.

We've been through so much together. It was you I could count on all those times when I reached out for a friendly hand. We've been each other's confidante on many an occasion. You've shown me an unconditional love and a loyalty beyond that of any other human being. You are a wonderful person and I'm sure God put you at my side to help me come through those difficult times.

Please believe me when I say that my life has been enriched just by you being there, showing your love and devotion. What I also loved was how you kept me in touch with your children through those phone calls every week or two. Thanks to your attention that that, I now feel beautifully close to my nephews.

I love you...
Thank you for your love,
Ana Cecilia

Marcela forever helping me, through her objectivity to see things more clearly and manage to get them done. It was through her that I first saw the possibility of becoming a mother. Holding her in my arms made me feel I had to take care of her, protect her and always be there for her. She allowed me to enjoy the pleasures of being a little girl for many more years than I would otherwise have done when we would play together for hours on end. Marcela is always a small light flickering in my heart.

The letter I wrote to Marcela some days before my second operation.

January 2008
Marcela,
The distance between us has made me value so many things. And I'm not just talking about the distance from my living in Puebla; it's also the many years you've been far away since I got married and you went to live in Europe. You are a wonderful person who I love with all my heart, and I thank God for having you as a sister.

I remember when we were little and I used to give you what I thought of "a piece of my big sister's advice", while we both perched on the bathroom tub. I'll never forget how much fun we had with our little games that went on for hours. How I loved playing with you! I know the age difference didn't always make it easy for us to share many things, but just let me say that, even though we are apart, I will always be your number one fan.

I remember changing your diapers and feeling that it was my job to protect you. How proud I was to have such a beautiful little sister. You probably don't know what a source of strength you were to me, as you so often made me feel as if I could actually be of use to someone, by protecting you, taking care of you and in some way guiding you in your life. And those times when I seemed to be racing through life

272

at top speed, terrified of it slipping through my fingers, just taking one look at you would halt the frenzy and calm me down. Probably that's why I often call Ana Paula by your name, Marcela. You were such an important part of my life when I was growing up.

Thank you for being my little sister and for giving me two wonderful nephews, as lovely as their mother. Thank you for keeping them close to us through photographs, videos and phone calls. That means such a lot and I cherish it like you can't imagine.

Marcela, you don't know how much you mean to me and how much I love you. You are like a precious treasure which I carry around hidden deep in my heart. It doesn't matter about the time, the distance or the ages; you will always be here with me.

I love you with all my heart,
Ana Cecilia

● FAREWELL

I know my life has been worthwhile when it leaves in its wake a spark of light to help others.

Once again, without actually realizing it, I was bidding farewell to everyone, just as before my first operation. I handed the letters I had written to my brother, my sisters and my daughter. That left my parents. As always, they were there, never leaving my side, but I just couldn't bring myself to put down on paper what I wanted to say to them. I knew that reading my words would bring them too much pain, and, once more, I wanted to shield them from the heartbreak.

I finally decided to write a separate letter to each of them, but they would only see these letters if I were to die. They were on my computer and only my daughter had the password to access them. I couldn't bear the thought of having to say goodbye to them and prayed that God would let me be the one to see them depart first. This still is my wish, but may it not happen for a very, very long time.

So, I devoted myself to simply enjoying my parents and making the most of this extra wait of three weeks. We talked and talked and I told them everything I was harboring in my heart: that I loved them and would be eternally grateful to them for the long-endured battle which they had lived and fought alongside me. We went sightseeing, had lots of laughs, watched movies and had fun with the friends who visited me.

I was delighted to have all this time with them, and particularly as I had them to myself in the house my uncle and aunt had lent us in Houston.

One day before the surgery, I phoned Daniel, who by then was 17 years old. We stayed in touch constantly but didn't speak every day. He was still living in a specialized institution and his father often picked him up so they could spend a few days together. At the time I phoned, he was with his father. I wasn't sure how much he had been told about the seriousness of my operation, but, in any case, I had to speak to him. His father had taken him to see me before I had moved to Houston and I couldn't help remembering how worried he looked. He had given me a flower and we had hugged like rarely before. I only knew that I missed him and felt that a part of my heart had stayed behind with him.

"Son, how are you?"

"Fine, Mom. Have they operated on you yet?" he said, in the faltering voice he used when he was frightened or upset.

"No, darling. They'll be operating on me tomorrow morning, which is why I'm phoning you. I just want you to keep me in your prayers and remember that we'll see each other soon."

"Of course, Mom. Thanks for calling."

"That's OK, sweetheart. Take care of yourself and never forget that your Mommy loves you."

"Yes, Mom.. Mom…" There was a long silence.

"Yes, honey. What is it?"

"…I love you."

"Me, too, darling, I love you very much," I said. "You'll be fine, sweetheart and before you know it, we'll be seeing each other again and chatting about lots of things."

"Yes, Mom."

He stayed silent, as if waiting for me to keep talking.

"The doctors have lots of experience and know what they're doing."

"Are you scared, Mommy?" he asked with the innocent voice of a 5-year-old child.

"A little, honey, but that's normal. None of us likes being operated on, but I'm happy because I know that, after it's all over, I'm going to enjoy many more years and be feeling better and stronger."

"Mm," he took in what I'd just said, and kept silent.

"I love you, son. Don't ever forget that!"

"I love you, too."

He hung up, and my heart shuddered.

Into my mind came the image of 18 years before when I could only think about my 9-month-old daughter. Now, my thoughts were of her and Daniel. I kept quite still in the room, trying to decipher exactly what I was feeling. Daniel was a child, emotionally speaking, and I always had the feeling that I couldn't get through to him. How would he be feeling now? Would he be calm? Would he have forgotten our conversation after a few minutes? No one knew.

I smothered my wet face deep into my pillows. I lay my fragile body back, took hold of a small blanket that was at the foot of the bed, and I wrapped it tightly around me.

I pictured in my mind all those things we went through when we lived together. He was sick, and totally dependent on the love and affection given him by his parents and family. I wanted to hold him tight and reassure that everything would be fine, like any mother would to her frightened child. But I couldn't. All I could do was carry him with me in my thoughts and trust we would see each other again soon. My soul wept, my body trembled and my heart embraced him.

"Mom, are you all right?" asked Ana Paula, entering the room.

"Yes, darling. I've just been on the phone with your brother."

She came up to me so lovingly and hugged me so tightly that I kept on crying. It was now she who was consoling me, who encouraged me, who held me up once more with her embrace. I told her what had happened and she found the words to calm me down.

How different it all was from 18 years ago! Now, I was joined by my daughter, my siblings and my friends, who didn't leave me on my own for one single moment. I could feel that Daniel was also thinking about me, and, in that way, he also was by my side.

Sandra arrived with her husband and Enrique Luis the day before the surgery. The doctors recommended I eat and drink whatever I liked best and that I should do my best to relax and take it easy. Not exactly an easy thing to do, considering what was to come. Enrique Luis organized a barbecue for me, as he knew how much I enjoyed that. We invited the friends who lived in Houston including Pamela, her mother and daughter. Pamela's husband, Fernando, wasn't well and couldn't make it.

Wine flowed and there were mountains of food. I felt we were celebrating my life. But it was a party, after all, and I intended to make the most of it. I ate all I could and just managed half a glass of wine. But what I enjoyed most was having around me all the people, or nearly all the people, I cared for most in this world: my family, my friends and, above all, Ana Paula.

I retired to bed earlier than everyone else. I was very tired, and the few sips I had taken of wine were enough to make me nicely relaxed. Ana Paula joined me a few minutes later.

We chatted a little and made plans for when I left hospital. We put on some instrumental music to relax me even more. This time, I didn´t spend all night writing letters as I had done nearly 20 years before, the night before the operation. I had already answered many emails and, thanks to technology, was in closer contact than before. This time, I had one of my greatest treasures in my life right by my side: my daughter.

That night, we slept with our arms wrapped tightly around each other, as if we were one. I relished her warmth, her scent, and stroked her as if she were a child. I rested deeply and felt at peace.

●THE MOST CRITICAL DAY OF MY LIFE

Practice the art of patience – when the storm has passed, the sun will appear and you will see everything clearly.

On the morning of February 27th, 2008, we all woke up before 5:00 a.m., as we had to present ourselves at the hospital by 6:00 at the latest. I had a glorious shower and took all the time in the world to wash my body, giving thanks for each part as I slowly sponged myself down, lingering luxuriously over every inch. This was very probably the longest shower I had ever taken in my life!

When we were ready, we all went to the hospital: my parents, my Aunt Martha, my brother, my daughter and I. Sandra and her husband met us there. I was given a warm welcome by some nurses and immediately put into the usual hospital gown and the little cap which is necessary before surgery. I asked them to sedate me as much as possible so as not to feel anything. The catheterization I had had some weeks previously had been very painful, and I would rather not have any pain if possible.

And that's exactly what they did. They gave me some pills and anaesthetized me through an IV, so that, by the time I entered the operating room, I was totally sedated.

Just before I went through the double doors to the operating room, I saw all my family. We said a prayer together. Well, they did, as I was already entering into another dimension, but I could hear everything. What I remember most was when the anesthetist arrived and spoke to me:

"Well, you have three large martinis inside you, so how are you feeling?"

"Fine, doctor, ready for the surgery."

"I just have one question for you. Why do you want to be operated on? Why are you here now?"

The question struck me as odd, but I understood that my state of mind when I entered surgery was crucial to its success and they wanted to make sure that I was emotionally ready.

"Because I want to get to know my grandchildren," I answered.

"An excellent answer. That's more than enough. We'll be absolutely fine."

My daughter came up and lovingly held my hand.

"Mom, I'm not in a hurry to give you grandchildren just yet. OK?"

We all laughed and cried at the same time. Tears flowed from my eyes and my daughter kissed my forehead and my hands. My parents, brother and sisters came up close, joined by my aunt. I'll never forget that also present was Dr. Elsa Echéverri, sister-in-law to my friend Pamela. Everyone was interested in this surgery, which, at the same time, was complicated and promising. When my bed was being moved to the operating room, I clearly saw my ghost *Ráfel* in front of me. He just had to be there. He looked at me with eyes of tenderness and love, just as when he had smiled at me before my first surgery. I knew he was always with me, but I could only perceive him in the difficult moments. This time, I didn't beg or beseech him for anything. I was calm and at peace.

THE PROCEDURE OF THE SECOND SURGERY

Family and friends are like the moon; they're always there even though at times they don't appear.

Enrique Luis has always been – and I know he always will be – one of my biggest supporters for many years. Without realizing it, he was the one who kept the family strong throughout my second surgery. He was there at all times, dropping whatever he was doing so that I was never alone and so that my parents weren't the only ones having to deal with what we were going through.

He took it upon himself to keep all our friends and family up-to-date with how the surgery was going. Thanks to the new technology, in just one moment, he could communicate by email with everyone and let them know how we were doing.

It was wonderful to have a brother like Enrique Luis, who acted as the official spokesman, amongst many other duties he took on. I shall always be grateful for his thoughtfulness, as the prayers which were sent up as a result of these emails made all the difference as to how I am today: alive and happy.

February, 2008. Texts transcribed exactly as he wrote them.

Feb 12th,, 2008.
Hello everyone. This is Enrique Luis, Ana Cecilia's brother, sending you the latest update. Yesterday, Monday, she was supposed to have the catheterization, but it didn't happen due to certain issues in the hospital. It was reprogramed for today, Feb 12th, at 12:00 p.m.
We had a meeting yesterday with the surgeon, who told us that, according to the result of the catheterization and consulting with the cardiologist, it will be decided whether the surgery will take place on Thursday 14th. as programed or whether it will be postponed a few weeks in order for her to take some medicines to strengthen the heart. The estimated time for the surgery is from 8 to 14 hours, according to

the surgeon, which means they have to pay attention to the slightest detail. The decision will be made later today or tomorrow morning. I'll keep you informed.
Thank you for your support and prayers.
Greetings.

Ana Cecilia UPDATE... Feb 12th.
On Tuesday, the cardiologist performed the catheterization which lasted four hours, much longer than normal. Ana Cecilia was left in a lot of pain, but they had to find out exactly what condition she was in up to that point. The results are as follows: it was concluded that the operation is far more complex than expected, and therefore, the operation on the 14th. Feb in St. Lucas Hospital will be suspended. It will be reprogramed and carried out in the Children's Hospital where the surgeon normally operates and has the equipment and personnel experienced in modified Fontan operations. Some time between Wednesday and Thursday, they will check availability in the Children's Hospital in order to program the surgery.
Thank you for your prayers for Ana Cecilia's recuperation and positive state of mind, and we just hope they'll be able to program the operation during these coming days as the Children's Hospital has few vacancies. Thanks for your support and prayers.

UPDATE 3... Wed. 13th.
No news today, still waiting for the operation date to be fixed at the Texas Children's. Ana Cecilia recovered well from the catheterization, but is still in a lot of pain. We're hoping that things will be finalized tomorrow. Ana Cecilia sends her best wishes to you all.

Ana Cecilia UPDATE 4... Thurs. 14th.
The doctors informed us that the operation is expected to be performed within the next 10 to 15 days, at the latest. Soon, they will give us the exact date as they are having to reschedule operations previously programed for other patients so as to free up the operating room. They estimate 8 to 14 hours for the operation. The doctors recommend that she shouldn't leave Houston as they need to keep monitoring her. Also,

they've prescribed the new medicine I told you about for strengthening the heart prior to surgery.

The plan is for Mom, Dad and Ana Cecilia to stay in Houston, and I will go back to Monterrey in the coming week.

Thank you for your prayers. God has been guiding the doctors to choose the best path to follow and this is all thanks to the prayers of all of us who love Ana Cecilia.

She is now feeling much better after her catheterization. She's in a good mood and as cheerful and optimistic as ever. Today, she celebrated St. Valentine's Day, eating what she hadn't eaten all week. Ana Paula came to see her and will stay on Sunday.

Ana Cecilia UPDATE 6...

Dear friends, today Tuesday 26th. February. The pre-operative tests were performed on "Anna" (as the Americans like to call her) and everything went well. The studies include: blood analysis, X-rays of the thorax, ECG, and others. She also had a word with the doctors and anesthetist, who said she should have a good dinner, whatever she fancied most, and they even said that a glass of wine (believe it or not!) would do her good as long as it's before 12:00 midnight. And so, I'm being forced to follow the doctor's orders by doing her a barbecue accompanied by a glass of wine. We know you will join us as we make a toast to her: thanks for your support. Ana Cecilia didn't put up any objection. Tomorrow, Wednesday, her last meal allowed is at 5:00 a.m. (transparent liquids) We shall set off at 5:30 to arrive by 6:00 a.m. The operation will begin at 8:00 a.m. and is still expected to last 8 to 14 hours, as I mentioned before.

Ana Cecilia is very calm, very confident, in the best of spirits and feeling the support of everyone. She sends you her best wishes as, like the good mother she is, asks that you remember her children, Ana Paula and Daniel, in your prayers.

Tomorrow, I shall write again.

Greetings, Enlugo

Ana Cecilia UPDATE 7... Wed. 27   1:30 p.m.

The operation started at 8:25 a.m. All is going well. At the moment, they're opening up the ribs and separating the veins and arteries so as *to leave the heart free for the modified Fontan operation. This takes a long time as they are going into places which are already scarred (bone and cartilage) from the previous operation (18 years ago).*

They tell us it's a very long, meticulous procedure. To sum up, the operation is going ahead smoothly.

I'll keep you informed, Enlugo

Ana Cecilia UPDATE 8... Wed. 27, 4:15 p.m.

The operation is still underway. She is now connected to a machine which oxygenates and circulates the blood. They found some calcification resulting from the previous operation which they are now removing. This will mean the operation will take a bit longer, but everything is going as well as can be expected.

Greetings and thanks for your prayers. Enrique Luis

Ana Cecilia UPDATE 9... 6 p.m.

We've just been told that the Fontan operation has been done, the heart is beating well, and she is no longer relying on the machine for the blood to be circulated. Right now, they are working on optimizing the heart's electrical signals by burning some nerve endings and thereby eliminating tachycardias (known as Maze surgery). After this, they will put in place a pacemaker to ensure that the heart rhythms are regular and continuous (this operates "intelligently", meaning it only works if it detects anomalies in the heartbeats.)

We shall stay in touch. We calculate at least another 2 hours still to go. Thanks for your prayers.

Ana Cecilia UPDATE 10... 8:00 p.m.

She's out of the operation, everything's fine and things went just as the doctor had anticipated.

* Undo the previous operation of 18 years ago (Fontan)

* Redirect the flow of blood directly to the lungs with a synthetic vein outside the heart (Revised Fontan)

* Optimize the heart's electrical signals by burning some nerve endings, thereby eliminating tachycardias. (Maze surgery)

* Put in place a pacemaker to ensure that the heartbeat is as it should

be and continuous (operating intelligently and only working if it detects anomalies in the heartbeats.)
The doctor pointed out that the previous operation was now in a bad state and it was a good thing that this was done now. He says if the recovery goes according to plan, this operation will see her through many years to come, and her quality of life will improve greatly.
She is now in recovery and will remain in intensive care for 2 or 3 days, after which she will be in a normal room for one week.
Thanks for your prayers. We thank Dr. Fraser as we know that without him and his incredible capacity; this surgery wouldn't have been so successful.
At 8:30 p.m., all of us, family and friends, will begin a rosary to thank God for everything and to ask for a prompt recovery.
A big hug to you all. God bless us all, Enlugo

Ana Cecilia UPDATE. Thurs... 28   9:30 a.m.
Good morning to you all. Ana Cecilia has started the day well, communicating with everyone and doing her breathing exercises. The doctors say she's doing very well and might even take her out of intensive care tonight and put her in a normal room (so that's a sign of a good and quick recuperation.)
Ana Paula is giving her ice cubes to eat as if it were Gerber (she's also fine and happy).
Ana Cecilia sends her best wishes to all.
A short while ago, she asked for her pillow to be changed, which means she's starting to be a nuisance, and that is a very good sign.
Thank God, in general everything's going well.
Greetings to all and thanks.

Ana Cecilia UPDATE 12... Thurs. 9:30 p.m.
Ana Cecilia is fine, still in intensive care. She occasionally talks but remains very dozy and in a lot of pain. She has a button which she can press in order to release a pain-killing medicine into the IV. She uses it a lot.
She's in very good spirits and jokes a bit when she's awake. She's working with a device to strengthen the lungs. She has to blow into it as hard

as she can 10 or 12 times per hour. She uses it regularly and even asks for people to pass it to her, which shows how keen she is to get better as quickly as possible.

Just as a comment: as from last night when we were talking to her, she was no longer intubated which was what had bothered her so much in the previous operation and made her quite scared this time.

I send you all greetings from the family and especially from Ana Cecilia. Thank you for your prayers.

Yours, Enlugo

Ana Cecilia UPDATE 13... Friday 2:30 p.m.

Ana Cecilia is still recuperating, but it's a slow and painful process. Anyway, she's doing fine, bearing in mind the kind of operation it was. It's highly likely that this afternoon they'll move her from intensive care to a normal room.

A short while ago she sat up and ate a little, but she's rather nauseous. We ask you to keep praying for her recovery.

Yours, Enrique Luis

Ana Cecilia UPDATE 14... Viernes 2:30 p.m.

Today was a very difficult day: she couldn't keep her food down several times during the day, and was in a lot of pain. She was moved out of intensive care in the afternoon and into a normal room. Tonight, she had a little supper and, so far, has kept it down. Let's hope that continues. Taking everything into account, it's normal for her to reject food after this kind of surgery, according to the doctors.

At this moment, she's asleep in her room and her sister, Sandra, and Ana Paula are keeping her company.

Thankfully, everything is normal or even better than normal from what the doctors say. Her vital signs are good and the recuperation is going well. The only problem is she's in a lot of pain and feeling nauseous. Let's pray that she has a good night's sleep, gets some rest and feels better tomorrow.

Warm greetings, Enlugo

Ana Cecilia UPDATE 15... Saturday 12:00 a.m.
Excellent news! She woke up feeling much better, chatting (telling jokes), has had two short walks in the past hours, they've taken the oxygen away for short spells, she's eating grapes, she's had a shower.
She's well in general; in fact, so well, she's worrying (only a bit!) because she wants to get back to work. She says the work's going to pile up. Ha ha!
The doctors estimate she'll leave hospital in a few days, which is earlier than expected.
To sum up, excellent, thank God.
We'll be in touch.
Fondest greeting, Enlugo
P.S. Dr. Charles Fraser has just arrived and said he'd been at a conference with other doctors in the morning and he'd brought up cases of Fontan in adults. And he gave her as an example, saying it is, in fact, possible for children with congenital problems to live into adulthood. Ana Cecilia's comment was that he should tell parents of children with congenital problems shat she is proof there is hope. The doctor then invited her to join a support group which gives conferences to parents of children with these problems to give them HOPE. She agreed happily.
The doctor says she won't leave tomorrow, but chances are they'll discharge her on Monday.
Finally, she's going to eat minced meat and rice that my Mom cooked for her this morning (hospital food leaves a lot to be desired.)
Greetings again.

Ana Cecilia UPDATE 16... Saturday 10:40
Three things:
The first, Ana Cecilia continues to be fine, thank God; she laughed a lot at the jokes "Good Humor"(adults) which an aunt sent whose name I won´t mention so as not to embarrass her, but I've attached them to this message. All of us: my father, Sandra, Ana Paula and I, killed ourselves laughing.
The second and third favors are to look at the pictures here. A phot says more than a thousand words.
Warm Greetings.

Can I remind you that if you want to send Ana Cecilia a few words of greeting, a joke or a bit of gossip, please send it to: acgfree@yahoo. com (someone will read it).
Bye for now, Enlugo.

Don't forget you're never too old to have fun and be happy.

MOM AND DAD

AUNT MARTHA AND SANDRA

ANA PAULA AND DR. FRASER

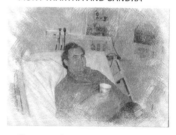

ENRIQUE LUIS ON MY BED

UPDATE 17..Sunday, March 2nd. 7 p.m.
Hello everyone,
Everything good, she ate well and walked several times, no news (she no longer had oxygen or IV). On Monday they'll decide if she goes home or not.
She's still laughing at the jokes, which is good for her lungs.

Letter that my father sent to a group of friends and family

02/03/2008
Hello,
We happily give thanks to God for Ana Cecilia's condition.
She gets better every day, eating well, walking, on the doctor's recommendation, in the hospital corridor, about 100 metres four times a week, and she's in good spirits.
Yesterday, 72 hours after the surgery, she was visited by the surgeon, the cardiologist and the anesthetistwho were totally astonished at her prompt recovery. Dr. Fraser, the surgeon, commented that, after such a complex and difficult surgery, her condition and general state of health were nothing less than a miracle. He invited her for next June to a meeting that's given regularly to parents of children with heart condition to offer them information and orientation.
We will never grow tired of giving thanks to God for the success of such a complicated surgery in doctor's Fraser hands, and to our friends for their prayers and shows of affection.
Warm greetings to you all.

●RECUPERATION

*Today my heart understands that there are answers which,
only with time, they may stop hurting.*

In this second surgery, I didn't live through the marvelous near-death experience as in the first one, but I was allowed to leave hospital quickly and, for me, that was extraordinary. My spirit felt strong, very optimistic, and I felt renewed. I could never thank enough to each and every doctor and nurse that made this possible. Despite the complexity of the surgery, and so many long hours with stress and standing up, they still manage to stay in one piece. They are like angels amongst us and I shall always be grateful.

The recuperation process was not simple. Even though I felt well in myself, the arrhythmias didn't leave me for over a year. I constantly had to go for medical checks and there seemed to be no way to get rid of them completely.

That was when I decided to keep writing. I was confined to the house, unable to work, and yet I felt strong enough to do many things. I spent my time reading, composing songs on my guitar, writing and getting closer to my friends and family. All of this made me feel truly alive.

As I wrote, I described again the wonderful near-death experience which I had lived almost 20 years before. My spirit now was so much more sensitive to everything that was happening around me. The time had come to tell the story which was inside my memory, my heart and my soul, more vivid than ever.

After a year and a half of being on sick leave, I had to resign from my job at the University of Monterrey. The law stated that after this length of time, for administrative reasons, they couldn't be kept waiting and had to finalize our working relationship. I could no longer return to work there. Because of that, I received a financial support from the University and Ana Paula retained her scholarship for the rest of her university studies, which was a great relief for me.

A short time afterwards, my arrhythmias miraculously disappeared. The medicine had finally done its job and my heart had now stabilized with the new circulation of blood. I felt much stronger and anxious to get going with my life again.

That was when Enrique Luis asked me if I would like to work with my father and him. I put up some resistance to start with, as I felt that nothing could be so satisfying as having contact with students and working in education.

But I was wrong. Very soon I was put in charge of one of the departments: Quality Control, amongst many other activities. I started to feel productive again, useful and in a position to help other people. Besides this, I had the peace of mind that I was not being a burden to anyone, which has been my intention all my life.

I started to go out again, have fun with my friends and get involved with some charity organizations. I also went to several reunions with my former university colleagues, and it was at one of these that I met up again with Carmen who I hadn't seen for many years. She was the friend who I had met at university and who told me that some day we would meet up again when we needed each other. It was as if we had never been apart.

"Carmen? Is it really you?"

"Yes, hello," she hesitated for a moment. "Ana Cecilia! I can't believe it. I've been thinking so much about you in the last years. I lost track of you and then moved out of the city. How are you?"

"Yes, I knew you weren't living here. I was operated on not long ago, but I'm fine. Well, this was my second surgery. The first one was many years ago, just after the birth of my daughter, Ana Paula."

CARMEN AND ME.

"Wow! You have a daughter? But weren't you meant not to have children? I suppose you had her after your surgery?"

"Ha ha. No, actually, it was a miracle, but I had her a year before. Carmen, we have a lot to talk about. I suppose you have plenty to tell me, too."

"I sure do. There's a lot for us to talk about."

From that day on, we became inseparable. We met up with our old university group, we went to different events together and shared the same interests for reading, helping others and devoting time to helping social causes.

One day, when we felt more comfortable with each other, she spoke to me.

"I must tell you that, many years ago when I thought about you, I just presumed that you were no longer with us. When I happened to mention this to friends who didn't know anything about your whereabouts either, they came to the same conclusion. It was the most logical thing, wasn't it? We all knew about your illness."

"What do you mean? You all thought I'd died?"

"I'm afraid we did. You had told me about how complicated things were for you and then, when I tried to get in touch with you at your old address, I was told you no longer lived there. I asked them if they could give me your new telephone number of wherever you were living, but they couldn't. I knew you'd got married, but I didn't know your telephone number or your new address."

"Who did you ask, who did you speak to? Didn't they give you my number?"

"No, they didn't. It might have been the woman who helps your mother, but she just said nobody called Ana Cecilia lived there and she didn't know who you were. She said that Mrs. Sandra only had two daughters. I just felt so bad I couldn't bring myself to ask her anything else."

I felt so bad for her. I can imagine how she must have felt at that moment.

"I can't believe it. I would never have believed that."

"To be honest, I didn't try to call you again. It was a long-distance call, and I just never thought of writing to your parents' house. I lost contact with you and with lots of other friends, too. It would have been so good to have internet in those days!"

Once more, I could confirm that her words had come true. We met again just when we needed to. Meeting up with her and with the rest of my old friends from my childhood made me reflect on my life. I realized that it wasn't only she who had thought that I hadn't survived; many friends who I had lost touch with over the years presumed the same thing.

That night, after thinking over what we'd said, I couldn't help having a big smile on my face when I went to sleep; Thank you God, I'm still here!"

Just how many times do we believe we know the truth about something because we make suppositions, but, in the end, we realize that, in fact, we were way off track? It's only with the passage of time that everything falls into place.

As time went on, I got stronger, but not without suffering some of the side-effects brought on by being that bit older. I was just coming up to the two-year mark after the second operation when I got sick again and was in and out of hospital various times in the course of the next year or so. There were serious complications after an operation on my uterus, and I had to go back into Intensive Care with heart failure. There, I underwent a minor surgery and ended up staying longer than expected in hospital.

I also had various episodes of arrhythmia which seemed never-ending and always meant another stay in hospital. Fortunately, this time the burden of taking care of me was not carried solely by my parents and family, but also my great Soulmates. They, as well as friends who had come back into my life, started to play an important part in my life as they helped look after my health and my wellbeing in general. I know I can always count on them; their friendship is truly unconditional. Friends can be found when you most need them. Thanks to them, I once again valued each stage of my life. I was alive, and with everything that had happened, and in spite of everything that had happened, I was still in the game. I was still here!

Ráfel still came and went during all these episodes. I was no longer afraid of him; I just held on tightly to his hand which now seemed to pull me in the direction of life rather than lead me towards death. I was no longer a little girl, I no longer played at being dead as I did in those days, but now *Ráfel* was more real than ever in my life.

I continued to write my life-story, but these episodes of sickness interrupted my writing and I would lose the thread and put it on one side.

Before long, Ana Paula graduated from university, which made me happy, proud and fulfilled. My daughter was concluding an important part in her life and I had been able to be at her side throughout. She finished with Honors and all the family was there to share the moment, including her father and her paternal grandparents.

ANA PAULA GRADUATION.

⬤ AND I'M STILL ALIVE

I hope the sunset of my life reflects the beauty of what I lived on my journey.

Fifty years have now passed and that little child who, it was first thought, would not live beyond a few months and who, in any case, would live in a very sorry situation, is still alive. Besides, this is the best time to tell my story. A story which has the sole intention of sharing with others how to survive in the midst of so many pessimistic voices and insinuations, all saying that her life would be short, full of pain and hardship; who, from an early age, learned to die by living intensely, instead of dying slowly and feeling sorry for herself; savouring life at each moment.

My way of dying has been to live in a constant state of gratitude for what I have. I learned to turn my enemies into my greatest allies and my allies into my path to happiness.

I feel like a very privileged woman. I live very close to my parents. My mother is an active

THE WHOLE FAMILY

ANA PAULA AND DANIEL

MY PARENTS

woman who always tries to help others. My father, as always, is a business man and constantly keeps himself busy. They both keep the family united through get-together and family celebrations. They are, indeed, the same fine, exemplary couple today as they were fifty-three years ago when they began their married life.

A short time ago, I had the chance to accompany my father to an international work convention in the city of Chicago, Illinois. He was invited to share his story of how he has come to be so successful in his business. I was also invited, to help with the presentation and any translation, were it necessary. I had never in my life imagined what a great gift it would be for me to be there. I realized not only how much his colleagues and work partners love him, but also how much they respect and admire him. I understood that tenacity, discipline and moral values are learned in the home because the parents set the example. This was always what they inculcated in us, their children, and it is how they have lived their lives outside the home.

When we returned home to Monterrey, my mother welcomed us with open arms. She kissed my father and congratulated him. She was proud of her husband and happy that our presentation had been such a success. I felt prouder than ever to belong to this family, and that these two people had raised me and dedicated years of their lives to me, years of struggle, every single day.

Today, I spend all the time available writing, always accompanied by my four beautiful Chihuahua dogs: Hansa, Nina, Lola and Kena. We go for walks and they are my constant companions. I feel productive as I have now been supporting my father in his business for several years. I have a wonderful group of friends, including, of course, my Soulmates, who fill my days with fun and light.

My sister, Sandra, and brother, Enrique Luis, live in the same city as I do. Sandra is happily married to her husband Tacho and they have five children: Tacho, José, Adrián, Pato and Sandrita. Enrique Luis married again and is very happy with Alejandra and is close to his three children: Enrique Luis, José Andrés and Juan Diego. Marcela has enjoyed living in Spain for various years with her husband Jaime and their two children: María Sofía and Isaac.

Daniel is still institutionalized. I speak to him on the phone several times a week, visit him whenever I can and we spend quality time together. He often goes out with his father or with me. He spends a lot of time drawing and is extremely gifted at that. We have him in private classes which he has greatly benefitted from, so passionate is he about his artwork. His progress is impressive and he is always coming up with a new cartoon strip to write and draw.

He has the emotional maturity of a small child, but in many aspects, he is a grown man and has learned how to develop his talents. He will never be able to provide for or take care of himself. As long as I live, I will make sure I do everything within my power to support him. I know that nobody comes into our life by chance. Daniel came into mine because I had something to give him, and he had something to give me. I sometimes think that God allowed me to live that extraordinary experience in Houston during my first surgery, in order to give me the necessary strength to endure, to be able to love my son in the way that he needed me to, and so that I could let him go when I had to without feeling guilty.

I think that, finally, he is ready to read the letter I wrote to him over fifteen years ago. We shall read it together. As someone once said: "Life is like a swing. You have to find the balance between holding on and letting go."

Ana Paula lives abroad and is the editor of a magazine. She is highly successful in her work. We speak every day and she brightens up my day with some of the stories she tells me. Bringing her into this world, and being able to enjoy her all these years, has been, and always will be, one of the greatest gifts that God has granted me. A short time ago, she became engaged to her boyfriend of three years, Gilberto. I know that their wedding day will be the happiest day of my life.

When I think about it, I believe that I have had many days which could be called the happiest days of my life, because I have lived each one as if it were the last. They have all been valuable to me.

Many things could have killed me off up to this point: my congenital malformation, my pregnancy, the infections and complications when I was operated on, my confusion when I almost disappeared in those vulnerable days after my operation, my sadness at losing Daniel, the difficult times living at the such a high altitude in Puebla. But nothing came so close to killing me as having stopped believing in myself. I came to my own rescue and I still do, every day. I managed to raise myself up when I looked deep inside and realized how much love I had received in those hard, hard days. I had the privilege to touch the sky, and all I had to do was share that experience with others. The answer lay within me. No prince, doctor, family member or friends could have accomplished for me something if I hadn't wished to do it for myself: live! And that is what I do every day: I live life to the fullest.

My heart has a physical defect, but it is no longer sick; it is a heart which, in every beat, expresses gratitude, and that is what keeps it healthy. I may still end up in hospital from time to time, as has already happened on many an occasion, but I will get up again as many times as is necessary whilst I have the strength to hold on tight to the hand which life offers me. And, without breaking the pact we made long ago, with the other hand I shall still resist the patient company of my ghost, my dear *Ráfel*.

He has been my most faithful companion, and today I feel a great affection towards him. A short time ago, when I visited my sister, Marcela, in Spain, I discovered that the name of my ghost, which I had called *Ráfel* from when I was small, is actually the name in Catalan for Rafael. I was also unaware that it was the name assigned to an archangel, and even less did I know its meaning: the medicine of God, medicine for the body and the soul. *Ráfel* has been my strength, my life, my hope, my health in many moments when faced with grim prognoses; it was only a few years ago I discovered all this. I have always been accompanied by the medicine of God.

Thank you *Ráfel*.

The love which I have received through my parents, my family, my friends; that which I enjoyed, and still do enjoy deeply, in my near-death experience, has been what has given life and strength to my heart. This love has been the best medicine of all. I have seen enough to know that the world in which we live, and the life that we live, is of our own making, and is the product of what we are inside and what we do. Even the way we experience those things which are beyond our control will depend on our way of facing up to them. I am sure that heaven is not a place; it is a state of consciousness, a reconnection with all that surrounds us. It is where I wish to live, always. I know it is within our reach before death. The key is how we love and how we think. I am convinced that one day my whole body will pass through that pale yellow circle, and in the eternal embrace, I shall receive a completely new heart which will, indeed, live forever.

I was born condemned to die, as we all are, but no death sentence, no crying or suffering have, so far, managed to stop this heart from beating; a heart that was faulty, yes, but a heart that was always full of hope. I know for sure that when I see the sun setting on my life, I shall be calm, at peace, and I shall enjoy the view until the sun, at last, disappears.

Getting old is not only a privilege, but a gift that not all may receive.

●CONTRIBUTIONS FROM MY LOVED ONES

My parents:

Right from the day she arrived in this world, Ana Cecilia showed an enormous vitality which would help her come through all the difficulties she has faced. She has been a great example for us, her family, and for those she has spent time with. We are enormously grateful to God for having given us the chance to be at her side when she most needed us, and, at the same time, this has been a great learning process for us, too. We admire her valor, her integrity, her strength to accept her pain, her devotion as a daughter, mother, sister and friends, and her always being there for us. For us, her parents, her life has been a gift which our Lord God has allowed us to enjoy, and we ask that it may continue to be so for many years to come.

With love,

Enrique Luis and Sandra Patricia Gonzalez

Ana Paula

Mother: an inspiration in my life.

My mother is proof that God exists, that a person can grow in the midst of pain and that nothing is impossible unless you allow it to be. My mother taught me that God knows why He made us in a certain way and why He put us in a certain situation. We have to accept ourselves and love ourselves exactly as we are, because that is the basis, these are the roots from the beginning of our life which will allow us to fight any battle.

I admire my mother like no one else in this world. She always made me feel protected and loved; she has taught me to pay attention to my intuition and to always try to see life from a different perspective, a more positive perspective, giving each situation and each person their due importance; and she has taught me to protect my heart (in my case, emotionally speaking) from the rest of the world and feel that I am special and to know that I am loved by God at all times.

Carmen Macossay

Your positivity, will to live and way of challenging adversity had given me life lessons during these years. It was interesting to see with what enthusiasm and energy you would give your opinion and, even more so, to see how you loved debating with everyone else. Without any shadow of a doubt, whatever assignment you took on, you achieved it.

Roma Ilkiw

Ana Cecilia's story is a testament to how much the body, heart and spirit can endure, and to one's capacity for recovery, rejuvenation and renewal.

She teaches us that a patient's recovery is dependent, not only on the skill of the physician, but also on the will of the patient. And that the source of this will is love.

Thelma Trevino

It's quite admirable how you always made it clear that you feared no one. Now I can see and understand many thing; it was as if you were in a race against time. You wanted to take on everything and didn't put any limits of yourself.

Scarlet Mireles

It was you who taught us to value friendship and put a high price on it. You must know that it is thanks to you that we are the Soulmates.

Carmen Castañeda

It is your destiny to leave your mark, and you are beginning to show that, not only to those of us who know you, but also to those who have yet to know you.

Morena de la Garza

You have come through all your physical and emotional obstacles which life has thrown at you with flying colors. You have shown that your heart might not be like everyone else's, but this has only served to strengthen your character, based on values and very clear goals.

Ma.Alicia Santa Cruz

Your inner fortitude and the great love you have FOR YOURSELF is what I admire most about you. I am absolutely sure that it is only because of this that you are here amongst us today.

Lilia Gomez

Ana had the ability to stop time itself whenever she got her guitar out and sang or read one of her writings. It was as if we must just enjoy the moment, savor it as if it was the last time one could have it. You didn't know this, but you invited me to walk towards my heart, my very core; I long to have a heart like yours, my dear friend… ."where everything can be and where everyone can be and where I can be at PEACE."

Gabriela Perez Maldonado

Ours has been a friendship in which we have lived beautiful things, adventures, we have shared our most intimate secrets. I am fortunate to have found you and to be your friend. Thank you for being part of my life.

Chely Araujo

I feel that you are a person who sees life as God would wish for us to see it, that we pass through this life in order to reach Him, and that we must LIVE IT.

Cecilia Villareal

I think you are an intense kind of friend, simply because that's the way you have had to live your life. You give of yourself completely if a loved one is in trouble or having problems.

Nancy Cruz

It's clear to me that we all have a mission in this life, and that you have shared yours with us so we can learn that with conviction and great faith in God, anything if possible.

Lucila Gama
I am so happy for this great project you are embarking on because you will see how valuable you are, not only for yourself but for everyone around you.

Adriana Lozano
The girl who wanted to devour the world, and for those of us around you, it was great because you transmitted to us your energy, enthusiasm and, as they told you in Houston, always with a smile on your face.

Chelo Lozano:
ANA CECILIA
Soul Mate

Clinging on to life
You grew from day to day
Amongst family and friends
As an exceptional woman
Illuminated by a Celestial light.
You have come through endless battles
Irradiating your joy.
We must celebrate, now and always.

Pamela Lombana
It is a story of hope and strength. When I met you, you were so alive, your smile made me know that you were going to live, and that no one would stop you. Your spirit was stronger than that of any of us who attended you. Your struggle was never to give up.

Nena Lopez
Meeting you has been a marvelous encounter with simplicity, humility, fortitude and an overwhelming human warmth. Our friendship is a great blessing!

Emma Gonzalez

As a colleague and a teacher, you have lit up my path. It gives real meaning to this journey we call life.

Lolys Villareal

When I got to know you in swimming classes when we were just little girls, I remember a girl who, physically, was fragile......in time, I discovered that your strength lay within you.

Gaby Carrera

We grew up, and your will to fight against everything grew with you. You are an example of tireless struggle, constancy and faith.

Myrna Ramirez

I have learned a lot from you, with your persevering character and your never giving up. No doubt, the Lord still has a purpose for you and, with Him as your guide, the best is yet to come.

Helen Rowland

Every page of this book is a testimony to love, in all its manifestations. For me, translating into English language the intimacies of Cecy's life has been a joy and a privilege, provoking laughter and tears, and a prevailing awe for the sheer, sometimes inexplicable, willpower of one person's spirit and her love for the miracle of life.

MARCELA, SANDRA, DAD, MOM, ME AND ENRIQUE L.

ANA PAULA AND I